the [barcode] W9-CWE-798 n

Patricia A. Wasley
Coalition of
Essential Schools

NCREST

SERIES EDITORS

Joseph P. McDonald
Annenberg Institute
for School Reform

School Change: The Personal
Development of a Point of View
SEYMOUR B. SARASON

School Work: Gender and the
Cultural Construction of Teaching
SARI KNOPP BIKLEN

The Work of Restructuring Schools:
Building from the Ground Up
ANN LIEBERMAN, Editor

Stirring the Chalkdust: Tales of Teachers
Changing Classroom Practice
PATRICIA A. WASLEY

Incorporating the following books from the
PROFESSIONAL DEVELOPMENT AND PRACTICE SERIES

The Contexts of Teaching in Secondary
Schools: Teachers' Realities
MILBREY W. MCLAUGHLIN,
JOAN E. TALBERT, & NINA BASCIA, Eds.

Careers in the Classroom:
When Teaching Is More Than a Job
SYLVIA MEI-LING YEE

The Making of a Teacher: Teacher
Knowledge and Teacher Education
PAMELA L. GROSSMAN

Staff Development for the 1990s:
New Demands, New Realities,
New Perspectives, SECOND EDITION
ANN LIEBERMAN &
LYNNE MILLER, Eds.

Teachers Who Lead: The Rhetoric of
Reform and the Realities of Practice
PATRICIA A. WASLEY

Exploring Teaching:
Reinventing an Introductory Course
SHARON FEIMAN-NEMSER &
HELEN J. FEATHERSTONE, Eds.

Teaching: Making Sense of
an Uncertain Craft
JOSEPH P. MCDONALD

Teachers' Work:
Individuals, Colleagues, and Contexts
JUDITH WARREN LITTLE and
MILBREY W. MCLAUGHLIN, Eds.

Team Building for School Change:
Equipping Teachers for New Roles
GENE I. MAEROFF

A Union of Professionals:
Labor Relations and
Educational Reform
CHARLES TAYLOR KERCHNER and
JULIA E. KOPPICH

Professional Development Schools:
Schools for Developing a Profession
LINDA DARLING-HAMMOND, Editor

Changing Teachers, Changing Times:
Teachers' Work and Culture
in the Postmodern Age
ANDY HARGREAVES

Chartering Urban School Reform:
Reflections on Public High School
in the Midst of Change
MICHELLE FINE, Editor

Unions in Teachers' Professional Lives:
Social, Intellectual, and
Practical Concerns
NINA BASCIA

Teacher Development and
the Struggle for Authenticity:
Professional Growth and Restructuring
in the Context of Change
PETER P. GRIMMETT and
JONATHAN NEUFELD

SCHOOL CHANGE

THE PERSONAL DEVELOPMENT OF A POINT OF VIEW

SEYMOUR B. SARASON

Teachers College
Columbia University
New York and London

Published by Teachers College Press, 1234 Amsterdam Avenue, New York, NY 10027

Copyright © 1995 by Teachers College, Columbia University

All rights reserved. No part of this publication may be reproduced or transmitted in any form or by any means, electronic or mechanical, including photocopy, or any information storage and retrieval system, without permission from the publisher.

Library of Congress Cataloging-in-Publication Data

Sarason, Seymour Bernard, 1919–
    School change : the personal development of a point of view / Seymour B. Sarason.
        p.   cm — (The series on school reform)
    Includes bibliographical references (p.   ) and index.
    ISBN 0-8077-3449-7 (alk. paper). — ISBN 0-8077-3448-9 (pbk. : alk. paper)
    1. Educational change—United States.   2. Education—United States—Philosophy.   I. Title.   II. Series.
LA210.S343   1995
370' .973—dc20   94-44041

ISBN: 0-8077-3448-9 (paper)
ISBN: 0-8077-3449-7 (cloth)

Printed on acid-free paper
Manufactured in the United States of America
02 01 00 99 98 97 96 95   8 7 6 5 4 3 2 1

To the memory of Esther (1918–1993)
who was always a part of my point of view.

CONTENTS

Foreword by Patricia Wasley   *ix*

Acknowledgments   *xi*

Chapter 1   Justifying This Book   1

Chapter 2   You Know More Than You Think and   9
               More Than They Give You Credit For

Chapter 3   Three Diagnostic Errors   21

Chapter 4   The Uneducated   36

Chapter 5   Aspects of a Community Program for   56
               Retarded Children

Chapter 6   The School Culture and the Processes of   65
               Change

Chapter 7   Jewishness, Blackishness, and the   85
               Nature–Nurture Controversy

Chapter 8   Some Observations on the Introduction   106
               and Teaching of the New Math

Chapter 9   The Overarching Purpose of Schooling   124

Chapter 10   Letters to a Serious Education President   147

Chapter 11   Governance, Power, and the   165
               Definition of Resources

Chapter 12   Experience In and Outside of School   190

Chapter 13   Reflections   214

References   *225*

About the Author   *227*

FOREWORD

For many years, Seymour Sarason has been a constant teacher of all of us who are working toward schools that are lively, engaging places for children and adults. In this volume, he provides a new kind of support. Organized as a kind of Sarason reader, essays from a variety of the books he's written are collected together into one volume that represents his most important understandings about school change. In some cases, he teaches old lessons, made fresh and important by recombination and the perspective of time. In other cases, new understandings emerge as a result of his airing previous insights in a new cultural milieu. In addition, the collection helps us to track the development of his own thoughtful and well authorized perspective about school change. This is particularly important at this point in the history of school reform because it lends important evidence to the emerging understanding that the creation of more powerful school settings takes considerable time and arises from a careful stew made up of contemporary circumstances, previous lessons, and best possible future predictions.

Professor Sarason's personal perspective is important for several other reasons. First, in examining the nature of his own intellectual development, he illustrates one of his own most constant maxims: If we don't understand our history, we will simply repeat it. This work collects his thinking over a 50-year period and draws on both the social and the scientific history of this country. In far too many instances he is able to point out lessons gone unlearned in one decade, resulting in the same mistakes being repeated in the next to no greater advantage.

Second, he comes to his own understandings by way of an interesting combination of personal experiences coupled with wide knowledge of the work of other scholars in a variety of disciplines. Far too often in education we claim that schools are unique—that what works in business or in medicine has no applicability to what we are able to do in schools—and so we ignore similar works being done in related fields. Wisely, Sarason draws on medicine, the arts, psychology, and mental health fields. Looking beyond the narrow scope of education enables him to see patterns that exist, thus building his understanding of the problem and broadening his access to potential solutions.

Third, his beliefs about schools and how they change are extracted from a broad spectrum of times, people, and places, many outside the common list of educational experts, most notable studies, and most often cited contemporary examples. As a result, he is able to provide us with additional fuel, and fresh sources.

This book is also important because it underscores several critical admonishments: Constant testing practices that suggest that intelligence can be measured by standardized tests out of the context of a child's own learning continue to undermine the capabilities of vast numbers of students. Professional training that continues to rely on remediation rather than a philosophy of prevention perpetuates many of the very problems teachers must try to fix. The fact that for the last 50 years, school practitioners and parents have made little headway in building better collaborative partnerships leaves children ever more confused about the value of school. Well-intentioned change agents cannot hope to improve the quality of educational experiences for children inside schools, without paying corresponding attention to instances of productive learning that go on outside schools. Each of these charges is well illustrated by all too familiar anecdotes. We are made ever more aware that until we grapple with these problems, little serious improvement is possible.

It is the intention of this series of books to illuminate paths taken to better schools and to point to routes as yet uncharted. This Sarason reader grapples with nearly all of the major considerations explored in his other volumes and reminds us of a number of paths not yet taken. At the same time he illustrates that constant professional curiosity, a willingness to look broadly for both questions and answers, and careful attention paid to the most fundamental hopes for good education can and do lead to a rich and challenging professional life, and to the development of a personal perspective that is of value to others.

Patricia Wasley, Co-editor,
the series on school reform

ACKNOWLEDGMENTS

I am grateful to Dr. Patricia Wasley and Carole Saltz for successfully provoking me to do this book. I learned a good deal from the effort, not the least of which is a glimpse of the obvious: memory is a sometime thing which, with the appropriate provocation, can expose connections you undervalued or never pursued.

In a preface to a book written thirty years ago I said that the two major problems in life were parking and secretaries and if as a society we could not successfully deal with them, we might as well forget about war, poverty, race, and injustice. I, as everyone else, have given up on the parking problem. In acknowledging here my affection and gratitude to Lisa Pagliaro for the help she has been to me over the past several years, I can no longer claim that all major problems in the world are irremediable.

1

JUSTIFYING THIS BOOK

When Dr. Patricia Wasley, a dear friend and an editor of this series, asked me to put together a book of selected papers that would trace the development of my thinking about school change, she advanced two justifications after I decisively said no. The first was that a fair number of my papers are not readily accessible, especially some written decades ago. I did not find that persuasive. The second justification was that there were people who were interested in how I came to hold the views I have written about in my books, a justification also advanced by Carole Saltz, the publisher of the Teachers College Press. I did not find that persuasive. I take satisfaction that the books I have written have been well received by some people, although if I had had to live on the royalties from those books I conceivably could have done so with the help of food stamps and public welfare assistance. Granted that some people would find how my thinking developed to be of interest, I could not believe their numbers would repay the costs of publishing such a book. Neither Dr. Wasley nor Ms. Saltz was persuaded by my estimate of readership. The fact is that nothing they said could be persuasive because shortly before our conversation I had finished and sent off a manuscript for what I honestly thought was the last one I would ever write about school change, *Parent Involvement and the Political Principle: Why the Existing Governance Structure of Schools Should Be Abolished* (Sarason, 1995). With that book I had said all I could justify saying. In fact, I would agree with the criticism that in my books on school change I had said everything I knew and believed at least three times, which may be an understatement. So, we parted with my saying politely that I would give it thought and call them with my decision. I find it easier to say no over the telephone than in person, especially with, as in this case, people I liked and respected. (Besides, how can you give an outright no after a lovely dinner paid for by people who had traveled to New Haven!)

There were three reasons I changed my mind. First, the day after the meeting I did something I have rarely done. I began to read some of my earlier papers as well as ponder over earlier professional experiences. That was both stimulating and unsettling. It was stimulating because despite the fact that those papers were clinical in nature and in no way dealt with school change, they clearly reflected a point of view that later informed all that I have written about school change. The words "point of view" do not capture my reaction to reading those papers. Beliefs, hopes, axioms are more appropriate but even what those words connote is not satisfactory or illuminating. Put it this way, *today* I can read those writings and discern aspects of my thinking that did not get integrated into what may be termed a point of view until years later because I had neither the knowledge nor the experience that would foster such an integration. To integrate is to bring things into relationship with each other. But to integrate implies a perceived need to integrate, and I had no such need. Why no such need? The general answer is that *professional* education (really graduate education) is both liberating and imprisoning: it expands your knowledge of a particular domain at the same time it puts blinders on you in regard to other domains of knowledge and action. In the course of one's training integration takes place within one domain and all else is foreign territory. Matters are not helped any by the fact that socialization into a profession is a form of indoctrination in which you "receive" the conventional wisdom about theory and practice. My professional training was in clinical psychology and fields like education, sociology, anthropology, and public health were truly unknown to me.

It is apparent, to me at least, that there are four thin threads or themes in those early papers that got increasingly connected once the nature and consequences of schooling became central to my interests. Here I shall state them very briefly:

1. Professionalism, as I said above, is a very mixed blessing, the imprisoning aspects of which can only be overcome or ameliorated if you do not take what you have been taught with a deadly seriousness or unreflective conformity. To be "open" to other domains or points of view requires, at the least, two characteristics: you want to expand your horizons, and you know, you truly know, that whatever truths you think you know are partial ones. I have always been impressed by how much I do not know and how easy it was (and is) for me to think and do stupid things. Someone once said that it is hard to be completely wrong. I agree,

although the wisdom in that remark was not easy for me to recognize. Too many professionals find it impossible to admit to errors and imperfections, thus rendering themselves incapable of capitalizing on mistakes.

2. If you want to understand another person or setting—or people in a particular setting—you should experience or become part of that setting. Better yet, nothing is more instructive or humbling than trying *to change* something about a person or setting. You can never comprehend the force or impact of a setting on its members unless, at the least, you have in some way become part of that setting, i.e., as long as you remain an "outsider" "looking in" you will disappoint yourself and others. A dogooder is a well-intentioned person who simply does not know with what and whom he or she is dealing. For every problem there is a simple answer that is wrong. That was said by H.R. Mencken and it applies to dogooders who may or may not be professionals.

3. To want to "repair" a person or setting requires no defense as long as you know that prevention is infinitely more effective than repair. That is a glimpse of the obvious but, as I can attest, giving more than lip service to the obvious is extraordinarily difficult in our individual and institutional roles.

4. In addition to death and taxes you can count on individuals and the settings in which they work to resist change very soon after they have requested help to change. That is true not only for "them" but for you and me. Change consists of unlearning and learning but far too many so-called change agents gloss over or totally ignore the turmoil that unlearning unleashes. Verbalizing the desire to change is easy; taking actions to change reveals how much we treasure our symptoms. That is as true for us as individuals as it is for a collectivity like a school.

What was unsettling about identifying those themes was that if a reader wanted to comprehend how and why they became important to me, I would have to include in this book writings that on the surface are not at all concerned with schools and school change. Would the diversity of groups comprising the educational community be interested in those writings? Even if I wrote extended introductions to each of those papers, would it be both interesting *and* helpful to those who in their daily lives are confronted with thorny, practical, frustrating, seemingly intractable problems. That it would be interesting and helpful to me I had no doubt. That it would be so for other than a few I had serious doubt. How could I justify the time such a book would require if it would have a very small audience?

That question got answered the next week as a result of two meetings with two remarkable individuals. The first meeting was with Jeff

Tseng who had just completed his first year at the Yale Medical School. Jeff had called earlier asking to meet with me because the medical school had received a grant to reform or redirect the curriculum of the school and he wanted to do his summer project on medical education. He had read my book *The Predictable Failure of Educational Reform* and he wanted to get my views about the relevance of what I had written for changes in medical education. That a medical student would have read that book was mystery enough and sufficient cause to see him, plus the fact that I was intrigued that a medical student at Yale would want to devote a summer project to examining medical education, this at a school taking pride in "scientific-research" training. The fact is that even if I had known nothing about Jeff other than he wanted to meet with me, I would have set an appointment because of my personal rule that I will see anybody who wants to see me, no questions asked. It is a rule that has paid handsome dividends. Indeed, I now realize it is part of my "point of view": you learn a lot about a lot of different people in a lot of different fields. It can be an antidote to your parochialism, to your belief that the truths you hold do not need amending or expansion, and to your smugness. That has been especially true when I have met with people coming from domains and with questions I knew little or nothing about until *they* presented me with "connections" that had never occurred to me.

It is probably the case that Jeff Tseng is unique among all medical students in this country because before this young man—I never asked him but he cannot be more than twenty-five years of age—came to the Yale Medical School he had been a public school teacher for two years. He had taught science in a middle school. He did not feel his preparation had been adequate, but most upsetting to him was the realization that he was not "reaching" his students, that although he knew his subject matter (extraordinarily well, I concluded) and by conventional standards his students "learned" it, he felt dissatisfaction with his teaching. So he decided at the beginning of his career to change careers.

In the first part of our meeting Jeff described what teaching and classrooms were like in the first year of medical school and the problems that were engendered in students who varied widely in interests and diversity of academic preparation. What, I asked him, was he proposing to study? He was not clear about how to proceed except to interview teaching faculty to find out what the purposes of the grant were and what they saw to be important issues. This is not the place to recount what the two of us discussed in a two hour meeting. What is relevant are several things I *heard* myself saying. I italicize heard because I was aware that what I was saying were aspects of a "point of view" I had come to over several decades. Let me very briefly state what I said:

1. You cannot understand why teaching is what it is in medical schools unless you understand the history and culture of the modern medical school which starts with Abraham Flexner's famed report in 1910 (Flexner, 1910/1960). Once you understand that culture you will comprehend why past efforts to change its pedagogy have failed, a comprehension my experience in and with medical schools convinced me was almost totally lacking in their faculties. To seek such a comprehension was not a summer project.

2. What would be both interesting and important was to obtain from medical students in a systematic way what Jeff thought were the dissatisfactions of students with *how* they were being taught, and *what* changes those students would recommend that would make their learning more productive, usable, and satisfying. After all, if the aim of the medical school was to initiate changes helpful to students, should it not know what students think and feel?

3. Why not capitalize on the fact that you, Jeff, may be *the* expert in the medical school on pedagogy? (In the land of the blind the one-eyed astigmatic man is king!) Why not put whatever you learn from the students in the context of your experience in a teacher preparatory program and as a public school teacher? Public and medical schools are different kinds of settings but they have at least one thing in common: they exist presumably to provide contexts for *productive* learning. Just as you don't need one theory to explain the oxygen atom and a different one for the hydrogen atom, you don't need different theories for productive learning for public and medical schools. Why don't you begin to put your experience in the two types of settings in relation to each other?

Jeff validly assumed that medical education had something to learn from public school education. What Jeff was downplaying was the significances of using his *personal* experience as a teacher as one basis for generating a position about his experience as a medical student. As a teacher he had developed a point of view about teachers and pedagogy. Why not apply what he thought he had learned in one setting to another that only on the surface appeared to be different? How else could that point of view be tested, expanded, amended? Why keep two worlds of personal experience apart? Why not take the plunge and say, "I have had valuable experience which my medical teachers should know about because no one else here can tell it to them, and if they don't know what I know, what they will recommend will support the maxim that the more things change the more they remain the same."

Understandably, Jeff regarded himself as "only" a first year medical student. At the Yale medical school he was *the* expert. From your students you are taught. In the abstract we agree, in practice we do not take it seriously. Who is really interested in what students think and feel? Seeing people through the prism of labels is easier than trying to understand them. When I went to my first convention of psychologists the identifying label on my jacket lapel read, Seymour Sarason, Southbury Training School. It and I meant nothing to the people there. A year later the label read, Seymour Sarason, Yale University. I became a someone worth talking to. Those experiences became part of my point of view (whatever those words mean): Maybe that is why I will see anybody who wants to see me?

Two days after I saw Jeff Tseng I met with Carl Ball who, I learned from materials sent to me, was a very successful scientist-businessman who owned a network of horticultural companies here and around the world. He had set up the Ball Foundation which, in recent years, supported efforts in educational reform. Dr. Steven Goldman, director of the foundation, arranged the appointment, telling me that Mr. Ball had on his own concluded that current efforts at school reform would be unproductive, and that Mr. Ball had read *The Predictable Failure of Educational Reform,* which is why he wanted to meet with me. I was intrigued, despite the fact that my experience with wealthy people who want to save our schools has always been disappointing. I feared that Mr. Ball would be another dogooder, although anyone who had on his own decided that current efforts to improve schools were doomed did not meet the more obvious criteria of a dogooder.

If my meeting with Jeff Tseng was refreshing (and more) the one with Mr. Ball was no less so. For my purposes here I need only note two things. The first is that *he had obtained a substitute teacher certificate and had spent time in classrooms in Chicago.* It's hard for me to be rendered speechless but I was, almost. Here was a man (in his early sixties, I would guess) who shared my point of view (I am uncomfortable with those words) that if you want to change a setting, you should become part of it in some meaningful way. The second noteworthy feature was that Mr. Ball took seriously that the preventive way of thinking and acting had been swamped by the emphasis on repair. That is why Mr. Ball was struggling with how to have an impact on elementary schools. There was really a third feature: Mr. Ball had learned to be skeptical of the conventional wisdom at the same time he truly tried to understand another person's differing point of view. He was not imprisoned within the boundaries of a narrow professionalism.

The two meetings led me to look more favorably on doing this book. For one thing, I realized that I had never tried systematically or in a focussed way to understand how I had come to see things as I do. My autobiography *The Making of an American Psychologist* had as its major purpose how my professional development was inexplicable apart from the times in which I had lived. That book describes "where I came and was still coming from" and parts of that book are relevant to the purpose of the present one but it does not come directly to grips with that purpose: how did ideas and experiences come together to forge a perspective on schools and school change? The more I thought about that question the more interesting it became to *me*, i.e., I could learn something about myself and my life, about how and why I think as I do. That was reason enough to proceed, given the fact that writing for me is a way of finding out what I have been thinking and doing and why. The fact that writing has as one of its several motives the satisfaction of narcissism does not necessarily impugn the effort. This is by way of saying that I overcame my fear that Teachers College Press may come to regret encouraging me to do this book. They could come to regret it, I would not. They were forewarned. Caveat emptor!

For reasons that will become clear the writings I selected are not ordered in a chronological sequence, even though I had unreflectively assumed that such a sequence was the way to go. The reason is that some of my most recent writings contain themes that I had long believed but I had not made explicit, a fact that surprised me but also mightily added to my interest in doing this book. In thinking about how to organize this book I learned something for the umpteenth time: what we call a point of view has explicit and implicit features and some of what is implicit is so obvious, so right, natural, and proper, so taken for granted, that you "forget" to explicate it. I like to call these implicit features axioms because they are the bedrock of the explicit.

A writer has obligations to the reader but the reader also has obligations to the writer. My obligation here is to try as best as I can to make clear how I have come to think as I do about school change. That, I can assure you, is easier said than done, subject as all of us are to the potholes in our memory, logic, use of language, and yes, self-serving tendencies. Self-examination is rough stuff and once you begin the process with the aim of putting it into words you find yourself pondering and reflecting in unexpected ways with unexpected difficulties and not infrequently wishing that you had not undertaken the task, that falling short of the mark is in the nature of things, and how many times do you want to fall short of the mark? The obligation of the reader is two-fold. The first is that if reading is not to be wasteful, it requires pondering and reflection, a truly personal effort, not "just" reading. The second, and part of the first, is that you are always asking the question: does what I am reading have the ring of truth for *me* (i.e., *my* experience, *my* per-

spective) and if it does not, how do *I* account for the differences. I have
not cornered the market on the truth, and neither have you, the reader.
A teacher can learn much from her or his students because their relationship is visible, palpable, and observable. Unfortunately, readers and
writers are not in that kind of relationship. Neither can learn from their
differences. A colleague and friend, Dr. Murray Levine, once wrote that
teaching is a lonely profession. Writing is a lonelier one even though it
is a continuous dialogue between two people who cannot see or talk to
each other. So let us begin to fill in the silence.

2

YOU KNOW MORE THAN YOU THINK AND MORE THAN THEY GIVE YOU CREDIT FOR

There is one reason I begin with a chapter in my 1993 book *You Are Thinking of Teaching?* Indeed, the basic theme in that chapter is why I wrote that book, a theme that in my mind helped organize everything else I say in it. When that theme got verbalized in my mind, I realized that it always had been in my head but I had never said or elaborated on it in anything I had written about school change. Stated most generally, the theme has two related parts: we respond to people in terms of labels we pin on them, and professionals have the tendency to see pathology or deficits and ignore or downplay the assets of people. I learned that in spades decades ago when I took my first job as a psychologist in a state training school for mental defectives (those were the days before the label mental retardation had replaced that of mental deficiency). And, I might add, it was a theme I learned the hard way in my clinical-therapeutic endeavors. As soon as you pin a label on someone—for example, calling him or her a student, a child, a patient, a handicapped person, an old man or woman, a blind or deaf person, or an uneducated or non-professional person—*in practice* we are far more set to see deficits rather than assets, limitations rather than capacities in that person. In education we are used to hearing that you teach children, not subject matter. Similarly, we should respond to people, not to the labels we give to them, but what we should do is not ordinarily what we do. How many times have educators dismissed what parents say with "They are just parents"? And in a similar manner how many times have physicians dismissed what patients have told them because they are "only" patients? The problem is not only that as professionals we tend to dismiss opinions of those without our credentials. More serious is that people learn in countless ways to regard themselves as unjustified in expressing opinions because they do not possess the right credentials, and that is often the case *between* professionals of differing specialties.

This hit me with full force when in the fifties Burton Blatt and I instituted an "observation seminar" for beginners in a teacher preparatory program at Southern Connecticut State College (now University). Through a one way mirror set-up, students could observe a classroom. What we told these beginners was very simple: "You cannot observe a classroom without having reactions, without questions occurring to you, without passing judgments of some kind. What we will ask you to do each time we meet is to observe for fifteen minutes to a half hour and then we will go to the seminar room where you will have the opportunity to state what your reactions, questions, judgements were." We were not prepared for the silences. These were not stupid, somnolent, uninterested students. But, we found out, they were intimidated students who did not feel entitled to have opinions, i.e., they were "just" beginners without any basis in experience (they thought) to say anything about the teacher and children they had observed, certainly not in the presence of two professors they regarded as knowing everything about everything. It was not easy for us to get them to overcome their stance of ignorance. It was that experience that started me asking the question: Why is it that these students who had spent twelve years in elementary, middle, and high school (and two more years in college before we met with them) considered themselves ignoramuses about productive and nonproductive contexts of learning? I had in a much more inchoate way asked earlier a similar question about people with whom I have worked; that is to say, I had already observed how difficult it was and how reluctant people were to bring their life experiences to bear on issues in their personal and professional lives that on the surface appeared new or foreign to them but, to me at least, were clearly usable and relevant. And not infrequently, it turned out, they knew those experiences were relevant but were fearful of expressing their opinions because others would regard their expression as trespassing beyond the bounds of their "credentials." Too frequently the educational process unwittingly produces "learned helplessness or ignorance."

I have already told the reader that I am uncomfortable with the words "point of view." Now (today) I know why. Those words sound too conceptual, too rational, too impersonal. The fact is that I have been, perhaps always have been, the kind of person who believes that what I have experienced and think I know I have a right to articulate and a right to expect that it will be given a hearing. I also have a right to be wrong and that being wrong is not sinful, however much being wrong injures my pride. What I have always resented—as a student and as a colleague with other professionals possessing expertise I did not—is not being taken seriously, being politely listened to and politely ignored. Sometimes it was not all that polite! That, I believe, is why I am regarded as a good listener, and some have said that I suffer fools gladly. Rarely, if ever (I hope), have I conveyed to a person that he or she is a fool. I truly believe in a gut sense that it is hard to be completely wrong and that it is my obligation to myself and the other person to determine the kernel of truth in their views. I am a person of strong convictions about damned near everything, at the same time that I know, and I do know, that I do not have anything resembling a monopoly on truth and wisdom. I try to get the best out of people because it has intellectual and personal payoff for me.

I grew up during times when to be a woman was to be a third class citizen. Far more often than not, when a woman expressed an opinion about an important social or professional issue—especially if it was said with conviction—the silent reaction was, "She is just a woman. What can you expect?" It is that kind of reaction I indict in what follows. Students have deficits which are remediable. They also have assets we overlook because we have learned to regard them as "just" students.

Something happened last night (May 26, 1994) after I wrote (and thought I had finished) this introduction. It tells the reader something about the way I think. The characteristic is that if I have reached a conclusion about a social phenomenon in one type of setting (e.g., schools) I am set to expect it in other seemingly different types of settings. I not only expect it, I look for it. So, I am watching the *MacNeill–Lehrer News Hour* and they are going to devote a segment to a current, controversial social policy issue: Should nurse practitioners be given the legal right to serve as primary care physicians, i.e., the patient's port of entry to other special medical services? Medical schools train relatively few primary care providers who charge much less than internists or other specialists. A few states, I knew, already have given legal sanction to such a role for nurses. It is a complicated issue. The point here is that early in my career I taught nursing students and had many discussions with nursing faculty at the Yale School of Nursing. I learned several things: nurses knew far more about *medical* care than physicians would publicly acknowledge; in the case of medical students, residents, and neophyte practitioners it was not infrequent that nurses "rescued" them from the untoward consequences of errors of omission and commission; physicians zealously sought to circumscribe the professional domain of nurses—a nurse could not write in a chart that a patient was dead because that was a diagnosis, but the nurse could write that the patient "appeared" to be dead because that was an observation. In those days nurses passively submitted to such a status and were intimidated from expressing their opinions; they played the role of handmaiden to the physicians, having been made to see themselves as having deficits and few assets by virtue of training and experience. When in subsequent decades nursing educators declared their independence of physicians, I was not surprised. It was that experience which forced me to recognize how easy and frequent it is to get people to see themselves as others do. That is to say, we define ourselves in terms of how others define us, and if they define us largely (and sometimes exclusively) in terms of our presumed deficits, we define ourselves in that way. I generalized from that experience. I assumed that it was a process of definition that was true beyond the confines of nursing. And, so, when I began to work with Burton Blatt in our observation seminar, I was surprised by the *strength* of their inability or reluctance to express their opinions, not by their inability or reluctance *per se.*

I should hasten to assure the reader that I am not asserting that in regard to nurses or students in a teacher preparatory program we are overlooking, or ignoring, or downplaying a gold mine of knowledge and experience. That we underestimate their knowledge and experience I have no doubt. And that is my point: they do have knowledge and experience relevant to *their* development and *our* pedagogy. Their knowledge may not be, indeed cannot be, wholly valid. They may have drawn unjustifiable conclusions from their experience. But is it not the teacher's obligation to get students to reflect on and exploit experiences clearly relevant to their future professional roles, to encourage them to overcome their reluctance to see themselves other than as empty vessels waiting to be filled with the knowledge and experiences of authoritative figures who succumb to the glories of an elevated status. I may change my mind in later pages of this book but as of right now I believe that what we call a point of view has deep roots in what we are as a person. It is not arrived at in a cool, rational manner. It may not be highly correlated with actions. How many people do you know who on the level of language are unequivocal adherents of a democratic ethos and who on the level of action are authoritarian?

My goal in this chapter is to convince you that its title has validity.[1] That is important for at least two major reasons. In the previous chapters, I emphasized that because of your inexperience and lack of relevant knowledge, you must make every effort to seek and digest as much knowledge as possible about what a career in teaching will require of you. That advice still holds good. You do have "deficits" in knowledge, but, as I shall endeavor to persuade you, you have some crucially important "assets" in experience that you should mine. You are far from being an ignoramus! The other major reason is that not only should your experiential assets enter into your decision, but once you have decided on such a career, you must use those assets as a basis for judging how well what you will be asked to learn in a preparatory program helps you make sense of those experiential assets. What you must avoid is falling into the trap of passively accepting attitudes about and conceptions of a teacher's role that conflict with your experience. I am not suggesting that you be argumentative with your college teachers but rather that you be true to yourself—that is, you will not lightly dismiss or forget or give up conclusions you came to as a student who spent twelve years in elementary, middle, and high school. Those conclusions inevitably will contain errors of different sorts, but they will also contain some important truths.

You owe it to yourself to listen to and reflect upon what you will be taught, but not at the expense of giving up all you have *learned about learning* in those twelve years. Some college teachers have the understandable but still inexcusable tendency to view students as having empty heads that need to be filled. As a college teacher, it took me years to realize that I vastly underestimated what students knew. After all, I was teaching *psychology,* and on what basis was I assuming that my students had empty psyches, that they had not had experiences directly relevant to what naively I assumed would be for them new knowledge? If I say such a stance is understandable, it is in large part because my students presented themselves as if they had no experiential assets I could or should exploit. And that is the point: students too readily assumed that they had no basis for using their experience to question in any way the

---

[1] The text beginning with this sentence and continuing to the end of this chapter is reprinted from *You Are Thinking of Teaching? Opportunities, Problems, Realities* (pp. 64–73), 1993, San Francisco: Jossey-Bass. Copyright 1993 by Jossey-Bass Inc., Publishers. Reprinted by permission.

"truths" I was giving them. When teacher and students collude in accepting that assumption, it is a recipe for nonproductive learning.

Teachers teach and students learn! Productive learning occurs when students and teachers teach each other. Teachers do know more than students, but unless that more takes into account what students know and have experienced, the students are robbed of the opportunity of examining, critiquing, and enlarging their personal and intellectual horizons. In the course of your professional education, you will frequently hear the maxim "You teach children, not subject matter." That maxim is intended to emphasize that you be sensitive to "what and where children are." Teaching should always deal with two subject matters: the world of the learner and the content and structure of the subject matter. That maxim is as valid for the individual in a teacher preparatory program as it is for a first-grade child. Too frequently, it is a maxim honored more in the breach than in the practice.

Let us start with the first major reason justifying this chapter's title, and let us do so by asking this question: When you review your twelve years as a student, which teachers come quickly to mind? Let me personally answer the question. Because I am undoubtedly a very senior citizen, I have to point out that the teachers I remember now are the same teachers I remembered when I was much younger. For example, when I was in graduate school—approximately six or seven years after being graduated from high school—a number of my student colleagues and I were discussing the nature of memory, in the course of which someone suggested that each of us write down the names of the teachers we had in our public school days. We were quite surprised at the relative shortness of our lists. (We could recall in our mind's eye several teachers whose names could not be dredged up.)

My list then was what it is today, and in this order: Miss Stephenson, Mr. Coleman, Miss Collins, Mr. Triest, Mr. Hunkins, Mrs. Schweig, Mr. McDonald. The last two names were not teachers. Mr. McDonald was the principal of my elementary (K-8) school and Mrs. Schweig was the assistant principal. But they were unforgettable because I and others viewed them as fearsome, punishing, if not child-devouring. The fact is that I can recall not a single instance when I interacted in any way with either of them, and I can recall no instance when I saw them in any way punish or discipline a child. But to the children in that school, Mr. McDonald and Mrs. Schweig were to be avoided like the plague. If you were in the hall and you saw either of them, your heartbeat mightily escalated, especially if they appeared to be approaching you. Why are they, who were not my teachers, on my list? For one thing, I cannot think of my elementary school days without their images being conjured up. I *feared* them. For all I know, they may have been lovely, decent, sensitive, supportive people, but you couldn't prove that by my testimony or that of my classmates. They never did or said anything to give students the feeling that they could be trusted. There is a difference between fear and respect. We *feared* them. We saw them as seeing us as potential criminals. We loved and respected Tom Kelly, the police officer who directed traffic at the busy intersection where the school was located. He was a delightful, friendly, joking, lovable person. When he was killed by a car at that intersection, we cried. If that had happened to Mr. McDonald or Mrs. Schweig, we probably would have been sad, but we would not have cried.

Why do I start with Mr. McDonald and Mrs. Schweig? For one thing, I wish to emphasize that how a child views an adult in the school may be dramatically discrepant with how that adult intends or would like to be viewed. I have no doubt whatsoever that Mr. McDonald and Mrs. Schweig did not want to be feared. But I can recall nothing said by either of them or any of my teachers to change my basic stance of fear, my belief that if they approached me, I was in trouble. (It was not until I was an adult that I learned that that is precisely what many parents believe: if they are asked to come to see the principal, they are going to hear bad news. Parents are not accustomed to being summoned to school to be told good news.) The more general point I wish to make is that young children, *like everyone else,* form impressions of others less on the basis of what they say or do not say and more (much more) on what they experience in their give-and-take with others. And by *experience*, I mean circumscribed instances in which the needs, expectations, and goals of a child are positively or negatively affected by the words and actions of an adult. It is not that actions speak louder than words but that actions are incomparably more fateful than words. I may very well have been told that Mr. McDonald and Mrs. Schweig were not to be feared, but there was nothing in my personal experience to lead me to change my mind. Fear is the enemy of trust, and trust is the interpersonal vehicle by means of which different personal worlds can begin to overlap. I had absolutely no basis for trusting Mr. McDonald and Mrs. Schweig.

As I have looked back and replayed my school days on my internal video screen, there were very few teachers I can say I trusted. Let me hasten to add that I never feared a teacher the way I did Mr. McDonald and Mrs. Schweig. Why, then, were there so few whom I did trust? Why when I think of trust do I think only of Mr. Coleman and Miss Stephenson? One reason is that I believed they were interested not only in my academic performance but in me; that is, what I thought and felt. When I gave a wrong answer to a question, they did not say "That is wrong" and call on another student. They tried to determine why and how I arrived at the wrong answer. And they did that calmly, patiently, as if I had piqued their curiosity, which they had to satisfy. With other teachers, I would not volunteer an answer unless I was *absolutely*, 100 percent sure my answer was correct. With Mr. Coleman and Miss Stephenson, I was relaxed and not fearful of appearing stupid. In fact, I enjoyed those give-and-take interactions. Their classes were interesting, they asked us interesting, even puzzling questions, they challenged us to draw on our out-of-class experience. And in doing so, they did one other thing: they revealed why and how *they* thought as they did. We learned a lot about them as people. If I had to put in one sentence what has stayed with me from their classes, it would go like this: "There is more than one way to think about and solve a problem."

When I think of these two people (they were more than the label *teacher* conventionally conjures up), the word *fair* always comes to mind. That is a hard word to define briefly. For my present purposes, let me just say that it appeared as if who you were, and how "smart" you were, were never grounds for ignoring or devaluing you. Regardless of who and what you were—and the students were very heterogeneous on any variable you can name—you *counted.*.

Let me now tell you about Miss Collins, whom I had in the ninth grade and who influenced my life. She did not have the "open," challenging style of Miss Stephenson or Mr. Coleman. I never felt I knew her or that she was particularly interested in me other than as a performing student. She was a prim, constricted, low-key, curriculum-oriented woman who in her quiet way ran a quiet class. If she rarely smiled or expressed any strong feeling, she was not intimidating. She taught Latin. In those days (shortly after the Civil War!), you took Latin if you were college-bound. You would be right if you assumed that students took Latin with the same enthusiasm they took a horrible tasting medicine. For the first month of class, it was all medicine. Then, slowly but steadily, Miss Collins began to demonstrate how some of the words we used every day derived from Latin. To me and a few other students, it came as a revelation that English mightily derived and developed from Latin. Yes, it was a Latin class, but to me it was also a class in the English language, *my* language. It was Miss Collins who stimulated us to look upon a dictionary as a kind of detective story. If Miss Collins was not an interpersonally interesting teacher, she was an intellectually mind-expanding teacher. She made "dead" Latin personally "alive."

Now to Mr. Hunkins and Mr. Triest (and many others whose names I cannot recall). The first word that comes to mind is *uninteresting*. Not only were they uninterested in me (or any other student), but they did not seem interested in *anything,* including the subject matter. It is as if they came to a class with a recipe (= lesson plan) that said "Do this first, that second, and that third, and if you follow instructions, you will end up with a palatable dish you will enjoy." There was nothing to enjoy! We were treated and felt like robots. More correctly, it is as if we had empty heads and hearts, but God forbid that I should put it into words. My job was to learn what I was told to learn even though in my "unformed" mind, I knew there was a difference between learning and understanding. And I learned one other thing: even if I learned but did not understand, do not ask questions, do not reveal your stupidity, do not ask "why" questions, do not take up valuable teacher time. By conventional standards, I was a "good" learner. By my own standards, I was a very poor understander. The classroom was no place to seek or expect to gain understanding. It was a place to get good grades, to appear as if you understood, not a place to ask questions that nobody else seemed to have (which, of course, was not true), but a place in which you had better be able to answer the seemingly scores of questions the teacher asked. None of these teachers *invited* questions. On the contrary, they made you feel that if you asked questions, you were either stupid or a show-off. None of the teachers responded to questions the way Miss Collins did. I said she was prim, low-key, undemonstrative of feeling. But when you asked her a question about whether a particular word in English derived from Latin, her eyes took on an excited cast, an ever so small smile seemed to struggle for expression, and she helped you to answer your question. I can sum up by saying that in these other classrooms, productive learning was defined by the number of questions I could answer, how well I could regurgitate what I was supposed to learn. That definition does contain a kernel of truth, but only a kernel. Another way of summing up is to say that the bulk of my classrooms were uninteresting, boring, and without much point.

Why do Mr. Triest and Mr. Hunkins stand out in my memory? Why do I remember their names and not those of similar teachers for whom subject matter was infinitely more important than what was going on in our hearts and minds? The answer is that I did not respect them. There were many teachers who were riveted on subject matter, but in some inchoate way, I concluded that they cared about the subject matter, if not about us. Mr. Triest and Mr. Hunkins, I and others had to conclude, cared about nothing except getting through class without once getting up from their chairs. Their classes were ones in which nothing seemed to make sense. Mr. Hunkins taught introductory chemistry, Mr. Triest introductory German. We ended up having no respect for or interest in Mr. Triest, Mr. Hunkins, chemistry, or German. There are people today who assert that the level of learning in a classroom is largely affected by factors extrinsic to the classroom, for example, family socioeconomic status. They never had the likes of Mr. Triest and Mr. Hunkins!

I could go on and on, but I do not see the point. I have revealed enough to buttress the conclusion that by the time I finished high school, I had had experiences quite relevant to conceptions of what makes life in a classroom interesting and challenging or boring and even deadly. Needless to say, I did not know that I had learned a lot about the ingredients working for and against productive learning. I was *just* a high school graduate. It could never occur to me that I had experiential assets relevant to matters educational. Who was I to pass judgment on teachers, classrooms, and the nature of learning? Is there any doubt whatsoever that my teachers would view me as without assets on the basis of which I was justified to come to conclusions? If after high school I had entered a teacher preparatory program—and in those days, you could do just that—it would have been with the attitude that nothing in my school years was of value in learning to become a teacher. I would have looked at my college teachers from precisely the same stance from which I had looked at my public school teachers: I knew nothing, they knew it all; their job was to pour in, mine was to absorb; I had only deficits, they would provide me assets; they were entitled to opinions because they had experience, I was not so entitled because I lacked experience.

What do you come up with when you review your school years? Which teachers stand out and why? Who turned you on or off? In which classes did you find yourself *willingly* eager to learn more? How frequent were boredom, lack of interest, and pointlessness? On which teachers would you confer sainthood because in some way or other you now know that something about what they were as teachers and/or people rang a bell you still hear? Is what I related about my school years (which were well over sixty years ago!) markedly different from what you recall? That there will be differences among us can be taken for granted. But are those differences of such a degree as to cause you to disagree with these statements?

1. In too many of our classrooms, children rarely, sometimes never, have what I will for the sake of brevity call a mind-expanding experience.

2. In too many of our classrooms, the structure and ambience do not encourage children to give voice to their questions about subject matter, personal experience, and the world they live in. Put another way, children live in two worlds, and the twain shall never meet.

3. From the standpoint of the student, there is no separation between

what is being taught and who is teaching it. To the student, the teacher is a person whose words and actions determine whether or not he or she will feel understood, fairly judged, valued, encouraged, as someone who counted, someone whose feelings and needs are not taken for granted, someone who wants to feel *interpersonally safe* to be expressive, spontaneous, even probing and "wrong."

4. Teachers, *all* of your teachers, contributed to your admittedly vague sense of the ingredients that make for productive learning. And that sense is always based on a comparison, a contrast between a Miss Stephenson and a Mr. Hunkins.

The point is not whether you find yourself agreeing with all, part, or none of these statements but rather that you have had valuable experience relevant to learning about learning (which is always social in nature). You do have assets. So, if you are contemplating a career in teaching, it should not be from the stance that you will be entering a completely new world for which you have no personal compass. That does not mean that these assets are a form of hands-on-the-Bible truths that will not require amending, enlarging, recasting. But it does mean that you know where you stand and what you stand for and that you will not easily give up your beliefs because someone says you are wrong. Your beliefs came from your experience, and you should change those beliefs on the basis of new experience and not because someone *says* you are mistaken. Your obligation to yourself and your teachers is to listen, to "hear" what they say, to reflect on it, not passively to assume that the voice of authority requires submission. Productive learning is a struggle, a willing struggle from which comes a sense of change and growth. It makes no difference whether you are a first-grader or someone entering a teacher preparation program. Productive learning has its joys, but they are a consequence of intellectual and personal struggle.

This chapter had a goal beyond trying to convince you that you have valuable assets. If I have, in part at least, been convincing, you will then better understand why being a teacher is among the most constructively impactful roles there are. *If you can do for your students what your best teacher did for you in the ways he or she did it, you will have justified your professional existence.* Your goal is not to become *a* teacher but to become one consistent with the personal style and intellectual creativity of those teachers whom you have cause to remember with gratitude.

It is easy to say "be true to yourself." Like all cliches, that saying contains a kernel of truth. The problem is to determine what you mean by "yourself." What I have endeavored to do in this chapter (and previous ones) is to suggest that in regard to becoming a teacher, "yourself" is, among other things, a condensation of attitudes, perceptions, and values forged in years of experience that led you, albeit vaguely, to define the conditions in which *you* came alive, in contrast to those in which *you* were going through the motions. *You* know when "yourself" was and is engaged. It is that engagement that you owe to your students. It is not a matter of imitation. It is a matter of personal-intellectual-professional *development*, and I italicize that word in order to make the obvious point that however clear the image of your best teachers is in your mind's eye, you are a unique individual who will have to find your own way to be true to that image. As a teacher, I undoubtedly looked quite different from Miss Stephenson, Mr. Coleman, and Miss Collins. I would like to believe that whatever my style, it reflected what these teachers stood for and did for me. If I was not the superb teacher they were, I have never forgotten what the best is. And if I have never forgotten that, I never have forgotten my worst teachers, who, in a strange way, were very impactful on my developing self.

3

THREE DIAGNOSTIC ERRORS

It was in the sixties and I and a graduate assistant were returning from a meeting at a community agency to which I was a consultant. During that meeting I had made some kind of flagrant mistake which I cannot now recall. My assistant, Brian Sarata, said to me that he was surprised and impressed that I had not appeared flustered, had admitted my error, and had gotten out of the situation rather well. I said to him, "Brian, among my few virtues are being able to own up to my mistakes and to capitalize on them, except, of course, when I have an argument with Esther" (my late wife whose track record for being right during fifty years of marriage was irritatingly high). I then went on to relate to him four experiences which well prepared me to teach Humbleness 101 and Modesty 102. The first was years before during a therapeutic hour when my psychoanalyst started a session by saying, "Two weeks ago I said something to you I should not have said. I was wrong." I was flabbergasted. In all that I read about psychoanalysis, and all I had heard about psychoanalysts and other types of therapists, the admission of errors was never even hinted at. Therapists were all knowing sages of the interpersonal incapable of making mistakes! What Dr. Mittelmann said and did that day forever influenced me. It was O.K. not only to admit to being wrong but that admission of error could have the effect of solidifying a relationship, of making it easier for others to own up to their mistakes, i.e., join the human race.

There was, as there always is, a history to what I said to Brian, and it has to do with three clinical cases where I had goofed but from which I learned lessons very much a part of my point of view. Briefly put, the lessons can be put this way:

1. Do not be taken in by first impressions regardless of their impact. First impressions or appearances are *not* to be disregarded, just distrusted, reactions consciously to be examined. That applies to individuals and settings. I am reminded here of Mrs. T who was an elementary school teacher in an inner city school where I was to be a consultant. In my initial group meeting with the teachers I quickly decided that she was a racist (and I subsequently had no reason to change my mind). The thought of spending time in her classroom was quite upsetting and it took me at least three weeks before I screwed up my courage to go into her classroom, expecting that I would be appalled at how she handled her students, and worrying that I would not be able to avoid explosions in our discussions which probably would mean terminating my agreement with the school. Mrs. T. was in her sixties, frail, intimidating, and sour. What I observed was as inventive, stimulating, fair, *and* demanding a teacher as I had ever seen. After numerous observations it became apparent to me that the only way I could explain what I saw was that, despite her racist views, it was as if she said to herself and implicitly conveyed to the children, "I do not care who you are and what you are, you are going to meet my standards of performance and I am going to help you, you can count on it." Her's was the only class, year in year out, in that school where students met or exceeded national achievement test norms. In short, my initial impressions were both right and (very) wrong.

2. However inadequate an individual appears, however obvious his or her deficits, do not blithely pass over the *possibility* that there may be someone who possesses the drive, ingenuity, and interpersonal skills to help that individual be more adequate. That is also true for settings (e.g., schools) which appear so disorganized, so rampant with conflict, seemingly so intractable to desired change as to cause you to throw up your hands and run for the exit. You may not want to deal with such a mess but it does not follow that there is no one with the motivation, ideas, hope, and organizational-interpersonal "street smarts" who could make it less messy. You may see only deficits, someone else may see usable assets. Hopelessness is one of the most effective barriers to seeking or participating in the change process. Hope is certainly no universal solvent but it is one of the necessary spurs to initiating change. When you hear yourself concluding that an individual or setting is beyond repair, you have automatically ruled out doing anything about it. You sustain, indeed reinforce, a bad situation by accepting "reality." Your reality is not everybody's reality.

3. It should be basic to your stance that the decision to initiate or not to initiate the change process should be based on other than a

superficial immersion and understanding of the context you seek to change. That decision cannot (should not) be made in your bailiwick, your office, your turf. However wise and knowledgeable we may be, there is no good substitute for what we can learn from experiencing the context containing the problems about which we have been asked to be of help.

 4. If a year from now your understanding of the change process is what it is today, you have not been thinking, you need a dose of Vitamin H (Humbleness).

 On the surface the three cases that follow do not involve schools but if you want to comprehend the development of my point of view about school change, these three cases are crucial. For example, I am frequently cited for my prediction and explanation of the new math disaster of the sixties, about which I wrote in *The Culture of the School and the Problem of Change* (1982). That was possible because (a) Esther took a workshop on the new math given for parents by our school system and (b) I sat in on the five day summer workshop for teachers (in an adjoining town) who were going to teach the new math when the new school year began. To be in on the first act of a tragedy is quite an experience. Unfortunately, the experts who developed the new math and whose disciples ran the workshops learned nothing. It did provide grist for their mill for scapegoating teachers. When in doubt project blame outward! Too many reformers, then and since, make that mistake. You cannot learn from mistakes you have not acknowledged. That may be protective of pride but it sure as hell short circuits learning.

 What I have just said explains why in almost everything I have written about school change I have emphasized that in the modal classroom in the modal school acknowledging ignorance by students and teachers is psychologically near impossible, and in the case of students the fear of making a mistake and being regarded as stupid renders them silent. Freud said that dreams are the royal road to the unconscious. Making and acknowledging mistakes is one of the roads to personal and professional change and in the case of students that requires a classroom context that does not penalize mistakes, that regards mistakes as an opportunity to learn. That is what I learned from Dr. Mittelmann to whom I was sent by one of my mentors who said, "He will be easy on you." He was not easy, he was truthful without being critical, supportive without being indulgent, and patient without ever manifesting frustration at my meanderings and resistances. He was a model teacher.

At its best, a clinical case report forces you to review and reevaluate your clinical experience because the report contains description and interpretation that either are discrepant with your experience or that seem to provide a key to clinical phenomena that have puzzled you.[1] A single case within a series of cases may not prove anything definitive (depending on what you mean by "proof"), but it can alter a field or open a new one. Itard's (Lane, 1976) report on Victor, Freud's (1925) report on Little Hans, and Kanner's (1943) report on a small number of autistic children are examples of case reports the reverberations from which can still be felt. I have no doubt that Blom's (Blom, 1979–80; Sarason & Doris, 1979) report on Heather will have a long life because of the challenges it poses for the way most people, professional and lay, think about mental retardation.

For my purposes here, Itard's report is most relevant because he failed in his goal to rehabilitate Victor. But the interest that his report has had across two centuries stems less from the fact of failure and more from its detailed, compelling, poignant descriptions about the effort to relate to and to change another human being. Indeed, his descriptions are so clear that it is not at all difficult to identify with each of the actors in the drama. And by the time one has finished reading the account, one is more impressed with what was accomplished than with what was not accomplished. One comes away inspired by Itard's persistence and ingenuity, by a doggedness that would not admit of the possibility that the Wild Boy of Aveyron could not be fully socialized and made into whatever was a normal French youngster of the time. Itard was disappointed with what he accomplished, but today we can only marvel at how much Victor changed from what he was when he was captured in the woods. Granted that Itard fell far short of the mark, and granted that the philosophical-conceptual basis for seizing the opportunity to work with Victor was wildly optimistic in its view of human perfectibility, but the following question remains: What are the conditions within which devotion and unflagging motivation will overcome what appear to be insuperable barriers? It is that question to which the following cases are relevant. If these cases do not flatter my self-image as diagnostician, I shall forever be grateful for what I learned from these errors.

---

[1] The text beginning with this sentence and continuing to the end of this chapter is reprinted from *Psychology and Mental Retardation: Perspectives in Change* (pp. 89–100), 1985. Austin, TX: Pro-Ed. Copyright by Seymour Sarason.

CASE 1

There were certain times during the week when "children" could be admitted to the Southbury Training School. Our offices were in the administration building, situated so that we could see the cars pull up to the entrance to deposit the child and the adult (or adults). Occasionally, case material was sent to us before admission, allowing us to make some preliminary judgments about a suitable cottage placement. More often than not, the case material accompanied the child on admission, and we had to make some quick decisions about cottage placement. We took cottage placement seriously because being in a "high grade" or "middle grade" or "low grade" cottage was a difference that made a difference. We could, of course, later change a placement, but that could bring in its wake complications for child and staff.

It was an admission day. A car pulled up and from the back seat emerged a rather large man carrying cradle-like in his arms what from our windows looked like an unusually large child of three or four years of age. But we knew that it could not be a child that young because at that time children had to be at least six years of age to be admitted. We went to the front door of the building to greet the party and only then could we see that what we had thought was a young child was in fact a much older male. The accompanying material (quite sparse) indicated that he was 30 years of age and had been taken care of from birth by his mother, who had recently died. The father had died years before. Why was he being carried like a baby? He was as gnarled and contorted, as muscularly and neurologically involved, as any case of cerebral palsy I had ever seen—and Southbury had loads of such cases. His body was constantly moving; he was almost constantly drooling; whenever he attempted what seemed to be a purposeful movement, the diffuseness of his body movement became more intense and widespread; and his disfigured face had a wild, "monster-like" quality to it. I looked at this man with puzzlement because I could not understand why he had not been institutionalized earlier. What little material was in the folder that accompanied him indicated that the mother had been opposed to institutionalization. If I was puzzled about that, I was not puzzled about the cottage in which he should be placed: a large, middle-grade cottage that, in truth, had as many low- as middle-grade individuals. Basically, it was a custodial cottage, unrelated to the institution's educational program. Mr. Humphrey (that was his name) was no candidate for an educational program. Of that I was sure!

It was our practice to do a formal psychological assessment within a few days after admission in order to make a final judgment about cottage placement, suitability for programs in the academic school, work assignment, special needs and cautions, etc. In the case of Mr. Humphrey, there was no need, I decided, to do an early assessment. Indeed, I was relieved that there was no particular point to a psychologic assessment in this instance. Those days were quite busy—the opening of South-bury's doors stimulated a stream of admissions (including children from schools that closed their special classes so that their occupants could be sent to Southbury where they became legal and financial wards of the state). Three weeks later, I was walking past the cottage in which Mr. Humphrey had been placed, and Mr. Rooney, the cottage "father" (there was no "mother" in that cottage) came out. Mr. Rooney was one of my favorite people and we began to talk about this and that and the state of the world. I remembered that we had not done an assessment of Mr. Humphrey, and I asked Mr. Rooney how he was doing. Mr. Rooney replied: "Now *there* is a smart person. He can read and he understands everything." I was surprised and my face must have shown it because Mr. Rooney, no shrinking violet and a rather good "natural" clinician, invited me to a demonstration of Mr. Humphrey's abilities. Inside the cottage, Mr. Humphrey was lying on the seat of a wheelchair; i.e., he was lying on the seat as if it were a bed. Mr. Rooney left us for a moment and soon returned with a checkerboard in each square of which was a letter of the alphabet, i.e., the top first square had a large A, the second a B, and so forth. The checkerboard had been one of the things accom-panying Mr. Humphrey to Southbury. "Now," Mr. Rooney said, "you ask him a question that requires a one-word answer, then move your finger slowly from one letter to the next and when you have reached the first letter in the answer he will let you know, and you do that for each letter in the answer." How could he let me know if he was in constant motion and if his attempts at vocalization were unintelligible and only increased the level of diffuse bodily activity? I cannot remember what question I put to him, but I do remember that when my finger reached the square containing the first letter of the answer, immediately it was obvious that that was part of the answer—his facial and bodily respons-es were like a pinball machine gone berserk. He did know the answer to that first question and to almost all of the subsequent ones. I was dumb-founded and I felt stupid, guilty, and quite humble.

I shall not dwell on my diagnostic mistake, which is as unforgivable as it is understandable. I should have known not to go by appearances, or by what a person cannot do, but rather by what a person can *learn* to do, i.e., by signs of potential assets rather than by exclusive reliance on deficits. I had reacted to Mr. Humphrey as if he were a thing, not a per-son. Instead of arousing my curiosity, challenging me to figure out how

I might relate to this individual, forcing me to keep separate what I was assuming from what was factual, Mr. Humphrey's appearance short-circuited the relationship between what I ordinarily believed and practiced. To someone like me, for whom Itard was a major figure in the pantheon of gods, my response to Mr. Humphrey was, to indulge understatement, quite humbling.

Once I was able to overcome (in part at least) my feelings of stupidity, guilt, and inconsistency, I realized that there were questions far more important than my diagnostic acumen. *How did the mother manage to accomplish what she did? What kept her going? What did she recognize in the infant as sparks that could ignite the fires that power learning? What was her theory and in what relation did this stand to her practices? What could we have learned if we had the opportunity to follow and study Mrs. Humphrey in the rearing of her son?* More about the last question after the other two cases are presented.

CASE 2

Not long after I left Southbury to come to Yale a friend-colleague asked me if I would evaluate his son, who was two years of age. My friend was a neuropsychiatrist who was known for two characteristics: He was top flight in his field of specialization, and he was quite unstable, if not volatile. I always found him to be strange, giving, sensitive, and internally pressured. His son had clear abnormalities at birth, and a comprehensive diagnostic workup at Yale revealed massive brain damage. My friend refused to accept the clear implication that the child was and would always be mentally retarded, requiring special management throughout life. He was so disdainful of the Yale workup that he took the boy for an independent workup to a well-known Boston center. Their conclusions confirmed the Yale findings, but they were more explicit about the severe restrictions the child's condition put on his future development. He was and would always be severely retarded. I had been told all of this by several people who were concerned not only about the father's inability to accept the findings but also about the obsessive quality with which he searched the literature for what could be done to help his son. So, when he asked me to see his son, my heart sank because I had every reason to believe that nothing I could find or recommend would be what he wanted to hear. I tried to tell him that, but to no avail. We agreed that my wife and I would visit his home the following Sunday and that I would make it my business to observe his son in the context of home and family. (There was an older child, a girl of six years of age who was both bright and pretty.) Three things immediately struck me when I first saw the boy: the speed with which he was getting around the living room on hands and knees (I knew he was not yet walking); the impression of constant movement his actions conveyed, what some people then would have called "organic drivenness"; and the size of his head, which not only was large but seemed to be as large as the rest of his body. I distinctly remember saying to myself: "If my head was as large as his, I would be unable to stand erect." We visited for a couple of hours. The boy had no speech, never seemed to be at rest, and did not respond to my attempts to gain his attention or to interact with him. His sister was the only person to whom he seemed to respond, by following her wherever she went. I saw nothing to contradict the conclusion that the boy was and would always be severely retarded. I told this to the father. If, I said, at maturity the boy had a mental age of six or seven, I would be somewhat surprised. Needless to say, the father did not hear this with enthusiasm. He was polite, thanked me, and, I think, knew that I felt very badly about having to say what I did. It was obvious that he was not about to accept my conclusions any more than he had accepted earlier ones. I never spoke to him again about his son. In fact, I hardly ever saw him. But through the collegial grapevine, I learned that he devoted a lot of time to the boy, including the administration of special medications that would stimulate development. The marriage had been a rocky one and culminated in divorce, the father continuing to maintain a close relationship with his son. From the rare times I saw him, he seemed to have become more unstable and volatile, an impression that the grapevine substantiated. He remarried, and one day a few years later, he threatened his second wife with a gun. She managed to get the police, and when he saw them arrive, he killed himself. Not everyone was surprised, but everyone was shocked. The local papers had a field day. In the course of conversation with someone who had been the father's neighbor, I asked about the son. I was told that he was headed for the state university. He went and was graduated from the university.

It was small solace to me that my diagnostic conclusions and predictions were as erroneous as those emanating from prestigious centers in New Haven and Boston. Countless times I have tried to replay my visit and observations in order to see whether I had overlooked or misinterpreted something, whether the mind-set with which I came to the visit blinded me to the child's potential. I had to conclude that I had made an error the significance of which was quite ambiguous. Was the error rooted in a faulty understanding of the developmental dynamics of brain-behavior relationships? Or was the error a function of the failure seriously to try anything—pharmacologic or psychologic—to test (i.e., challenge) the diagnosis? Were the father's efforts irrelevant to the outcome? How could we answer that question without knowing what the father did pharmacologically and psychologically? I could not conclude that his efforts were irrelevant to the outcome. As in the case of Mr. Humphrey, we lacked crucial information. Aside from the diagnoses and prognoses, the one thing we knew was that this father's obsessions led him to actions and interactions that few seriously retarded persons experience.

CASE 3

Not long after I had observed the boy in Case 2, a colleague called to ask if I would, for purposes of assessment, visit a retarded five-year-old boy in a residential nursery in another state. A friend of my colleague, the boy's grandfather, requested an evaluation because the nursery felt that the boy, Andrew, should be moved to another setting. I was reluctant to make the trip and told my colleague that I would prefer seeing the boy in New Haven. This, it turned out, was not possible for several reasons. The boy's parents had been divorced two or three years earlier, and the father had never visited the nursery; the mother, who lived hundreds of miles away, visited once or twice a year during her shopping expeditions to New York; and the grandfather, who footed all the boy's bills including my fee, had never visited the boy in the nursery. The grandfather had arranged for a pediatrician in the local community to be available to Andrew. Again reluctantly, I agreed to visit.

I arranged to meet with the pediatrician before going to the nursery. He told me that Andrew had had a mild polio attack from which he had recovered; there was some nonspecific brain damage associated with a "sugar-loaf" shaped skull and with an awkward gait and other motor movements. Andrew was a nice, likable, obviously retarded child.

The nursery was a large ranch house in a residential neighborhood. I rang the bell, and the door was soon opened by a young boy who, from the pediatrician's description, had to be Andrew. He did have a markedly pointy skull and seemed both distracted and anxious. He said something that was hard for me to comprehend because his articulation was not clear, and he ran back into the house and quickly returned with the chief nurse. The nurse and I talked for a while in one corner of a large living room. Andrew was almost always in sight, not because he was asked to be but, it seemed, because he did not want to be far from the nurse. She told me that Andrew was the only ambulatory child in the nursery, all the others being bed patients. She, it turned out, was the one prodding the grandfather to move the boy to a more socially appropriate and intellectually stimulating environment. She obviously liked Andrew and would miss him terribly, but she could not justify his continued residence there. In fact, she asserted, it had become harmful to his development because there literally was no one there, aside from her, with whom he could have a relationship. After indicating that from time to time she had taken Andrew for a visit to her apartment (she was unmarried), she related an incident from several months earlier. She had to go to the local drugstore for supplies and, for the first time, took Andrew with her. She had started to go into the drugstore when she became aware that Andrew was not at her side. She looked back and there was Andrew, paralyzed by fright and unable to take a step forward or backward. Instantly she realized that Andrew had never been in a store and was fearful of what awaited there. Aside from the handful of times he had been in her apartment, Andrew had not been out of the nursery and its immediate environs. She took him by the hand, went back to the car, and returned to the nursery. That incident was crucial in leading her to contact the grandfather to convince him to consider placing Andrew elsewhere.

Prior to testing, I tried to interact with Andrew. For one thing, I had trouble making out what he said. No less interfering was his clear reluctance about interacting with me. It seemed to be a reluctance powered by anxiety, which at the time mystified me, although the thought did occur to me that Andrew did not view my visit as being in his best interests. There was something very likable and pathetic about him. As soon as I tried to administer some intelligence test items, his anxiety noticeably increased and, in the most indirect ways, he let me know that he wanted no part of what was going on. It was as if he sensed that I was somebody who could be harmful to him. He whimpered, became tearful, and once or twice got up from his chair to depart. I stopped my efforts at formal testing. I had already concluded that Andrew was markedly retarded, although I did not know how seriously. I had also concluded that, regardless of the degree of retardation, this nursery placement had become dramatically counterproductive and that he had to be placed elsewhere. Finally, and crucially, what concerned me most was the implications of the fact that Andrew had one and only one significant relationship with another human being: the nurse. Psychologically, she was his mother. That is the way he related to her and she felt about him. Theirs was not a nurse-child relationship. I related all of this in a report to the grandfather and urged that it was essential that the nurse accompany Andrew to the new setting and stay with him until he had made some kind of positive adjustment. The thought that Andrew would be picked up at the nursery and taken (psychologically alone) to a new setting interfered with my sleep! I received no reply from the grandfather.

A year or so later, my colleague called me up to say that the grandfather was requesting another evaluation. The nurse, my colleague related, had been persuaded by the grandfather to give up her job and devote her time and energies to caring for Andrew. He had been placed in a public school and the immediate question was: *Should he be promoted to the first grade, which the school recommended?*

I did not need to be urged to visit the nurse and Andrew. Obviously, somebody was selling somebody else a bill of goods! What fool or knave was recommending that the Andrew I had seen a year or so earlier was ready for first grade? The nurse had moved into a garden apartment development. When I steered my car into the development, I had to go at about one mile an hour because the area seemed to consist of more children than blades of grass. I parked the car very near their apartment and, as soon as I got out of the car, a young boy approached. It was Andrew, but what a different Andrew! There was that pointy skull, his motor movements were not graceful but they were far more smooth than when I had first seen him, he spoke with a clarity that amazed me, and he seemed to know and to be on very good terms with the other children. He guided me to the apartment, chit-chatting with me. However, even in those early moments, I sensed that he was very ambivalent about my visit, as if he wanted to be his usual giving self but was suspicious about what my agenda was. This became more noticeable later when I tried to test him and, again, I stopped because it seemed upsetting to him. We did enough to establish he was within the normal range. Whereas on my first visit there was a question about how seriously retarded he was, the question now in my mind was how bright he might be. If on my first visit I intuited a mother-child relationship, I did not have to resort to intuition on my second visit a year or so later. She was a mother constantly seeking ways to stimulate the boy and to help him overcome a pervasive anxiety and self-depreciatory tendency. She told me that within a year or so she would like to move south and take Andrew with her. What did I think? I, of course, said that Andrew should go where she goes. As for promotion to the first grade: of course. Two years later I received a call from the nurse. She and Andrew had moved south and they were both happy and doing well. The reason for the call was that Andrew's mother had visited a number of times in the past years, developed a real interest in the "new" Andrew, and now wanted him to come live with her. How should the nurse respond? I was explicit in recommending that she try to avoid such a change. I also wrote this to the grandfather.

I shall assume that no reader will accuse me of stating or implying that parental love, devotion, and energy are unmixed blessings and that, if these characteristics could be appropriately channeled, scads of retarded persons would become "unretarded." Nor do I wish anyone to conclude that parents possess knowledge and wisdom that professionals do not, as if parents possess a productive interpersonal sensitivity and "natural" clinical acumen that is in short supply among professionals. These are arguable issues, but they are irrelevant to the reasons why I have presented these cases. The first reason why I have presented the three cases is that they raise this question: How frequent are these kinds of cases? Far more often than not, we write about our successes, not our mistakes. Also, we feel more secure in our explanations of our successes than of our failures. After all, our successes presumably confirm us as thinkers and doers; our failures clearly say that we have earned the right to be humble. The second reason is to suggest that the unusual degree of involvement and commitment demonstrated in these cases is rare among parents. Their commitment and involvement are far from typical; rather they are very atypical and, therefore, there is all the more reason to focus on them. But it might be argued, I am confusing rare with infrequent. That is to say, the outcomes associated (not in any simple cause-and-effect way) with such parental dedication may not be as rare as I am suggesting. They certainly are not frequent, but, the argument might continue, they are less rare than published cases would indicate. Parents of these children rarely write up their experience, and for obvious reasons professionals are hardly in a position to see such cases. There is a difference between incidence and prevalence; the incidence of these kinds of cases may be greater than their prevalence in the literature suggests.

But why is such parental dedication rare or infrequent? That question brings us to the third reason for presenting these cases: Professional and societal conceptions of attitudes toward the biologic basis of severe mental retardation and its implications for prognosis are obstacles in the way of parental activity and creativity. If in diverse ways a parent is told that his or her child has a damaged brain and that there are very definite limits to what can be expected developmentally, and if these communications are unaccompanied by any concrete suggestions about how to stimulate and manage the child in regard to eating, sleeping, playing, crying, vocalizing, locomoting, etc., it is not surprising that these parents often are fearful, feel helpless, and are uncreative. I have known scores of parents at or around the time they took their severely retarded infant or young child home from the clinic or hospital after a definitive diagnosis has been made. As one of them said, summing up beautifully what almost all such parents experience: "I came home with a child and a diagnosis.

But as soon as we opened the door and entered the apartment, the question popped into and remained in my head: What do I do *now*, this minute, the next hour, tonight at bedtime? No one told me anything about those kinds of very practical questions." That brings us to the fourth reason: Brain-behavior relationships have to be conceptualized within a complicated matrix of relationships bearing the stamps of the societal attitudes and their history; the status, knowledge, and influence of the professionals involved; individual experiences among parents; and the degree of compatible matching between characteristics of the child and the capabilities, interests, and temperament of the parent. So, today we know, to a degree that Itard could not, how what went on between Itard and Victor is comprehensible only in terms of what happened and was continuing to happen in France, a society in which changes in the social order had altered theories and practices about what the human animal was and could be. That is as true for how we theorize and act today as it was in Itard's time. For example, today it is most unusual for a retarded child to be observed on his or her turf, i.e., in the context of home and family. A very elaborate rationale can be developed to support the practice of the child being seen on the professional's turf. That rationale has, among other things, an economic basis that tends to be downplayed—obviously you can see more patients by schedule in your office than if you visited them in their homes. But the practice also rests on the assumption that you can validly deduce what is going on in the home from what you are told and what you observe in the office. In fact, the available evidence suggests that acting on that assumption can create as many problems as it may ameliorate. The fact is that in the past half-century an enormous change has occurred in terms of where patients are seen, the number and variety of professionals who will see them, and the economic factors associated with these changes. We would like to believe that this change is due to advances in knowledge and technology brought about solely because they are in the best interest of patients (independent of economic considerations), the self-interest of professionals and the societal zeitgeist. But that is never the case, however much we all collude in the myth that it is. I would maintain that the failure to observe the retarded child in the context of the home and family leads us frequently to erroneous conclusions the detection and correction of which are made difficult by current practice. Moreover, this failure has robbed us of opportunities to be more helpful than we have been.

The final reason I presented the three cases is that they mightily influenced and altered my outlook on mental retardation and our society. This reason is best conveyed in the following story. Not long after I saw the last of the three, I received a call from someone in charge of a foundation devoted to mental retardation that was now seeking to have national impact. The person wanted to meet with me to get my views on what I considered the important problems in the field—the problems that the foundation ought to address. We met twice, each time for several hours. I iterated and reiterated the following points:

1. To my knowledge, there has not been a single longitudinal study of retarded infants.
2. By longitudinal, I mean periodic visits made to the home during which systematic observations are made of the child and family members. In addition, these members are interviewed, with the overarching goal of describing and understanding family structure and dynamics as they conceivably impinge on the infant's or child's behavior and development. (It may sound immodest, but I understood and articulated the conceptual basis of family therapy long before that clinical field became fashionable. That one could understand and program for *any* child without secure knowledge of home and family made as much sense as studying the earth as if the sun did not exist.)
3. Longitudinal studies might provide us with important clues about individual differences in development and about child-environment relationships that either positively or adversely affect a child's progress. If we know anything about brain-behavior relationships, it is how risky it is to predict one from the other and that we must look to other types of interactions to better explain individual differences.
4. When will we begin to take seriously the fact that whatever the justifications for longitudinal studies, they are no less applicable to the area of mental retardation than to normal development?
5. Longitudinal studies are not easy to carry out, they are beset with diverse methodologic problems, they are conducted in a world we cannot control, and they are not panaceas for our ignorance. But, potentially, and at their best, they force us to alter our thinking and actions.

I told this person about my three diagnostic errors and how they drove me to questions that could only be studied by a longitudinal approach. I concluded by saying that the absence of these studies said far more about societal and professional attitudes than it did about their importance for a better understanding of different conditions giving rise to mental retardation. He was not impressed. But he asked me to send him an outline of the kind of study I was recommending. I did, but never heard from him. That was in 1954. Today, the situation has not changed. In fairness to this man, I should point out that he was (and is) not alone in his lack of enthusiasm. For a period of 10 years (beginning around

1954), I was a member of different advisory committees to the National Institute of Mental Health on funding for research grants. Those were years when longitudinal ("womb to the tomb," as we called them) studies were fashionable. Not one research proposal demonstrated an interest in mental retardation. Mental retardation has never been in the mainstream of the mental health fields, a fact not explainable in terms of the number of afflicted individuals, their impact on their families (and vice versa), the economic costs, the moral sensitivity of the society, or the challenge this field poses to theory, research, and practice.

4

THE UNEDUCATED

No one will deny that you cannot describe and/or understand schools without coming to grips with tests: their nature, uses, and attitudes toward them on the part of those being tested and those who use their results. Long before I became interested in school change my training and professional experience had convinced me of several things. First, most people, and even psychologists who should know better, use test results as if they reflect little or nothing about the interpersonal or group context in which those results were obtained, as if the results "mea- sured" an uncontaminated essence. That is nonsense, of course, but in "real life" that nonsense is by no means infrequent. Second, in school settings tests are rarely used to understand individuals but rather to make decisions about placement. There is nothing wrong with that as long as you are aware that your goal is not understanding, and it is that aware- ness that is so frequently absent. Test scores are just that: numbers the psychological significance of which are never self-evident. And the problem is not "solved" by collecting several test scores from an individ- ual. I will never forget what a teacher of a gifted class (IQs of 140 or above) said to me: "Each of these kids has an astronomical IQ but some are smart and some are dense, some use what God gave them, others cannot, some require direction and support while with others you get out of their way and they find their way." Third, the correlation between the level and quality of problem solving in the testing situation and level and quality in naturally occurring, non-testing situations is far from perfect.

It was these conclusions that stimulated me to initiate a long term project on the role of test and general anxiety in elementary school chil- dren. If my hypotheses were proved correct, we would be able to pro- vide educators with information useful for understanding individual children. At the least, that information could prevent them from uncritically accepting intelligence and achievement test scores as having the meaning they unreflectively ascribed to those scores. Our hypotheses received robust confirmation, i.e., we were able to demonstrate the conditions in which the performance of high anxious children was negatively affected, as well as the conditions in which their performance was the same as or even exceeded that of low anxious children. That research was reported in numerous articles, monographs, and a book.

That research had absolutely no practical influence on anybody or any school practice. In the several decades since that research I never met a teacher, administrator, or a teacher of teachers who had ever heard of the research we did over twelve years. That did not surprise me because during the time we were carrying out that research, Burton Blatt and I had begun to examine teacher preparatory programs and we quickly learned that these programs hardly prepared their students for how they should understand and deal with the individual differences among students in their classrooms. That may sound both strange and harsh to some readers in which case I urge them to do what Dr. Blatt and I did: we talked to scads of new teachers, asking them how they were prepared to deal with the more obvious kinds of individual differences any classroom contains, e.g., the shy, or impulsive, or dependent, or hyperactive, or anxious, or aggressive, or daydreaming child. To deal with such children requires more than pinning a label on them. To deal with them means that you have some idea of the whys of their behavior on the basis of which you adopt an action strategy that will help them acquire internal controls over their self-defeating behavior. That kind of understanding is not something preparatory programs do, or do well. Their emphasis is on how you organize and deal with *groups* of children; understanding individuals is on the back, unlit burner. By virtue of the anxiety project I spent hundreds of hours in scores of classrooms. Generally speaking, the teachers were bright and highly motivated but I had to conclude that most of them were psychologically unsophisticated. I shall have more to say about this later in this book. I have brought it up here to indicate that before school change became my central concern I already had a particular point of view: schools can be desirably changed by a number of strategies but the degree of change will be small if preparatory programs are not drastically revamped.

The above are glimpses of the obvious noted by many people before I came on the scene. With one exception: the problematic relationship between level and quality of performance in formal testing situations and level and quality in naturally occurring situations. If that relationship is far from perfect, it requires us—I would argue that it obliges us—

to ask this question about performance in the formal testing situation: under what conditions can the level and quality of test performance be improved? Put in another way, before we accept performance in the testing situation as a "true" indicator of the capacity to learn, should we not create and alter conditions to determine whether our initial conclusion is as valid as we think? In the course of a day every teacher makes decisions about what children can and cannot do. Those decisions may be made on the basis of knowledge of test scores provided the teacher or on the basis of tests he or she gives or the answers children give to oral questions. It is one thing to use such data, it is quite another thing to accept such data as indicative of capacity to learn. That, of course, is what the nature-nurture, heredity-environment controversy has always been about. What happens when you change the conditions of learning? I am not arguing that heredity is more or less important than environment. Such an argument is a red herring because it in no way absolves us from determining in this or that instance whether the test performance we have observed would have the same quality and level as performance outside the testing situation.

This issue was forced on me when I worked in an institution for the education and training of mentally retarded individuals. I did not grasp its general significance, especially for education, until 1954 when I had already been at Yale for eight years. It was then that I read Ginzberg and Bray's *The Uneducated* (1953). That book, based on analysis of and experience with the test and non-test performance of World War II recruits, confirmed what I had learned from my clinical experience. But it did one other thing, it described an educational experiment that required drastically altering the conditions of learning, with results that were, to say the least, very instructive, I would say startling. What I learned from that book, together with my own experience, made me confront what should have been obvious but was not: classrooms and schools were not places where alterations in the conditions of learning were or would be warmly embraced. They were places where things were done the way they had always been done, and changing them would be, to indulge understatement, very difficult if only because both educators and the general public agreed that the way classrooms and schools were organized and run was the best way to achieve educational goals. They (we) had, so to speak, inherited a tradition that seemed right, natural, and proper. If it ain't broke, don't fix it. It was broke then and it is, as all of us now know, more broke today. I was beginning to formulate interrelated conceptions that a decade and a half later were contained in my book *The Culture of the School and the Problem of Change* (1971/1982).

At this point it is appropriate to say that what we call a point of view has numerous sources each of which may have impact (or emerges) at different times in your life and, not infrequently, remain apart, unconnected with other sources until in the strange ways of the human mind "connections" are made. In my case reading has been a major vehicle for making connections. I am a somewhat indiscriminate reader but it has paid off because sometimes I am reading an article or book ostensibly unrelated to what are my major interests and I become aware that the writer is describing an event, or posing a problem, having kinship to my concerns. Unreflectively, I learned early on to be set to see similarities between events and ideas that on the surface appeared to be unrelated. So, for example, late in my career I became interested in the governance of schools, i.e., its inadequacies and resistance to change. For years I had read a fair amount about the constitutional convention of 1787: why that convention was necessary, the issues with which it struggled, and the compromises that got worked out. But that reading was, so to speak, off by itself in my head. When school change became my central interest, I found myself reading (for recreation!) Clinton Rossiter's *1787: The Grand Convention* (1966), a historical account that reads like a gripping novel. "Suddenly" I saw connections I never could have imagined, and those connections will be apparent to anyone who has read my books on school change.

As I read what I have just written I am aware that I am reluctant to say something because I may appear to be presumptuous. But if I am to convey how and why I have the point of view I hold, I have to overcome my reluctance. Without pretending to know its origins, I have, in my career years at least, always believed that what I have experienced and thought has general significance, i.e., it is applicable to arenas which I do not know or have experience with, that I should not be intimidated from assuming that what I have experienced and learned must not stay within the narrow confines of those experiences. Because different arenas have different labels and ostensibly circumscribed boundaries does not mean that what I have learned in one arena *ipso facto* means that I cannot and should not transfer that learning to "alien" arenas. That, I know, is a dangerous belief, a fact I never forgot at the same time that it has not prevented me from seeking to make those transfers. Now, dear reader, you may understand why I chose as the first of my writings to be reprinted in this book a chapter titled "You Know More Than You Think and More Than They Give You Credit For." Yes, students in a teacher preparatory program have a lot of experiential assets but they intimidate themselves and are intimidated by others from transferring those assets. They are students. They are also potential teachers of their teachers. It is a situation in which self perception and the perception of that self by others collude to make transfer of experience virtually impossible.

PROBLEM SOLVING IN NONTESTING SITUATIONS

How do you account for the fact that the behavior sampled and observed in a formal testing situation can be so different from problem-solving behavior in a nontesting situation?[1] What has permitted us to assume that the style and level of performance in a formal testing situation predicts style and level in a nontesting situation? The issue, I must emphasize, does not involve prediction from one testing situation to another (e.g., from an intelligence test to grades or achievement tests). Indeed, there is a prior issue: Why has there been such a paucity of research on problem solving in naturally occurring situations? The answer, in brief, is that it is very hard to conduct such research. Besides, educators and psychologists needed means to make relatively quick judgments about many, many individuals. In short, society (through its representatives—educators, psychologists, and social policymakers) defined the problem in terms of the needs of a mass society, and one of those needs was for relatively quick and efficient means to get information about those who comprised that mass society (e.g., schoolchildren). This definition was not in itself unjustified during the decades of a burgeoning population, unprecedented waves of immigration, the legitimation of compulsory education, and the transformation of schools into bureaucratic organizations. But in a strictly scientific or logical sense, these factors did not excuse the absence of research on the validity of the assumption that scores on formal tests permitted prediction of problem-solving ability in nontesting situations. If that assumption has less validity than current theory and practice require, it would have enormous consequences for current practices. It would also cast the cyclical nature-nurture controversies in a new light.

---

[1] The text beginning with this sentence and continuing to the end of this chapter is reprinted from *Psychology and Mental Retardation: Perspectives in Change* (pp. 102–117), 1985. Austin, TX: Pro-Ed. Copyright by Seymour Sarason.

THE UNEDUCATED

An article I wrote in the early forties (Sarason, 1944) very briefly raised the issue of the relationship between problem solving in formal and naturally occurring situations:

> A more recent manifestation of the limitations of the intelligence test results is the number of so-called defectives who have not only successfully adjusted to the Armed Services' program but who also have become noncommissioned officers and in some instances been cited for bravery. While it is true that there are many defectives who have been inadequate in the Armed Services, the fact still remains that the intelligence quotient is unilluminating in regards to the reasons for success or failure of defectives of similar mental level. (p. 242)

The problematic nature of that relationship was far more dramatically described by Ginzberg and Bray in their 1953 book, *The Uneducated,* an analysis of World War II soldiers who were illiterate and/or mentally retarded by a psychometric criterion. That book never received the attention it deserved, so the fourth edition of *Psychological Problems in Mental Deficiency* (Sarason, 1969) devoted a section to the implications of their descriptions and findings. That section is reprinted here.

In 1953 Ginzberg and Bray published a book entitled *The Uneducated*. This book contained a searching and illuminating analysis of men who were rejected on the ground of mental deficiency for military service in World War II. It also contained a study of a sample of men who had been accepted by the armed services but who were illiterate or semi-illiterate. The men in this sample had been through a special education training program set up by the military. We shall discuss this book not only for the data it contains but also because we feel that it can serve as a basis for raising some of the most important research problems in the area of mental retardation.

From the beginning of selective service until the end of the war, there were 716,000 individuals who were between 18 and 37 years of age and were rejected on the grounds of mental deficiency. Some of the problems associated with the interpretation of this figure may be seen from the following quotation:

> Relatively little research has been devoted to ascertaining the number of individuals in the population who cannot meet a minimum performance criterion as workers and citizens. Some authorities estimate that approximately one per cent of the population can perform even unskilled work only under close supervision in a protective environment. It is believed that another one per cent of the population are able to work effectively

only if they have some type of special supervision. According to these estimates the percentage of persons who would not meet a minimum performance standard because of intellectual deficiency would be 2 per cent. The more than 700,000 men rejected for military service under the general heading of "mental deficiency" amounted to about 4 per cent of the men examined. On the surface this might be taken to mean that the screening standards used were somewhat tight but approximately correct. Again, however, a national average obscures the truth, for nearly 14 per cent were rejected in some states and only one-half of one per cent in others. The fact that the national rejection rate was only a little higher than the theoretical rate of true mental deficiency cannot be taken as an indication that the screening validly assessed either mental deficiency or ability to give satisfactory performance. The regional patterning of the rejections indicates that the screening assessed primarily the individual's educational background. (p. 41)

We turn to Ginzberg and Bray's study of a group of men who had been accepted by the armed services but who were illiterate or semi-illiterate. These men had been through a special education training program set up by the military, a program that became increasingly larger as the standards for acceptance into the armed forces became progressively lower. The men sent to the Special Training Units were of two kinds: those who were formally classified as illiterate and those who scored low (Group V) on the Army General Classification Test. Re the latter Ginzberg and Bray state: "These men were considered `slow learners' but in reality were mainly those who had had only a little more education that those called illiterate." The problem of illiteracy confronting the military can be seen from the following:

> More than 400,000 illiterates served within the Armed Forces during World War II. The combined group of illiterates and poorly educated who saw active duty totaled almost 700,000. To this must be added more than 700,000 additional persons, the vast majority of whom were rejected outright for military service because of serious educational deficiencies. In short, the findings which emerge are directly relevant for appraising a group of almost one and one-half million persons out of a total of 18 million registrants who were screened. Clearly we are dealing with a significant sector of the nation's manpower resources. (p. 77)

In setting up the Special Training Program certain specific goals were sought:

1. To teach the men to read at least at a fourth-grade level so that they would be able to comprehend bulletins, written orders and directives, and basic Army publications.

2. To give the men sufficient language skill so that they would be able to use and understand the everyday oral and written language necessary for getting along with officers and men.
3. To teach the men to do number work at a fourth-grade level, so they could understand their pay accounts and laundry bills, conduct their business in the PX, and perform in other situations requiring arithmetic skill.
4. To facilitate the adjustment of the men to military training and Army life.
5. To enable the men to understand in a general way why it was necessary for this country to fight a war against Germany, Japan, and Italy. (p. 69)

The maximum amount of time that an individual could remain in the course was 120 days. "Approximately 40 per cent of the men graduated in less than 30 days. Almost 80 per cent graduated in less than 60 days. Only a very few, less than 11,000 out of 255,000 graduates, remained in a Special Training Unit more than 90 days."

Let us make the following assumptions: (a) more than a few of those formally classified as illiterates were not intellectually retarded; (b) more than a few of the "slow learners" were diagnostic errors—their true IQ was above that indicated by Army test scores; (c) more than a few of the graduates did not reach the goals previously indicated and did not in fact pass the examination in reading and arithmetic required for graduation. Making the allowances indicated by these assumptions we think it not unreasonable to make the further assumption that the above figures suggest that the rate of learning of more than a few men was far beyond that which one would expect from their potential as inferred from test scores. Put in another way: the performance of more than a few was better than an evaluation of the potential or capacity had indicated. Here again one cannot avoid inquiring about the possible factors which can produce an apparent discrepancy between capacity and functioning. In order to do so it would be helpful if one described some of the background characteristics of the sub-sample of 400 men whose Army records were scrutinized by Ginzberg and Bray:

> Our sample, it will be recalled, consisted of 400 men: 200 white and 200 Negro, half drawn from the deep South and half from the border states and the North, half inducted in the latter part of 1943, and the other half in the last six months of 1944.
>
> All but three of the 400 men were born in the United States. Since, at the time of the 1940 Census, almost three-fifths of the 1.5 million draft-age men with less than four years of schooling lived in small communities or on farms, it is not surprising to discover that most of our group

also came from rural backgrounds. Almost three-fourths were born in communities of under 5,000 population. More than one-third, however, had migrated from their birth places. When inducted, 56 per cent lived in communities under 5,000 population; a little more than a fifth were inducted from cities of more than 100,000.

Slightly under half, 179, were 20 years of age or less when inducted; 275 were 25 or less; and just under 85 per cent of the entire group were 30 or less. Thirty-nine were between the ages of 31 and 35, and 14 between 36 and 38. The median age for the entire group was 21.5 years. The median age for the Negroes, however, was 2.4 years higher than for the whites.

There were no conspicuous differences between the years of school completed by the whites and the Negroes, but the "northern" group (Camp Atterbury, Indiana) showed a higher average than the "southern" (Camp Shelby, Mississippi, and Fort Benning, Georgia) group. The men inducted in 1944 also had a higher average number of years of schooling than the group inducted in 1943. The most striking fact about the educational background of the group is that 55 per cent had completed more than four years of schooling. Only 3 per cent had never attended schooling. Almost 5 per cent had more than eight grades of schooling, and more than 25 per cent had reached at least the seventh grade. In light of these facts, it is surprising to find that of the men for whom information was available, 228 were designated as illiterate, while only 69 were classified as literate and sent to special training because of a low score on the Army General Classification Test.

More than half of the group, 226 men, had once been farmers, although less than half were farmers when inducted. Just more than two-thirds of the whites had farming backgrounds, but less than half of the Negroes. Only about a third of the Northern Negroes but almost 80 per cent of the Southern whites had been farmers at some time. (p. 80)

Not only is it clear from the above that these men came from rural areas where educational resources are generally inferior, but also that many of these men either learned nothing or did little from their schooling, or that whatever they did absorb during school was of no significance in their later lives and consequently was "unlearned." *That an individual can go through eight grades of school and then at the age of 20 appear to be illiterate may be explained in different ways; that the same individual at age 20 can in a very short period of time demonstrate a fair amount of educational progress increases the complexity of the problem. We feel that we do not have a basis for choosing among different explanations. We do feel, however, that it is justified to suggest that we are not dealing primarily with an educational problem in the narrow sense of the word but one of motivation and attitude both of which cannot be understood unless studied in the cultural matrix in which they arise.*

Table 1 contains information concerning the occupational status of the men at induction. Since we know that these men were either illiterate or low scorers on an intelligence test, it is not surprising that they had the kinds of jobs they did. However it is one thing to say this is expected and another thing to provide an explanation. In one sense it is perfectly correct to say that these men held the jobs they did because of their intellectual and educational status—these are the kinds of jobs available to them. But this brings us back to the recurring question: What are the factors determining the intellectual and educational status of these men? Again leaving this question aside—primarily because our current knowledge only permits us to suggest, as indicated earlier, what some of these factors and their interaction might be—we would like to pose another question: How does one evaluate an individual's problem-solving behavior outside of a test situation? Throughout the course of the day in the life of any individual he is presented with problems the solutions to which vary in the complexity of response they require for resolution. Not only may we commonsensically assume variation through the course of a day but also among problem-solving activities in different spheres of func-

TABLE 1. *Occupations at induction of men assigned to special training units*

Occupation	Total	White		Negro	
		North	South	North	South
Farmer	173	43	60	22	48
Non-Farm					
Laborer	90	22	13	29	26
Janitor, porter, busboy, etc.	36	3	4	21	8
Truck driver, chauffeur, auto mechanic, etc.	44	12	6	15	11
Factory operative	26	11	8	5	2
Coal miner	13	7	2	4	0
Craftsman	7	1	3	0	3
Other	11	1	4	4	2
Total non-farm	227	57	40	78	52
Grand total	400	100	100	100	100

From Ginzburg and Bray.

tioning, e.g., educational, vocational, social, etc. Although more often than not there is a fair degree of variation or "scatter" within an individual's own test performance, it is surprising how frequently we assume that the level of problem-solving behavior outside the test situation is fairly even. When it is remembered that our discussion concerns those men whose performance in the Special Training Units suggests a capacity beyond that indicated by their test scores and educational status, we think it justified to raise the possibility that the previous non-test problem-solving behavior of these men was in some spheres or activities better than their test scores or educational state suggests. Unfortunately, there have been no systematic investigations of this problem. It is apparent that there are extremely thorny problems involved in the observing, sampling, and recording of non-test problem-solving behavior—aside from the problem of quantifying samples of behavior obtained in situations over which we have no control. But if problem-solving behavior in test situations cannot be assured to be representative of all problem-solving, the lack of research in this problem can no longer be excused.

> To check on the reasonableness of our evaluation of the military performance of the uneducated, the graduates of the Special Training Units were compared with a control group consisting of average soldiers whose education and mentality were sufficient to enable them to enter basic training immediately after induction into the Army. This control group was constructed by selecting the man of the same race whose serial number was next higher than that of each man in the Special Training Unit group. If the man with the next higher number had also been assigned to a Special Training Unit, the man with the nearest higher number was selected. The control sample was not representative of the Army as a whole, but permitted a comparison between men inducted from the same localities who differed primarily with respect to their level of education.
>
> While 26 per cent of the 400 Special Training Unit men had less than four years of schooling, this was true of only one per cent of the control group. Only 2 per cent of the whites and 8 per cent of the Negroes in the Special Training Unit group, but 55 per cent of the control group had attended high school. Five per cent of the control group had attended college. Obviously, there was a significant difference in the educational background of the two groups. With respect to occupational background, the size of the communities in which they had been born, the extent to which they had migrated, and their place of residence at the time when they were inducted, however, the differences between the two groups were not substantial. . . .
>
> In order to judge the relative over-all performance of the Special Training Unit and control groups, a summary card was prepared for each man. Care was taken that the cards would contain no hint whether

the case was a Special Training Unit graduate or a control case, or whether the man was white or Negro. These cards were then shuffled and sorted into five groups: very good, good, acceptable, not acceptable, and non-chargeable. . . .

This objective comparison showed that just under a quarter of the men of the control group were very good, a third were good, another third were acceptable. Only 7 per cent of this group were not acceptable, and 3 per cent were non-chargeable. Only 9 per cent of the men of the Special Training Unit group were very good but slightly under a third were good, and almost half were acceptable. Twelve per cent were not acceptable, and 3 per cent were non-chargeable.

This comparison demonstrates conclusively that, granted our criteria, the control group contained many more very good soldiers than the Special Training Unit graduates. One of our criteria, however, was rank, and it is to be expected that those with more pre-service education would more often qualify for higher non-commissioned-officer assignments. It was, in any case, not expected that the Special Training Unit graduates would include a great many outstanding soldiers. The question was rather whether any appreciable number would perform adequately and represent a clear gain to the Army. This question is answered unequivocally. Eighty-five per cent of the graduates performed acceptably or better as compared to 90 per cent of the control group. Clearly, at a time when the Armed Forces needed men badly, they were able with a small investment to turn many illiterates and poorly educated men into acceptable soldiers. (pp. 31–32)

It should be noted that Ginzberg and Bray were quite aware of the many problems involved in utilizing and categorizing military records. Even if one were to assume that the "true" picture of the records of the men from the Special Training Units was not as favorable as Ginzberg and Bray describe, it would still be reasonable to conclude that the problem-solving behavior of many of the men was better than objective educational and test data indicated. It would repay the reader to study the 22 case records which Ginzberg and Bray present in one of the chapters in the book. In more than a few of these cases the discrepancy between problem-solving behavior in and outside the test situation is marked.

We have previously noted that the rate of learning of many of the men of the Special Training Units was surprising. Unfortunately we do not have the data or observations with which to evaluate such a conclusion. However, the following partial description of the Training Unit has some important implications for future research on this problem.

A "cadre" or staff of enlisted personnel form the basis for all instruction in the Special Training Unit. Each man has been selected for the position on the basis of his academic background as well as being a capable military instructor. With but few exceptions, all of the instructors are college graduates, many of them possess Master's degrees and a few holding various Doctor's degrees. Formerly they were connected with civilian school systems, ranging from the elementary through the college level. The unit is staffed by 26 officers qualified both academically and militarily.

Experience has shown that men of the calibre that are received in the Special Training Unit learn more and faster if they are allowed to absorb the training given with the same group of men for the entire period they are here. For that reason, men are assigned to barracks and remain there until they leave. One classroom is set up on each of the two floors of the building and provided with tables, chairs, blackboards, and other instructional aids pertaining to the type of work being covered. For a short period of time after entrance into the barracks, some men are prone to exhibit shyness due to the fact that they have never associated closely with other men.

Gradually the spirit of teamwork and cooperation are developed and within a few days the men have made an adjustment sufficient to enhance learning. Since changing from one group to another would tend to prolong the period of adjustment, that method is not employed. The military instructor, a Corporal or Sergeant, lives in the barracks with the men, eats with them and works with them and it is rare that he fails to gain the complete confidence of his men almost immediately. The instructor's job lasts 24 hours per day. During the off duty hours much of his time is taken up writing letters for the trainees or giving them advice on their personal problems. Also he will devote considerable time to additional instruction for men who are learning slower than others. (p. 81)

The implications of this excerpt might be put in a series of questions: What significance did these men attach to being sent to the Training Unit? Did they view the education they were now receiving differently than when they had previously been in school? What were the kinds and strengths of motivations engendered in these men by this experience? To what extent was their progress due to the fact that instruction was specifically geared to their needs? Were the attitudes of the instructors to the men different from those of the teachers they had in their previous school experiences? Was there a change of attitude on the part of these men toward education as a result of experiences after leaving school?

In a real sense part of the previous discussion has begged a question which, while central to any analysis of the problem of subnormality, has received surprisingly little attention. We refer here to the question: What do our available intelligence tests measure? From the previous chapter one could conclude that these tests to a marked degree measure educational opportunity and achievement. While it is encouraging to know that these tests are significantly correlated with these variables, the implications of such correlations are both far-reaching and disturbing. Since the contents and goals of our school curricula are extremely narrow in terms of the skills and contents encompassed, we are faced with the possibility that our intelligence tests measure a very restricted range of problem-solving stimuli and intellectual activities. Let us put the problem in cross-cultural terms: if one were to observe daily learning activities of an urban American 10-year-old and his counterparts among the Navaho or the Alorese, one would be struck by the differences in the kinds of problem-solving stimuli and intellectual activities which would be observed. Although the differences on the stimulus side would probably be greater than on the response side (i.e., the kinds of thinking sequences required for problem solution), the important point is that any conclusion about the "intellectual performance and capacities of 10-year-olds" would be limited and even misleading if based on the observation of any one of these cultural groups. In this connection it should be recalled that in the previous chapter it was pointed out that for many children in our culture, particularly those that have been labelled mentally retarded or slow-learners, there is reason for raising the possibility that the kind of intellectual stimuli and activities which one observes in a test or school situation may be of a different level and/or kind than one would observe outside of such a situation. In other words, there is no a priori basis for rejecting the possibility that the range of differences we observe cross-culturally may be found, to a lesser degree, between and within certain groups in our own culture if a representative sample of their problem-solving behavior was obtained. It should perhaps be made explicit that we are not equating problem-solving with all intellectual activity or thinking behavior. We stress the problem-solving situation, because it is a standardized one as in a test or one observed in a free situation, not only because of what we learn about the adequacy, level, and varieties of problem-solving behavior but also because it allows us to make inferences about kinds and characteristics of thought processes. Equally important is the fact that the problem-solving situation, being a clear instance of goal-directed or motivated behavior, gives us the possibility of studying the relationships between intellectual and personality variables.

That intelligence tests may be excellent indicators of educational achievement and poor indicators of non-test or non-academic intellectual activity is something to which the practicing clinician, particularly the one who has worked in an institutional setting, will readily attest.

More recently, in 1980, I was asked to review Jensen's (1979) *Bias in Mental Testing*. That gave me another opportunity to restate the issue. That review (Sarason, 1980) is reprinted here:

I have never regarded Arthur Jensen as a racist, and always felt the epithets hurled at him to be unwarranted. He is a very sophisticated psychologist who surveyed a vast literature and had the courage to state conclusions he knew would be unpopular and controversial. His earlier monograph created a storm that has not yet subsided. That blacks view him with disdain goes without saying, but his critics go far beyond the black community and include diverse kinds of scientists no less sophisticated than he. Unlike combatants in nature-nurture controversies of earlier times, Jensen's critics seem to accept the fact that there is overwhelming evidence that blacks score lower than whites on intelligence tests. They accept the "fact" but argue that its "truth" lies elsewhere than in the genetic framework where Jensen places it. He has been attacked on the grounds that he does not really understand genetics, that he simply does not comprehend the influence of an adverse environment (sustained over centuries) on its victims, and that not all of his "facts" are facts. For example, in his book *The Cult of the Fact,* with the subtitle *A Psychologist's Autobiographical Critique of his Discipline,* the British psychologist Liam Hudson spends somewhat less than ten percent of the book criticizing Jensen's use of a study of people with Turner's syndrome, a chromosomal anomaly in which there are forty-five chromosomes instead of the usual forty-six. According to Jensen, this is "a genetic observation, clearly identifiable under the microscope, which has quite specific consequences on cognitive processes. Such specific intellectual deficiencies are thus entirely possible without there being any specific environmental deprivations needed to account for them." Hudson demonstrates that Jensen's reporting of this study is both incomplete and misleading and that the "facts" hardly justify Jensen's conclusions. (Long before Cyril Burt's faking of data was exposed, Hudson asserted that Jensen was accepting that research too uncritically.) Although Hudson is extremely critical of Jensen, he ends the discussion with the following statement:

If my interpretation is approximately correct, and if one may be forgiven a cheap pun, Professor Jensen's impulse is to call a spade a spade. And, under the influence of this impulse, he has not merely misinterpreted evidence but also confused the purposes to which it can logically be put. One's initial reaction is that of high-minded indignation—followed quickly by a wave of fear lest you have blundered equally publicly yourself. But in the light of truths about the nature of psychology now dawning, both responses seem inadequate. Our perception of meaning in our own research is a subtle affair, related only in a complex way to fact and logic. Transgressions as blatant as those surrounding Turner's syndrome one can still condemn in the conventional way: but more baffling are the processes of selective attention that involve all of us, as soon as we relate factual evidence to some more generally interpretive theme. Jensen's article could be dismissed as lying—at least in part—outside the normal confines of scientific debate; he could be discredited as someone who has fallen from the straight ways of Science. But this, I am now convinced, would be to miss the exemplary point he unwittingly affords us. Namely, that the search for meaning in data is bound to involve all of us in distortion to a greater or lesser degree. Psychology should be pictured not as a society of good men and true, harboring the occasional malefactor, but rather, as one in which everyone is searching for sense; in which differences are largely those of temperament, tradition, allegiance and style; and in which transgression consists not so much in a clean break with professional ethics, as in an unusually high-handed, extreme or self-deceptive attempt to promote one particular view of reality at the expense of all others. On this second view, Jensen is certainly not alone, and his company may prove to be very numerous indeed.

Hudson is obviously a person who does not take himself and his field (and the "facts") with deadly seriousness. Jensen does, or seems to, and that characteristic, I suggest, is what has been most bothersome to his critics. I do not offer this as an argumentum ad hominem but as a way of saying that it is puzzling how deadly serious Jensen can be about issues and conclusions that at this time cannot be solved in the natural-science sense of solution. It would be one thing for Jensen to raise a question and suggest an answer. It is quite another thing to raise the question and insist on the answer. One could argue that if Jensen (or anyone else) were so sure of the answer, it would have been worse than hypocritical not to have said so. Besides, the argument could continue, Jensen's deadly seriousness and insistence will sharpen the issues through controversy and research and, with the passage of time, the field may come around to accepting the validity of his position. But that argument concedes the point: at this time Jensen's interpretation of the facts has not been persuasive to many people and, therefore, cannot and should not be the basis for any social action. It may turn out that Jensen was right; it may turn out that he was wrong. We are not dealing with quantity and quality of facts, and with clarifying explanations of those facts, to justify any public policy. Have we not learned anything from the arrogance and failures of the field of economics?

The above is by way of prologue to comments about Jensen's *Bias in Mental Testing*. It contains 786 pages, weighs about five pounds, and is not bedside reading. It is, without question, the most serious and boring book I have read since the days long ago when I tried (unsuccessfully) to read Talcott Parsons. It is an unremittingly humorless book that in countless ways tries to convince one that there is a psychometric science, that it is based on many discoveries about the nature of intelligence and its measurements, and that those who oppose mental testing simply do not know what they are talking about: they confuse fact with myth, wish with reality. Jensen always presents two sides (sometimes more) to an issue: his side and the wrong one. There is, however, a good deal in this book that anyone with an interest in mental testing ought to know. If the critics of mental testing understood much of that material, they could marshall their arguments far better than they do. Similarly, some of the people who are unreflective partisans of mental testing would become less certain of their position if they absorbed much that is in this work. This is not a book one should ignore. One has to contend with it. Jensen, far from being a fool, is a very astute person who tries to be fair. The problem is that in reading this book, I get the feeling that when Jensen is stating positions opposed to his own, he is trying to be fair but his heart is not in it. When he states his own position, it is obvious where his heart is. But, as Hudson indicated, that characteristic does not differentiate Jensen from the rest of us.

I shall not attempt to review the contents of this book for reasons that I hope will become clear. Suffice it to say that as soon as one takes on Jensen on his grounds, one has accepted a very restricted view of the concept of intelligence in terms of its nature and measurement, social history, and societal uses. The Achilles heel in Jensen's position, as well as in those of his critics, is the significance they all attach to standardized tests and testing conditions. The question I wish to discuss is: what is the relation between problem solving in test situations and in non-contrived, naturally occurring situations?

I came to ask myself that question shortly after I took my first professional job testing individuals in a new institution for the mentally retarded, a very innovative institution in the middle of nowhere. There was a certain problem with runaways. Although people ran away infrequently, there was always the fear when they did so that they would get lost in the woods and get hurt. Although I do not know how many of these runaways succeeded in not getting caught at all or only being found days later in their homes miles away, I did become aware that some of them had exhibited a kind and quality of problem-solving behavior that was simply not predictable from my testing of them. For example, I routinely administered the Porteus Mazes, which are scaled in difficulty from simple to complex. Some of the runaways who had done poorly on these mazes had managed to plan and execute their flights successfully: i.e., they demonstrated a level of planning and foresight quite at

variance with their test performance. Part of my job was to make recommendations, on the basis of tests, for job placement within the institution. I began to learn that in a fair number of instances there was little relationship between the problem-solving behavior of an individual
in testing and non-testing situations. I do not want to exaggerate the
number of these instances; but their occurrence was frequent enough,
and the discrepancies often dramatic enough, to make me wary of predicting from testing situations. This wariness received further support
from the literature on what happened to mentally retarded individuals
after they left special classes in the schools. They became part of the community in ways and at levels of competence that were at variance with
their problem-solving test behavior.

In 1953 Ginzberg and Bray wrote *The Uneducated,* an analysis of
World War II soldiers who were illiterate and/or mentally retarded by
a psychometric criterion. That book contains some extraordinary descriptions of discrepancies between problem-solving behavior in test and
non-test situations, the latter occurring under conditions of battle stress.
Here is one example from Ginzberg and Bray:

> E.H., a white soldier, born and still living in rural Kentucky when induct-
> ed, represents perhaps the clearest case of a man who should be classi-
> fied as a very good soldier. He was inducted at the age of 19 in the sum-
> mer of 1943. . . . Shortly after induction, he was sent to the Special
> Training Unit at Camp Atterbury, Indiana, where he spent two months.
> The date is not given, but when E.H. took the Army General Classifica-
> tion Test, probably prior to his assignment to the Special Training Unit,
> he received the very low score of 42. After completing the special train-
> ing, he was sent to the Infantry Replacement Training Center at Camp
> Blanding, Florida. Although many men receive ratings of excellent for
> character and efficiency during their basic training, E.H. was graded
> very good in character and only satisfactory in efficiency. He was trained
> as a rifleman. Immediately after "D Day" he was en route to the Euro-
> pean Theater as a member of the 8th Infantry Division. He received the
> Combat Infantry Badge, which made him automatically eligible for the
> Bronze Star Medal. Moreover, he earned three Bronze Service Stars for
> the Campaigns in Northern France, the Rhineland, and Central Europe.
> But his most important achievement was the award of the Silver Star for
> gallantry in action, which carried the following citation.
>
> Sgt. H., a squad leader, exposed himself to enemy small arms, mor-
> tar and artillery fire to work his way within 25 yards of an enemy
> machine gun position which was holding up their advance. He threw two
> hand grenades and then overran the position, killing one of the enemy
> and wounding two others. Later, during the attack, his squad account-
> ed for more than 30 Germans. Sgt. H.'s great courage, coolness under fire,
> and devotion to duty were an inspiration to his men. (pp. 87, 122)

Although I do not know the kinds of intellectual activities or prob-lem-solving behavior involved in being a squad leader, more particular-ly, a successful squad leader under conditions of stress, it seems not unrea-sonable to conclude that this man's intellectual activity is not predictable.

Jensen is quite aware that one of the major criticisms of mental tests is the restricted range of cognitive functions they sample. But in making that criticism, the critic is saying that we need better, more encompass-ing standardized tests. Neither Jensen nor his critics ever seem to con-sider the problems of the relation between problem solving in and out-side of the test situation, although the importance of this problem is implied in their writings. For example, when one finds that there are pervasive differences between social or ethnic or racial groupings, are there similar differences when the everyday problem-solving behavior of these groups is studied? Phrased alternatively, are the differences in level of problem-solving behavior in the test situation observable in all problem-solving behavior outside of the test situation? While it should be necessary in constructing a test to observe non-test behavior as a guide in selection of items, it should also be essential to demonstrate that the level of problem solving elicited by these test items is highly correlated with behavior toward these items when they are met with in everyday life. In constructing a test to select certain machine operators, one selects items which clearly reflect what these operators actually do or will be required to do, and one endeavors to construct the test so that it will dif-ferentiate between levels of performance. Similarly with our intelligence tests: implicitly and explicitly they have been validated on the basis of scholastic achievement and the content of these tests reflect such an aim. If one's goal is to construct a test which will predict problem-solving behavior outside of school-like situations, then it would seem necessary to study and demonstrate the relationship between performance in such situations and in response to the test.

The question I am raising goes far beyond mental testing. Indeed, it has been explicitly raised by a highly sophisticated group of experi-mental cognitive psychologists led by Michael Cole at Rockefeller Uni-versity. I refer specifically to their monograph bearing the delightful title: *Ecological, Niche Picking: Ecological Invalidity as an Axiom of Experi-mental Cognitive Psychology.* On the basis of their studies of test and non-test behavior, these researchers are forced to the conclusion that at the present time, "laboratory models preclude the operation of principles essentially to the organization of behavior in non-laboratory environ-ments (and that) theories and data derived from the laboratory cannot be used as a basis for predictions about the behavior of individuals once they leave the laboratory."

Cole's studies and conclusions should be alarming to both Jensen and his critics because they point to a severe limitation, and possibly semi-lethal defect, in the practice of validating performance in one standardized testing situation by another. I raised this issue a quarter of a century ago and Cole has raised it again in a more systematic, data-based way. Some day, perhaps, psychologists will start looking at performance in naturally occurring situations. That will be the day!

————————————————

It has never been my position that formal psychologic tests are evil inventions that ought to be made illegal. I think of tests as somewhat like a body thermometer in that in the face of presenting symptoms, abnormal and normal "readings" are no basis for inaction but require one to look elsewhere to understand what the symptoms may reflect. But where does or should one look? In psychology the emphasis has been on other tests and trying to see a pattern among their different findings. That can be productive—or at least not misleading—in the case of problem-solving behavior, but only up to a point. That point is reached (and very quickly) when an extrapolation is made from what is observed in formal, contrived, standardized testing situations to what one infers would be observable in informal, nonstandardized, or naturally occurring situations. That kind of extrapolation is unwarranted—or should be made with more than lip service to the underlying assumption—in view of the fact that there is no existing body of literature to warn one of the cautions that should be observed. Cole's work is a real beginning to an examination of these kinds of extrapolations. What he reported is almost of the nature of pulling the rug from under a superstructure of assumption and practice.

5

ASPECTS OF A COMMUNITY PROGRAM
FOR RETARDED CHILDREN

When I started to read my early papers, the one that surprised me the most is the one reprinted here. It was a paper I gave at a meeting in 1951, a quarter of a century before the passage of Public Law 94-142, the so-called mainstreaming legislation which impacted on every school in the country. The title may put off some readers not especially interested in mental retardation. But if the reader is interested in tracing my point of view about school change, this paper may be illuminating. It was to me because it contained aspects of my point of view which only in later years got connected in my head. I could say that this paper was a "switching point" because up until I wrote it I was a more or less conventional clinical psychologist and researcher primarily interested in individuals. It is true that I had always been interested in the relationship between the individual and his or her culture and/or family context. But those relationships were globally conceptualized by me. They lacked a concreteness; they were not a basis for practical actions.

Why was I surprised? The answer is in the major themes this short paper contains.

1. *The preventive orientation.* The problems schools and their communities encountered with "special" children derived in large measure from their stance of "repair," i.e., these children and their families presented complex and difficult problems for conventional educational practice and policy. These problems need not have arisen with the turmoil they did if there had been a preventive orientation. Although that paper focussed on mentally retarded children and their families, by implication at least I was advocating the superiority in general of the preventive over the repair stance.

2. *The insensitivity of educational, psychological, and medical personnel.* By insensitivity, I did not refer to a personality trait but rather to the fact that the training of these professionals inculcated in them attitudes that, more often than not, created problems or made them worse than they should have been. It took me several years after writing that paper to recognize that their training was inadequate for dealing with problems even more numerous than those of mentally retarded individuals. In brief, that paper tells me that I was being steered to issues of professional training, how that training contained so little about the practical significances of the preventive orientation. Decades later I wrote *Caring and Compassion in Clinical Practice* (1986) which concerned the preparation of physicians in general, psychiatrists, clinical psychologists, educators, and lawyers in family practice. And then I wrote *The Case for Change: Rethinking the Preparation of Educators* (1993). The paper reprinted here was the forerunner of those two books, although that paper had a far more narrow focus. In those early days I had neither the knowledge, or experience, or chutzpah to see the larger significances of professional training.

3. *Schools and their communities.* I was already dimly aware that schools were encapsulated, walled off, bounded places for whom communities were alien territories, even though schools were affected in countless ways by community attitudes and perceived responsibilities. I was already aware that the typical school stance was engendering resentment among parents of handicapped children. I was unable at that time to draw a more general conclusion: the ways in which school personnel judged and reacted to parents aroused a good deal of resentment. Not long after I wrote that paper my research in schools and my work with Burton Blatt increasingly convinced me that one of the oldest cold wars was between parents and educators. (A colleague of mine once pointed out that that war probably is historically younger than that between students and teachers.)

When I wrote this paper in 1951, it could never occur to me that a quarter of a century later the rights of handicapped students (and their families) as well as the obligations of schools to them would be radically altered in Public Law 94-142. I knew well the resentments of these parents and the blatant ways in which their children were the objects of discrimination but I saw nothing to suggest that anything would change, least of all the attitudes of and practices of educators. But when in 1954 the Supreme Court rendered its desegregation decision, I immediately saw that the logic and morality of that decision were clearly applicable to handicapped children, and so did leaders of parent groups who nationally were a small lobbying group but in an amazingly short time became very powerful in state legislatures and the Congress.

I was almost alone among my friends and in my professional community in predicting that the desegregation decision would have stormy, destabilizing consequences. My perspective about school (and societal) change had sufficiently developed to the point where it became inconceivable to me to expect that as traditional a setting as a public school could change its attitudes and practices other than over a long, long time during which there would be conflict after conflict, within the school and between the school and the community. As was implied in the 1951 paper, schools not only did not know how to reach out to the community but they had never been interested in doing so. Let us remember that the forces that led up to the desegregation decision hardly (if at all) had the explicit support of the national educational leadership. Schools were unprepared for that decision. They had no welcome mat in the wings to roll out.

As in the case of racial segregation, the parents of handicapped children quickly learned that they would get nowhere by pressuring schools and boards of education. They devoted their efforts to lobbying in state legislatures and the courts. They essentially bypassed the schools, quite understandable in light of what I suggest in the 1951 paper.

What I hope the reader takes away from what I am saying is that the development of my general point of view about school change benefitted mightily from my specific interest in and experiences with how schools viewed handicapped children and their parents. And that experience began in the early months after I took a position in Connecticut's new state training school when I learned that there were more than a few towns and cities eager to close their segregated special classes and send those students to Southbury, whether parents liked it or not. From my earliest professional days I was drawn, really forced, to ask why schools do what they do or do not do what they should do. It took me decades to gain clarity on some of the answers and when I grow up I hope that clarity will get broader and deeper. Hope does spring eternal!

I have never scapegoated schools or educators because to do so assumes that their shortcomings or inadequacies are perversely willed, which they are not. Whatever are the dominant attitudes in the larger society are present in school personnel. School personnel, like the rest of society, do not take kindly to change. None of us does. I learned that in my personal life and learned it again and again in my professional life. I may become frustrated and even angry at the resistance of schools to change but I cannot bring myself to blame them for being by my lights wrong, stubborn, or contentious. That goes with the territory, and there are too many reformers and school administrators who respond to the resistance of others with authoritarian, do-what-I-say, shape up or ship out directives, thus strengthening the resistance. All this is by way of saying that because you want to change schools does not mean you have the temperament or understanding to get to first base. In regard to school change there are no home runs. You are never dealing with problems you can solve in a once-and-for-all way. To engage in school change requires courage, persistence, patience, frustration tolerance, and a lot of masochism. Those are the parts of a job description that few reformers, past and present, had or have. I do not say that hostilely or even critically because I understand that their hearts are in the right place, they know what they want to change, and they want to be alive to see those changes. The problem is what is in their heads: a catastrophically oversimplified conception of what they are up against. I do blame reformers who are obviously unable or unwilling to learn from the experience of others, who in more than a few instances cannot or do not read. The world was not born yesterday and it will not be remade by tomorrow. We really need a vitamin for humbleness deficiency.

Two weeks ago I received a call from the secretary of a local organized group of parents of cerebral palsied children.[1] It seems that one of the mothers had been trying to get her seven-year-old daughter into the kindergarten of one of the public schools. The school had refused admission because the child was not considered eligible. The mother, believing that the child was eligible, took her for a psychological examination to the out-patient clinic of one of the state training schools. The psychological report was sent to the secretary who was calling me, and who had suggested that the mother have the child given a psychological examination in order to use it as evidence for her belief that the child should be in kindergarten. The psychological report contained the following: (a) a diagnosis was deferred because the child did not talk and the suggestion was made that the child should be seen again when she had learned to talk; (b) on those test items which could be given to the child her mental level seemed to be around three years; (c) the child should not be institutionalized at this time; (d) she should be entered

---

[1] The text beginning with this sentence and continuing to the end of this chapter is taken from a paper given at the New York City chapter of the Association for the Help of Retarded Children, November 28, 1951.

into a kindergarten class if she was considered eligible by the school. The problem with which the secretary of the parent group confronted me was what should she tell the parent?

The above situation is by no means infrequent, and in my own experience is the rule rather than the exception. In trying to understand these frequent situations we might ask this question: How do these situations come about? Before trying to answer this question we first have to ask other questions: What is the nature of the situation here and now? What are the problems with which we should be concerned? Briefly stated, here is what I think are the important aspects of the situation:

1. We are dealing with a parent who has certain beliefs about what her child can learn to do.
2. The mother's beliefs are not shared by school authorities.
3. It is very likely that the mother has a very hostile attitude toward the schools because she feels that they are being unfair and discriminatory.
4. It is also likely that the school authorities consider the mother to be unrealistic and aggressive—in short, a nuisance.
5. It is a fact that the schools do not consider this child to be *their* problem.
6. The psychological report does not support the mother's beliefs about the child's capacities.
7. The psychological report contains a recommendation about kindergarten which makes little sense in light of the earlier refusal of the school to admit the child.
8. The psychologist did not discuss his report with the mother.
9. No one, except the local parent group, considered the parent to be their problem, or understood, let alone tried to handle, the deep anguish she undoubtedly was experiencing.

Let us now make one assumption: the mother has an unrealistic conception of her child's capacities. If this is so, it is difficult to see how anything done—by the school or the psychologist—was oriented toward helping this mother achieve a more realistic attitude. Telling a mother that her child is not eligible for school may be a valid statement, but in no way does this solve the mother's problem. In fact, making such a statement to a mother is evidence of the fact that the school assumes that only the child is a problem. Telling a mother that her child is not eligible for school without at the same time making concrete proposals concerning the child's training obviously does not help the child, but, just as obviously, increases the severity of the mother's problem. In the case of the psychological examination apparently no attempt was made to convey anything to the mother. The function of a psychological examination is not only to collect data about a child and his problems, but to use these data to help parents react realistically to the child. If the psychologist, for example, had only conveyed to the parent that the child was severely retarded, then he would have been as superficial in his approach to the problem as were the school authorities.

In short, in these instances we are dealing with unhappy, frustrated, conflict-ridden parents who have no one to whom they can turn for help. It is little wonder that they become hostile and direct such feelings toward those who gave them facts but no help. By help I mean a sustained attempt on the part of some trained person to understand the motivations of the parents, as well as by previous training, enable the parent to accept more realistic and satisfying attitudes. It is worth repeating: in these situations to convey facts should not be taken as synonymous with giving help.

There are other comments one can make about the kind of situation we have been discussing:

1. In most instances, our schools do not understand the psychological ramifications of these situations and it is, therefore, not surprising that they usually do not have the facilities for handling the child or the parent. To handle the situation properly presupposes an understanding of the problems which most educators do not have.

2. The fact that our teacher training schools prepare students in an inadequate way for meeting the problems in this area is but a reflection of an absence of community consciousness about the problem. Too many communities are content to have the handicapped child institutionalized. Too few communities make an attempt to utilize their own facilities or to set up new resources for the handicapped child. I have seen countless children who, after spending several years in an institution, were returned to a community which had little or nothing to offer them in a social, educational or vocational way.

3. The most discouraging feature of these situations is that there usually have been countless earlier opportunities when the parents could have been given a realistic understanding of the problem, prepared for the future problems with which they will be faced, and a concrete program of action formulated. The great bulk of these children have been previously seen by a variety of medical specialists who, for one or another reason, failed to see the social-psychological ramifications for the family, the school and community.

This last point deserves elaboration. There are cases, probably a small minority, where the seriousness of the child's retardation was simply not caught. Sometimes this is due to the incompetence of the physician or psychologist, and sometimes to the fact that our diagnostic methods are not perfect. That our instruments for evaluating intellectual capacity in very young children are not as good as we would like is no reason for not using them. What these imperfections mean is that we must be cautious in assigning weight to a single examination and make provision for a series of examinations with appropriate time intervals. If a series of examinations point to a certain conclusion, we can be more sure of the validity of that conclusion than if it were based on a single examination. One implication of what I have just said is that in the case of very young children the diagnosis should be made by a person with special training in this area. Because a person is a physician or psychologist is no reason for assuming that he has competence in this particular area.

In the great majority of cases, however, the seriousness of the child's retardation was recognized when the child was still very young. If so, one might ask, why does the situation I described earlier arise? There are several reasons:

1. The physician feels that it is not wise to tell the parent until the child is older. The logic behind this unhappy procedure is not always clear. One physician said: "If they can be happy for a few years, why should I stand in their way? They will have enough trouble later on." Some physicians feel that one should not discuss the problem until the parents themselves become aware of it. Whatever the logic the consequences are unfortunate. Ignorance may be bliss, but there are more than a few parents who gladly would have liked to have been spared the bliss. In some cases the awakening is so rude that parents strive (consciously or unconsciously) to prove that the blissful period is not over. They may become hostile to the physician for withholding the information, question his competence, and seek help from others.

2. Frequently the physician does tell the parents about the child's condition, but because he finds this obligation such a painful procedure (it is indeed not a joyous task!) he talks out of both sides of his mouth. At one point he gives glimpses of the true condition, but at another point he reassures the parents with unwarranted optimism. He cannot bring himself to reveal the unvarnished truth which can then serve as a basis for a realistic program for both child and parents. It is to be expected that parents will remember the optimistic and forget the pessimistic aspects of the information which have been conveyed to them.

3. Although the physician may tell the truth to the parents, frequently he fails to relate the educational problems which will confront them in the future with their child. It is easy to tell parents that their child will be able to go to school, but do the parents know that this may mean that the child conceivably might go only as far as the fourth grade? That the schools in the community may not have facilities for their child? That the child may be able only to learn to recognize a few words and do only the simplest of arithmetic tasks? In short, the parents are rarely told what kinds of educational problems they will probably have to face. Unfortunately, too few physicians know the educational system of their community in a way which would allow them to be of more help to parents.

What has all this to do with the setting up of a community program for the mentally retarded? Let me answer this question by giving what I think the aims of such a program should be. First, to detect as early as possible the mentally retarded child; second, to help parents gain a more realistic understanding of their child so that his capacities can be realized; third, to begin to plan with the parent the future program of the child; fourth, to bring our educational system into the picture long before the child is of school age so that the clinic, parent, and school can gain a much better understanding of each other's problems than they now have. In short, the aim of such a program is to prevent personal unhappiness, mutual distrust, self-plaguings, and misdirected use of energies. *At the present time we spend the large proportion of our time working with problems which never should have been allowed to rise.* For example, in the case I described earlier we found a psychologist, a parent, and a school system expending time, effort and money with one result: the parent is probably now more desperate, hostile, confused, and unhappy than before. The point I want to stress is that such an unfortunate situation could have and should have been prevented.

A community program would seem to require the following:

1. A mass educational program the aim of which is to urge parents to bring their children to appropriately staffed clinics for evaluation of their mental and physical growth. The emphasis should be on the preschool child especially those between two and six years of age—ages at which defects become most apparent.

2. The setting up of clinics comprised of medical, psychological and educational specialists. The problems of the handicapped child as well as those of his parents cannot be handled by any one specialist. The emphasis in each case should be on formulating, as soon as possible, a concrete training program and supervising the execution of the pro-

gram, *even if that means that the clinic comes into the home.* When you tell parents to give their child a particular medication three times a day, the chances are that this will be done. In the case of a handicapped child, however, the prescription is a complicated one, not only to understand but to carry out. Parents need support, encouragement and advice, not only during the clinic visit, but when they are faced with and responding to their problems in the natural setting in which they arise.

3. The community must meet its obligation to provide appropriate educational, occupational and recreational facilities for these children. In providing such facilities attention must be paid to the fact that some day these children will be adults with special problems due to their mental handicaps. The aims of a well-organized program for the childhood and adolescent periods can be defeated by failure to meet the problems of later life.

4. There must be an effort made to get the various professional personnel in this area better acquainted with (a) the need which they should have for each other, (b) the limitations of their own training, and (c) a more keen awareness of the psychological, educational, and community aspects of the problems with which they are dealing.

5. There are many problems in this area for which we do not have answers. Some of these are medical problems, others are problems in psychological measurement and treatment, while others are concerned with the educational process. Any program in this area, therefore, must stimulate and support research. If there is any lesson we can learn from the history of science, it is that in the long run research pays off. It is not enough to say we *should* support research in the same way as we say we are for virtue and against sin. We *must* stimulate and support research programs because not to do so guarantees a sterile program, inadequate solutions, and the continued despair of all concerned.

CHAPTER

6

THE SCHOOL CULTURE AND THE
PROCESSES OF CHANGE

In educational circles I am best known (I think) for my book *The Culture of the School and the Problem of Change,* published in 1971 (a second edition of which appeared in 1982). Someone said it was the right book at the right time. To younger readers who may not even have been born at the time, it is hard to convey why and in which national and international contexts school change was put on the societal agenda as never before, on which agenda it has remained. When in 1956 the then Soviet Union orbited the first Sputnik, it is not exaggeration to say that all hell broke loose. We had become Avis to the Soviet Union's Hertz. As was (and still is) the case when national pride has received a narcissistic wound, blame had to be assigned and our schools were sitting ducks. The scientific leadership of our country seemed to be imperilled, the number of young people interested in or knowledgeable about science seemed alarmingly low, and the future supply of scientists was drying up. Thus began the era of curriculum reform, e.g., the new math, new biology, new physics. Money for these and other school reform efforts began to flow, all of this taking place at the same time that the social consequences of the 1954 desegregation decision and the vigorous civil rights movement guaranteed that schools would be at or near the center of social concern and action. No major societal institution—political, military, business, religious, educational—escaped criticism and attack, least of all our public schools. As someone said, it was in the turbulent, sizzling sixties that schools and educators got their comeuppance; they had been asleep at the switch, they had been smugly mired in suffocating tradition, they were unchanging in a changing world, unaware that their practices and outlooks were anti-educational in their consequences.

It was in that context in the very early sixties that I, Esther Sarason, and Murray Levine created the Yale Psycho-Educational clinic, one of its major aims being to get us into schools in ways that would permit us to understand what I called the culture of schools. We confessed openly that neither by training or experience were we sophisticated about schools but we were certain that if efforts to change schools were to stand a chance of being effective, schools had to be understood far better than existing knowledge allowed. Although I never said it openly, I believed that our lack of training and experience were deficits that could be turned into assets. That is to say, we would be experiencing schools relatively uncontaminated by what tradition said was right, natural, and proper. I knew that what we wanted to do would be seen by some people (in and out of schools) as arrogance or dogoodism. After all, what credentials did we possess entitling us to seek to understand schools by developing roles that would be helpful to educators within the confines of classrooms and schools, not by "seeing" or dealing with the problems of students and teachers on our turf? The Psycho-Educational Clinic was not going to be a place to which schools sent us their problems. We were going to do whatever we were going to do in classrooms and schools.

The helping role inevitably involves changing someone or something. We made one basic assumption: in our role of trying to be helpful to students and teachers on their turf we would learn a lot about the culture of schools: how their structure, practices, regularities, goals, and rationales combine as justification for what is and rejection of alternatives about what could or should be. Esther, Murray, and I were by training and experience clinical psychologists in which roles we had learned the obvious: people do not take kindly to departures from their accustomed ways of thinking and acting even when they proclaim they are motivated to do so.

If others saw what we proposed to do as professional arrogance— and their perception was understandable to us—we knew that what was going for us was what I can only call a mixture of honesty and anxiety. We never presented ourselves to schools as experts, we emphasized in a well rehearsed "speech" that we wanted to help, we did not know how or in which ways we could be helpful, but we wanted to learn. What that introductory speech did not say was that we were scared, we knew we would make mistakes, please be forgiving. Basic to my point of view, as person and psychologist, is that knowledge of myself and my world will never deepen or expand if I do not risk the dilemmas, pot holes, and anxieties that moving in new directions entails. So, what the reader needs to know is that the creation of the Yale Psycho-Educational Clinic was in a most conscious way a reaction to the fact that in the previous decade I had directed a research project on test anxiety, which by conventional standards was unusually productive and respected. I was a "successful" researcher. I had also stopped thinking! It all came to a head one day during our weekly research meeting when one of our group reported data on his most recent study in which he found the predicted differences in learning between high and low test anxious children, another of scads of similar studies we had done. I heard myself saying to the group, "You know, if we filmed high and low test anxious kids drinking bottles of Coca-Cola, I bet we would see stylistic differences." When I heard myself smugly say that, I knew that I was in trouble and that I had to move in new directions, that I needed to change. That was unsettling. I was like a patient who knew that he or she could not continue in the same way, that the price for standing still would be too high. I was that patient! The process whereby the clinic got organized and started, what went on in me and it during its first two years, were the most instructive, mind expanding, wonderful, anxious, turbulent experiences of my life. There were times I was sorry I had ever entertained the idea that I needed to change. Better I should have remained a successful research academic than a fearful explorer of new experience! Change is not easy, it never is.

An example. To get the clinic started I applied for funds to the National Institute for Mental Health. In that grant request I said what I indicated above: we wanted to study and understand the culture of schools by getting into a helping relationship with them on their home grounds. I said that we were not clear, and could not be clear, precisely how that would develop, what problems we would encounter, or even what we would learn. What I emphasized was that unless the culture of schools was better understood the effort to change schools would be ineffective. The NIMH sent a visiting team of outside consultants to discuss questions raised by our grant request. The visiting team consisted of two psychologists and one psychiatrist. I knew them and they knew me. The reason for the visit was puzzlement about what we intended to do and how—the why they did not question. We told them we could not honestly say more than we had in our application. They asked us to try to be more specific and submit a new grant request. We did, and they visited us again with the same concerns. Our grant was turned down, albeit, as one of the team later told me, with reluctance because of their respect for my previous work.

I am not lacking in self confidence but those visits and rejection for a brief time made me wonder whether I was justified in doing what I wanted to do. Was I biting off more than I could chew? Was I being naive, arrogant, presumptuous? Shouldn't I stick to what I was familiar with, what had worked so well for me? By that time I was hoist by my own petard, I had to change, I could not go back although part of me wanted to retreat.

The paper in this chapter was given as the Brechbill lecture at the University of Maryland in 1966; it was written in 1965 three years after the clinic started and years before I began to write *The Culture of the School and the Problems of Change*. When I reread that paper I was flabbergasted by three things. The first was that I had forgotten how much I had learned and experienced in the first three years of the clinic. The second was that the guts of the later book were already in this paper. And the third was that I had already concluded that efforts to reform schools would fail. I have been used to saying (without satisfaction) that I am the only person who, in public or in print, predicted as early as twenty five years ago the failure of reform efforts. I was wrong. I said it thirty years ago. Indeed, I said it more clearly in this paper than in many subsequent writings, perhaps because it was a delivered paper and I was less cautious about expressing the certainty of my conclusions. And that reminds me that a year or so before I delivered that paper, I had given a talk at Boston University where I said that Headstart could not be other than minimally successful because it assumed that the Headstart experience would be sufficient to inoculate children against all of the factors that made school experiences so extinguishing of motivation, curiosity, and personal meaning. In summary, I already knew back then that any effort to change schools that was not informed by an understanding of the culture of schools was doomed. And, I should add, I already was unlearning the belief or attitude that there was nothing about schools that could not be changed if only we were willing to spend money. Yes, money was and is an issue, a very important one, but quite secondary to gaining an understanding of the culture of schools. We have spent billions of dollars to improve schools. It has not bought us what we wanted and needed, the lessons from which we have hardly learned.

In this chapter Dr. Sarason uses the introduction of the new math as an example of how change tends to be viewed and handled in the school culture.[1] One of the several reasons why the Clinic developed services for schools was the opportunity it would provide for understanding the culture of the school (see Sara-

---

[1] The text beginning with this sentence and continuing to the end of this chapter is taken from the Brechbill Lecture, University of Maryland, January 10, 1966. Reprinted from *The Psycho-Educational Clinic: Papers and Research Studies* (pp. 6–20), edited by Frances Kaplan & Seymour B. Sarason. Boston: Department of Mental Health, Commonwealth of Massachusetts. Undated Public Monograph.

son, Levine, Goldenberg, Cherlin, & Bennett, 1966). Basic to this approach was the assumption that attempts to change a setting have to be based on an understanding of how those in the setting view the setting and themselves. This chapter is an initial attempt to state that problem of change from the standpoint of the culture of the school and to describe the usual ways in which attempts to change the school are viewed and implemented. This chapter discusses the problem of how one goes about understanding and describing the culture of the school. In a real sense this monograph is a prologue to the study of this problem.

I approach this discussion with some trepidation since I am not at all sure that I am seeing the problem whole or that I am asking the right questions. I believe that a comprehensive understanding of the culture of the school is absolutely essential for anyone who wants to introduce change into the school. We live in a day and age when everybody is an expert on education and ignorance is thus no barrier to the expression of opinions. This would be of no special concern were it not for the fact that billions of dollars are going to be spent in the next decade in the attempt to change our schools in diverse ways. I am anticipating one of my major conclusions when I state that there is not good reason—in past experience or available theory—to expect that these intended changes will be successfully introduced or maintained in the schools, except in some small measure.

A BASIC ASSUMPTION

In approaching the problem of change, I am making an assumption that the school is a subculture in our society since it has traditions, goals, dynamics, organization, and materials which set it apart from other settings in our society. Let us put it another way: Those who are part of the school setting see themselves as different in numerous ways, from those who work in or are a part of other settings, e.g., a factory, a mental hygiene clinic, or a political club. What is involved is not merely the feeling of being different, but the awareness that one possesses special knowledge, values, and obligations which have a history not only in the life of the individual but in the larger context of history. There is a sense of individual and group identity derived from a past that gives structure and meaning to the present and future. Those in the school culture "know" what they are in the same way that a newspaper reporter knows what he is, or an Australian bushman knows what he is, or a physician knows what he is.

The school culture is, of course, a highly differentiated one. There are elementary, junior, and senior high schools; there are superintendents, teachers, principals, and supervisors; there are urban, suburban, and rural schools; and there are boards of education. In addition, the school culture has many points of contact with the larger society—parent groups, schools of education, business, law enforcement, and mental health clinics. Despite the differentiation within the school culture and the fluidity of its boundaries with the larger society, I assume that those within it possess values, self-perceptions, goals, technical skills, training, and expectations which have a distinctive organization or patterning. It needs to be emphasized that the distinctiveness resides in not just one of these characteristics but in their overall relation to each other.

Is it warranted to make this basic assumption? It could be argued that schools and school personnel vary so fantastically on so many different levels that attempts to arrive at communalities or distinctive patterns of behavior and attitudes are rendered meaningless or fruitless. From this standpoint each school, or even each classroom, is a unique entity which can only be understood in its own terms and which has little or nothing in common with what goes on in other schools or classrooms. There is truth to this in the same way that there is truth to the statement that no two people are alike. But the fact of uniqueness in no way invalidates the perception of similarities. The significance of uniqueness or similarities depends on what one wants to do. The fact that no two teachers are alike would in no way impede one from predicting similarity in response to an increase in pay or a reduction in class size.

The fact of the matter is that the assumption of a school culture has hardly been examined or studied. This is not to say that there is not a good deal to be learned about schools from the many studies which have been done on scores of educational issues, problems, and practices. For example, one can devote one's life just to reading what has been written about reading—one lifetime probably being in the nature of a gross under-estimate. What bearing does the literature on reading have on our understanding of the culture of school? Asking that is clearly to beg the question of what I mean by culture. It is realistic self-appraisal rather than modesty that compels me to say that far wiser and more knowledgeable people than myself have asked this question and have left it unanswered or have given answers which left them and others far from happy. I will not attempt a definition but rather will give examples of the kinds of things to which the concept of the school culture refers.

Example 1

There is a physical education program in every school I know or have heard about. In almost all instances there is a particular place in the school where this program is conducted. Those who conduct these programs are expected to have special training. What happens, as I have done on numerous occasions, when I say to groups of teachers that I simply do not comprehend why there should be physical education programs in the schools? As you might imagine, the most frequent response is staring disbelief followed by a request to reformulate the statement. Without going into the details of the discussion—which is usually quite heated—I shall indicate the significance I attribute to the initial response and the ensuing discussion. First, there is the implicit recognition both by the teachers and myself that we operate in different worlds, i.e., I perceive them and they see me as having different backgrounds and experiences. Second, it is inconceivable to the teachers that a school could or should be without a physical education program. They have a conception of a school which, if subject to change or challenged, they strongly defend. Far from being indifferent to the conception, they defend it to a degree which illuminates the extent to which their sense of identity is related to this conception. Third, they justify the physical education program in terms of what they think children are and need; their justification is both psychological and philosophical.

Example 2

The concept of the school culture refers to those aspects of the setting that are viewed by school personnel as "givens" or essential features, which they would strenuously defend against elimination or marked change, and which to them reflect psychological concepts and value judgments. It is important to note that the frequency or regularity of an activity does not inform one as to its significance in the school culture. For example, I have been in many elementary school classrooms at the beginning of the school day, and in each instance the day began with the salute to the flag. On several occasions I have said to groups of teachers that I did not understand why children had to salute the flag each day. The responses to this statement are much more varied than to my statements about physical education. Some teachers respond by saying that the daily salute to the flag is an empty ritual which they would like to dispense with or reduce in frequency. Others say that it reinforces feelings of patriotism and contributes to the school's goal of making good citizens. Some teachers go on to point out that the salute to the flag is mandatory by law or administrative regulations. Rarely has the response been one of bewilderment or disbelief.[2] Aside from suggesting that frequency of an activity is not in itself a revealing characteristic, this example suggests that not all activities, however frequent, are considered by school personnel as equally important or relevant to their conception of the school or of themselves as professional people in the school.

There is one other thing that can be said about these two examples and again it is not something that is discernible from observing and recording ongoing activities in the school. I refer here to those activities which school personnel feel they must perform or engage in regardless of personal views, in contrast to those activities for which no such feeling is experienced because it is so syntonic with their view of things. It is interesting to note that although some teachers say explicitly that they are required to have their children salute the flag daily, no teacher says that about physical education programs even though in most, if not all, instances these programs are also required by law or administrative regulation. In other words, the culture of the school cannot be derived by examining laws and regulations just as it cannot be derived from knowledge of types of activities or their frequency.

Let me summarize what I have said thus far. One of the ways to get aspects of the school culture is to focus initially on activities that characterize the setting. The next, and more important and difficult step, is to determine how each activity is justified, and its centrality to the individual's conception of a school and sense of identity with it. It is not enough to determine the different bases for justification. One must determine, in addition, the degree to which the presence or absence of, or a change in, the activity is capable of affecting the individual's equilibrium.

I would expect two major consequences of the approach I have described. The first would be a clearer picture of what school personnel consider to be essential activities in the setting without which they would not apply the label *school* to it. The second consequence would be a much more explicit statement and understanding of the thinking and reasoning of the school personnel. Finally, and this is crucial, what we would learn about school personnel would differ in important respects from

------

2 It has significance in understanding the school culture that the private views of teachers to certain school activities are by no means similar to those they may voice in public. Whenever I have raised the flag-salute question with teachers, it has been after we have established a working relationship and a situation of mutual trust has developed.

similar studies by nonschool personnel, since school personnel characteristically view and think about school activities in a distinctive (although not necessarily unique) way.

Some may regard what I have said as a glimpse of the obvious. I do not think so, of course, but if it is obvious it will not be the first time that the obvious has not been taken seriously.

RELATIONSHIPS

There is much more to the concept of the school culture than can be discerned by focusing on activities. Of crucial importance are the different kinds of people who work in a school and the significance of "kinds of people" to the nature of relationships. To a person outside the school setting a principal is not a very differentiated kind of person. To someone in the school setting the principal is a very complicated kind of person because he is perceived and judged on factors that only become explicit when one becomes part of the setting. His years in the position, the help of an educational kind that he gives to teachers in classrooms, the help that he gives to teachers in regard to the management of children, the degree to which he "fights for" his staff in matters of salaries and working conditions, the quality of the evaluations he makes of his faculty, the degree to which he establishes personal as contrasted to professional relationships—all these are some of the factors which should prevent one from assuming that the relationship between the principal and his staff is a simple one or that the principal's role is not a very differentiated one. You undoubtedly noted that I omitted a very important characteristic—the sex of the principal. Is there anyone who would deny that the sex of a principal makes a difference in the culture of a school? Is it fortuitous that the significance of this factor is rarely raised or discussed in educational literature and research? Is this an oversight or is it a symptom of the fact that too little attention has been paid to understanding the school as a social system?

I would like to make clear that I have not been talking about the personality or other factors (race, religion, or political affiliation) about the principal which may be of great importance by virtue of their interaction with the factors I have mentioned. My focus has been on those aspects which are inherent in the job of principal and which make for the variety of relationships he has with others in the school.

Let me now ask another of those apparently, and perhaps truly, silly questions. Is it necessary for each school to have a principal? I have put this question to friends who are not connected with schools. There are three types of responses to this question. The first is one of mild surprise that the question should be asked. The second response is that the individual simply has no basis for considering alternatives, although in principle he would not be opposed to alternatives. The third and least frequent response is one in which alternatives are stated and the pros and cons evaluated. If I have sensed anything common to these responses it is that the question is an open and interesting one. Now, how do teachers respond to the question? As you might expect, their response is far stronger than it is to my question about physical education programs. Once emotions are relatively out of the way, a variety of answers are given although they tend to have one thing in common: There are "practical" matters of an everyday sort (that do or could occur) which could bring the operations of a school to a halt if the principal were not present. Who would keep the attendance data? Order supplies? Handle behavior problems and sick children? Supervise fire drills? Talk to parents when they phoned or visited? One could go on listing housekeeping matters which are considered to require the presence of a principal. What is most interesting to me is that teachers rarely, if ever, respond in terms of the factors I presented earlier—the principal's educational or leadership role, his evaluation functions, his role as representative of the teachers to other administrative bodies, and the importance of personal as contrasted to professional relationships with him. In other words, teachers tend not to respond in terms of the variety of relationships they actually have with the principal. And yet I have the distinct feeling, although perhaps without external evidence, that the teachers have a strong need to have *one* authority figure in the school who is "above" everybody else.

How does this shed light on the culture of the school? Again I would want to emphasize how inconceivable it is to teachers to think of a school without a principal. I confess that I stress this because it is conceivable to me that a school does not require a principal to attain its educational objectives. What I think, however, is far less important than what teachers think, rightly or wrongly, if one is interested in bringing about changes—*and this is what most innovators fail to realize.* Of equal significance is the possibility that the relationships which teachers have with the principal—relationships which stem from the duties and obligations of the principal—are far less important to the teacher than one might suppose. That is, the importance which teachers attach to the role of the principal does not reflect relationships they have with him in his role as an educational leader.

This conclusion receives a good deal of support from our work in schools and is summarized in our book (Sarason, Levine, Goldenberg, Cherlin, & Bennett, 1966) in a chapter titled "Teaching Is a Lonely Profession." Very briefly, we give a number of examples illustrating the point that teachers are alone in the classroom with their problems and are not given, and do not expect to receive, help and advice from the principal. That is, teachers do not tend to look to the principal as an educational leader who is capable of providing help in matters of teaching techniques, classroom organization and management, and the nature of the learning process as it relates to educational and psychological objectives. In fact, rather than look to the principal as an educational leader and expert, teachers tend to shy away from meaningful discussions of these matters with the principal. I should quickly add that it is our distinct impression that principals feel most uncomfortable in their role as educational leader, that they prefer to have teachers solve their own problems, and that they infrequently visit classrooms to ascertain what is going on and its relationship to educational-psychological goals.

The principal-teacher relationship is but one means by which one can begin to understand the realities of the school culture as opposed to what may be deduced from job descriptions or untested statements of practices. Far more complicated than this relationship are those which exist among teachers. Age, years of teaching, marital status, perceived competence, sex, the grade being taught, psychological and educational orientation—these are some of the lines along which teachers vary and which affect their relationships with each other. I think there is a tendency for those outside a particular social organization to view those within it as a cohesive and interacting group, particularly if they share a common label, e.g., teachers. This naive but understandable view prepares the way for the surprise one feels when one learns that relationships within the system are otherwise. I am sure that it is akin to bringing coals to Newcastle when I say that in any one school the relationships among teachers are quite complex. I cannot go into detail about these complex relationships since they have hardly been the object of study. I will only state, but not expand upon, the assumption that when important human relationships occurring within a particular social system have not been the object of study, it is symptomatic of the need either to deny reality or to hide it from outsiders. When one considers the vast amount of educational research done in this and previous decades, is it not surprising that the relationships among teachers have received little attention? I cannot believe, and our experience clearly contradicts, that these relationships are not among the most revealing features of the school culture.

There is one aspect of teacher relationships which happens to fascinate me and which also relates to what was said above about principal-teacher relationships. I think I can make the point most clearly if I tell you something about the Psycho-Educational Clinic, more specifically, about our Fridays.

All members of the Clinic are expected to be there all day on Friday. We are the type of Clinic in which staff members and interns spend a good deal of time in the schools and in other community settings. Consequently, Friday is set aside for group discussions, and for staff members and interns to have smaller meetings as the need may be. From 9:00 to 11:00 A.M., a member of the staff usually presents something about his work to the entire group. His presentation may be concerned with any problem to which he wants the group to react, i.e., it may concern a teacher, a child, a school, or a research problem which poses some kind of issue. At the end of this meeting there is a short break after which a second two-hour meeting is held. During this meeting, a staff member or intern presents his work with a child at the Clinic. Whereas the focus of the first meeting is a problem encountered away from the Clinic, the second is more narrowly focused on a child as seen in the Clinic. Between 1:00 and 3:30 P.M., there are no group meetings but there are informal discussions, planned and unplanned. Between 3:30 and 5:00 P.M., there is another group meeting, but this time devoted to some ongoing group work being conducted by a staff member in one of the community settings in which we work.

Obviously we are very verbal characters. If I had the time to go into detail I could no doubt convince you that these meetings tend to have a "no-holds-barred" quality and that whatever other consequences they may have, they serve to make clear how each of us thinks and approaches common problems. We influence each other and recognize that we become changed by virtue of these meetings. We do not seek controversy but we do not avoid it. Personal feelings enter into or are reflected in discussions that can be quite stormy. We do not seek to be a happy family at the expense of candid discussion.

The major reason for the above description of our Fridays is to give you some idea of the importance we attach to the presentation and discussion of what we think and do. Aside from crowding everything into one day, we are probably no different from other clinical settings devoted to understanding and helping other people.

What does this have to do with teacher relationships? It serves as a contrast to the relative lack of meaningful, open, and sustained discussion among school personnel about their work, goals, professional problems, and explicit or implicit theoretical orientation. Let us not forget that everyone in the teaching and helping professions has an explicit or implicit, variably organized theory about human behavior which, in part at least, governs their professional actions. "Sharing" among teachers tends to be as productive of learning and communication as the "share and tell" periods are for elementary school children.

This state of affairs raises three questions: Why should this be so? Do school personnel wish it to be otherwise? What are the direct and indirect effects of this lack of communication on teachers and children in classrooms? I am not prepared to attempt to answer the first question. As for the second question, our experience at the Clinic, which is discussed at length in our earlier book (Sarason et al., 1966), indicates that school personnel are ambivalent about the aloneness of teachers. In regard to the third question our experience is quite clear, particularly in relation to the neophyte teacher; the beginning teacher (especially in our large urban settings) tends to anticipate failure, is plagued by all kinds of doubts, is fearful of a negative evaluation, is thankful for her relative isolation due to fleeting and infrequent visitation by administrative superiors, and yet is acutely aware that she needs and wants help, guidance, and support uncomplicated by the implied threat of a negative evaluation. We have seen numerous beginning teachers and their pupils suffer the consequences of a state of affairs in which help through candid and meaningful relationship with professional colleagues is distinctive by its absence. That such relationships are indeed rare says something about the social system we call a school.

The Complexity of the Problem

There is much more to the school culture than can be described by a discussion of activities and professional relationships. As we describe in our earlier book (Sarason et al., 1966), there are "peripheral personnel" (nurse, secretary, custodian) in the school whose activities and relationships with the children and teachers are not as simple or as uninfluential as their titles might suggest. There are, of course, the material or instrumental aspects of the school culture—those aspects through which information is communicated, skills are learned, traditions are explained, and attitudes are inculcated. Through the written word and other sensory media one can see most clearly that which the society considers its most prized traditions and significant historical events and movements, its expectations of its citizens, and its conceptions of human nature and development. It took, among other things, a Russian Sputnik and a civil rights movement to force many to the realization that the curriculum in our schools was based on philosophical and psychological assumptions which needed scrutiny and change.

Many other complex factors comprise the school culture. I have attempted in this chapter to convey to you that the school setting is a highly complicated and highly organized social system which we are far from understanding. On the surface it looks like a self-evident type of social system, aspects of which can be delineated by organizational charts, job descriptions, budgets, goals, and materials. This naive view could be tolerated if it did not serve as a basis for introducing change into the school, i.e., the way you effect change is to spend more money, erect more buildings, hire more people, add new services, and change what is between the covers of our textbooks. Lest I be accused of cynicism at best and of nihilism at worst let me state clearly that I have no doubt that changes introduced in these ways will have some positive effects. But, as I said at the outset and shall elaborate upon below, the degree of desired change will be much less than expected because of the failure to take into account some of the characteristics of the school culture I have discussed or alluded to.

PROCESSES OF CHANGE

I will illustrate my point by a "case history" which although taken from the past has relevance for the present. I learned a lot from this instance and still have feelings of guilt because my role, however well intentioned, produced some unhappiness in others and failure was the end product.

A number of year ago I was asked by a Superintendent of Schools to visit him and his Board of Education in order to discuss his proposal to organize a department of research in the school system. After a two-day visit I learned the following things. First, the Superintendent felt very strongly that it was an obligation of a school system to evaluate the effectiveness of its program. Second, he had many doubts about certain ongoing programs but had no firm basis for making decisions about their continuation. Third, he felt that a school system should support not only applied educational studies but basic research in the learning process. Fourth, the Board of Education (which seemed on all counts to be unusually interested and informed) basically supported the idea of a department of research but was uncertain as to how to justify the necessary expenditures—this being a time when our school systems were already overwhelmed by the great number of children born during the years following World War II. Fifth, the Superintendent was a bright, decisive, energetic individual who was in the process of finishing his research for a doctorate, perhaps an irrelevant but nevertheless interesting fact. I returned to New Haven with the feeling that it had been a good visit. After all, I had heard people say what I wanted to hear, and they had listened respectfully to what I had had to say. To add material pleasure to personal joy they had also paid for my time. The decisive reinforcement to my self-esteem was a letter from the Superintendent stating that approval for his ideas had been obtained and asking me to recommend someone for the top position. I quickly got in touch with a former student of mine, explained to him the excellent potentialities in the situation, and urged him to apply for the position; he did so and was chosen for the job.

Permit me to review the beginning of the story from the vantage point of subsequent years of experience in schools because what I have thus far related to you set the stage for later failure, my ignorance being an effective barrier to seeing the obvious. I shall list and discuss very briefly four related factors in the situation.

1. The decision to innovate was not only made from on high but by one individual.
2. There was no indication then, and this was subsequently confirmed, that the decision was other than cursorily discussed with other directors or supervisory personnel in the system. It need hardly be said that nobody below the supervisory level had even an inkling that a department of research was to come into being.
3. There apparently was no consideration or anticipation of the possibility that a department of research would be viewed as a threat to school personnel. That is, a department of research presumably evaluates ongoing programs and there is always the possibility that these programs would be found ineffective. The important point is that most school personnel take a dim view of research and researchers.
4. The fact that the person who was given the position was not in the narrow sense of the word an educator but rather a clinical psychologist was not viewed as a potential source of difficulty for the psychologist or the more traditional kinds of school personnel. The fact that there would be a "stranger" in the system, both in terms of role and training background, was not thought of.

What does the above indicate about the culture of the school? It is, in my experience, characteristic that decisions frequently are made at the top of the administrative hierarchy without regard for two likely consequences: the reactions of individuals and groups to the *manner or means* by which decisions are made, announced, and implemented, and equally as important, their reactions to the *contents* of the decision in light of prevailing attitudes, relationships, and ongoing activities. Decisions are made as if there is no means-ends problem and as if one were not dealing with a social system in which the introduction of change is no small matter. I think it important to emphasize that decisions are made by people who are part of the system but who act in ways which suggest that they do not know the system in some of its more socio-psychological characteristics.

What happened to my poor student? A less selfish question would be to ask what happened to all the actors in a drama which had not been written but was nevertheless being enacted? My former student came to the situation unaware that he was entering a social system which he did not understand and for which his training did not prepare him. Ignorance is one thing but when it is accompanied by a strong motivation to change and influence people and settings—and there is no doubt in my mind that too many research psychologists have an insufferably superior attitude to people in general and educators in particular—we have the necessary but not sufficient basis for interpersonal disaster. The near sufficient basis is provided when the individual is viewed by those within the system as unwelcome, potentially harmful, unnecessary, and an alien within their midst.

What happened, very briefly, was that the psychologist (who in this instance was a relatively humble and unaggressive individual) got caught up in a never-ending series of political maneuvers having diverse aims, e.g., to circumscribe his activities and prerogatives, to influence his choice of research problems, to saddle him with the most time-consuming and meaningless types of data collection, to stay out of the schools and classrooms, to "prove" that certain existing programs were ineffective, and, finally, not to really rock the boat. By the time he resigned his position, many within the system felt their worst fears had been confirmed while he felt that his status had deteriorated from that of a stranger to that of an outcast.

One could say that the situation I have described is not peculiar to a school and that one could find countless similar stories in other types of settings, for example, business, industry, and so on. There is truth to this, of course, and I shall return to this point later. Wherein then does the situation reveal the distinctive culture of the school? The distinctiveness is contained in the fact that the participants, each in their own ways, were stating and defending attitudes, beliefs, theories—call them what you will—about the purposes of education, the nature of teaching, the role of teachers, how children learn, and how the school settings should be organized. It would be missing the point to view the situation as resulting only from personality clashes and resistance stemming from the operational fatigue characteristic of bureaucratic structures. Equally as important as these features are the points of view about people and learning which have histories and traditions that give meaning to activities and to the sense of professional identity. It is these points of view which are distinctive to the school setting. The attempts to innovate or change which do not take these points of view into account are inviting failure, assuming that such an invitation has not already been extended through autocratic decision-making and a confusion between laudable intent and self-defeating actions.

Another story concerns the "new math" which was being introduced into this school system at the same time my former student was starting in his position. The new math had been introduced to the teachers in the previous summer through specially arranged workshops. From the standpoint of the administrative personnel, the introduction of the new math was considered the hallmark of their progressiveness, especially since at that time there were not many school systems which had made the transition from the old to the new. The psychologist was in his element; *he* wanted to learn the new math, observe it being taught in classrooms, and ultimately to devise studies comparing it to the old math. To his puzzlement there was little positive response to his interest and enthusiasm. It would be more correct to say that in diverse ways he was encouraged to focus on other problems. It was not until months later that he found out the following.

1. The teachers were never consulted about the change to the new math.
2. Although it was stated verbally that attendance at the summer workshop was not mandatory, it was the teachers' view that they had no alternative but to attend.
3. For some, perhaps many, teachers the learning of the new math was far from easy and was accompanied by much concern about their ability to teach it to their pupils when school opened.
4. The manuals which the teachers were to use were not considered by them to possess the virtue of clarity.
5. After the workshop and at the beginning of the school year most of the teachers were tense, anxious, hostile, dependent, and semi-mutinous about the new math. Weekly meetings with supervisors were instituted in an attempt to handle the problems the teachers were having, but with little apparent success.
6. There was apparently a marked discrepancy between what teachers said in public and what they said in private about the new math.

And my poor former student, coming from another world, could not understand why his desire to learn and evaluate the new math received a cool reception!

And what light does this anecdote shed on the culture of the school? In my experience, it is representative of numerous instances and allows for the following generalizations.

1. Innovations or changes practically never reflect the initiative of teachers but rather come from the highest level of administration. As a group within a single school, or as the largest subgroup within a system, teachers are remarkably unrelated to the initiation of change. I can think of no other professional group which in its own setting takes as passive a role in the initiation of change. Teachers react to change, they do not initiate it.

2. Those who initiate change generally adopt means which maximize the strength of reactions which in turn only dilutes or subverts the intent of the innovation. Although this is not peculiar to the school setting, I think it occurs with a frequency which makes it a distinctive characteristic of the school culture.

3. In practice, schools and school systems are authoritarian social systems in which their "proletariat" (the teachers) overtly conform to what is expected of them but covertly resent their lack of power. This is particularly true of the urban school culture. One frequently hears teachers state that the public no longer has the degree of respect for teachers that it once had. *What teachers tend not to say publicly is that they do not feel that they are accorded respect by those in administrative or supervisory positions in the schools.*

4. Pervasive in the school culture is a suspiciousness of, hostility toward, and derogation of formal attempts to evaluate the effectiveness of educational activities and programs. It is true, but nevertheless a misleading oversimplification, that these attitudes and reactions are unfortunate as well as obstacles to change. What is so frequently overlooked by critics is that reality frequently confirms the teacher's view that research and evaluation studies are initiated without seeking their opinions or suggestions, that these studies are inadequate or irrelevant, and that in one way or another these studies will serve as a basis for explicit or implicit criticism of teachers. From the standpoint of teachers they are the most frequent and convenient objects of criticism (from within as well as without the system) in regard to policies and programs which are not of their making.

Some might say that what I have been describing is not peculiar to the school setting and could in principle be found, for example, in business and industry. It is certainly not my position that schools are unique settings in that they are governed or explainable by principles which hold for no other social setting. The school setting is one in which, by virtue of traditions and the larger society, there are distinctive relationships among people, role attitudes, values, materials, and goals; and these distinctive relationships have a content, strength, and dynamic quality which crucially determine the fate of attempts to change any aspect of the culture or setting. Although these statements may be in the nature of the obvious, it is my contention that the failure to recognize the obvious or take it into account is primarily responsible for past and present resistance to change and for the tendency of change to fall far short of its intended mark.

Let me illustrate a few of my points by reacting to some statements by a proponent of the new math (School Mathematics Study Group, Stanford University, 1961). In concluding a presentation on student achievement in SMSG courses the following is said:

> Suppose a school administrator asks, "Can I use SMSG or similar courses in my school? My teachers are inexperienced, or their background is poor. Few have attended summer institutes." On the basis of our present evidence we must answer, "We know of no reason why you cannot, providing your teachers have the proper attitude. If they are willing to try new courses, and if they try to judge the materials critically, there is no reason to expect trouble. If you can arrange for a mathematical consultant or an in-service program during the first year, so much the better!"

I interpret this statement to imply that the success or failure of the program will be a function of the *teachers' attitudes* and the teachers only. No caution is given to the school administrator about *his* responsibilities and attitudes, *his* way of presenting and carrying out proposals for change. There is no recognition that there is a means-ends problem which, when overlooked, can produce trouble, independent of teacher attitude and capability. In recent years I have had numerous opportunities to observe the teaching of new math and to have prolonged discussions with teachers about their experiences with and attitudes toward it. My experiences unequivocally support two conclusions: (1) Many teachers are in trouble with the new math. (2) The sources of trouble are many but among the most important are the consequences of how it was introduced to the teachers; the difficulty the teachers have in voicing questions, problems, and doubts which they fear will be construed as a lack of intelligence and competence; and the tendency on the part of administrators and supervisors to relate to teachers in a way not conducive to two-way conversations. When will we take seriously the blatant fact that a teacher is part of a complicated social system and that her effectiveness as a teacher must, *in part* at least, reflect her place in and her relationship with that system? The disadvantage of this way of thinking is that it removes the teacher as the convenient scapegoat for the ills of our schools.

One final point. My observations on the teaching of new math have convinced me that children learn the new math in much the same way they learned the old math, i.e., by drill and rote memory which is also the way many teachers had to learn it in a workshop. Most children can learn the new math. However, if you are one of those people who does not equate learning with thinking, and performance with competence, it must become clear to you that we must also be on guard against the dangers of equating change with progress.

7

JEWISHNESS, BLACKISHNESS, AND THE NATURE–NURTURE CONTROVERSY

This is the most personal paper I have ever written. Neither its title nor its contents in any explicit fashion say anything about school and school change, but that is precisely what literally forced me to write this paper in 1972. It was written not long after Arthur Jensen's monograph on racial differences in intellectual performance created the social uproar it did, arguing as it did that compensatory educational efforts were misdirected because they glossed over those differences. And those were the days when it was becoming apparent that the goals of the multifaceted school change effort were not being achieved, indeed the downward trend of conventional achievement test results was not being reversed, indeed it was still plummeting and no convincing explanation was at hand, unless, of course, you accepted Jensen's explanation that the "cure" was exacerbating the "disease." Even if you accepted Jensen's conclusions, they by no means explained the downward spiral.

I had already written the *Culture of the School and the Problem of Change* which was a critique of the conceptual and procedural inadequacies of reform efforts, leading to the conclusion that nothing would change. I said little or nothing about racial differences or compensatory education because they were not directly relevant to my central purpose which was to show the relationships between the culture of schools and its resistance to change. However, there was one theme in that book that was not as prominent as it deserved to be, which by the time I finished writing the book I realized needed elaboration. That theme was: we, people generally and school reformers specifically, were dramatically unsophisticated about how to develop a time perspective that took seriously complicated problems of social and institutional change. That is to say, our time perspectives are unrealistic in the extreme, setting the stage for disappointment, disillusionment, and unwarranted pendulum swings. How you understand a problem in institutional-historical terms should determine your time perspective, i.e., how long it should take you to reach your goals. I already knew that the time perspective of school reformers not only grossly underestimated the complexities with which they were confronted but, even leaving their oversimplifications aside, their time perspective reflected wish fulfillment more than reality.

My point of view in this regard—less a point of view than thoughts in need of connection—was forged by virtue of a personal experience. It was just before jets became commonplace. I was flying on a four engine, propeller plane from New York to Dallas. When we began the long taxi to the take off point, our pilot, who was obviously a frustrated disc jockey, began a series of announcements. First, we *would* take off, please be patient. Second, this was a wonderful airplane. Third, the plane had four marvelous "Evinrudes" that would give us a smooth ride. And more, much more. We did take off. The sky did not contain a cloud. I was sitting in the window seat on the right side of the plane. About an hour or so into the flight, black smoke, clouds of it, poured out of one of the motors. How I managed not to pee in my pants, I do not know. The disc jockey cheerily came on and said, "Those of you on the right side of the plane can see that one of our Evinrudes is in trouble. We knew that ten minutes ago and "feathered" the motor (fortunately not explained). We can fly to Dallas with three Evinrudes but that is against American Airlines regulations. We will put down in Louisville." Five minutes later he is back on, "We will not put down in Louisville. We will put down in Cincinnati. Now, when we get there, you will see the landing strip surrounded by a lot of fire fighting equipment. That is standard operating procedure. Don't worry, we will put down safely." I have abbreviated his commercials! And we landed safely. During the three hour wait for another plane I met the pilot and told him how my mind had been flooded by the movies I had seen in my younger days about World War I planes going up in smoke, plunging to earth. To which he said, "The one thing you cannot do with these four engine monsters is put them down quickly." It was that statement, then and there, that brought poorly connected ideas about time perspective and school change into a meaningful integration. A school, let alone a school system, is a very complicated institution, conceptually a monster, reflective of a past that is still in the present, comprised of human relationships locked in institutional concrete, and distinguished by practices and outlooks honed over scores of decades.

What the reader must bear in mind is that when I agreed to write and give this paper, public awareness of the failure of compensatory programs was expanding and there were segments in that public who cottoned to Jensen's writings. School reformers were also disappointed and puzzled, although as a group they pronounced anathema on Jensen. I made two decisions before writing that paper. The first was that it was strategically inadvisable, really impossible, to deal head on with Jensen in the format of a paper. I did not want to get mired in a discussion of his data and logic of his argument. From my standpoint Jensen's position was amazingly ahistorical, acultural, and insensitive to how culture and history shape the phenomenology of psyches, features that have long stamped the thinking of psychometricians. Psychometrics is a legitimate and important field and Jensen is among the best in that field, but he suffered from the defects of his narrow virtues.

The second decision was that having critiqued school reform efforts there was no point in repeating what I had already said. I had raised the time perspectives problem but not in a compelling (to me) way, and I had said nothing about all of the issues surrounding race and education. How to write such a paper? I knew I would be saying things that would not sit well with some black people, as well as with many other people who understandably preferred near term solutions. Too many people have to believe that in the societal arena we are dealing with problems that have "solutions" in the sense that four divided by two is a solution. In that arena we are always dealing with problems we have to solve again and again. That fact is hard for the American psyche to take because we have been schooled to believe that with a deep and sincere national resolve, plus the right amount of money and resources, no problem is intractable, no problem is unamenable to foreseeable eradication. I was going to be saying that in regard to the improvement of the performance of blacks, our usual time perspective was utterly and unfairly inappropriate. And I also knew that in some quarters I would be seen as a Jewish chauvinist, perhaps a patronizing one, someone who had "made it" and was now advocating "Be patient, some day your descendants will make it too." Today, more than two decades later, I would alter nothing I said in that paper.

So, although the title and substance of this paper said little or nothing about school change, it represented a decisive step in my emerging point of view. I am indebted to that disc jockey pilot for uttering that sentence about the impossibility of putting a monster airplane down quickly. School change is a monster problem. When in his inaugural address President Kennedy said that by the end of the decade we would put a man on the moon, that time perspective was warranted by a long past of experience and research, successes and failures, i.e., the basic problems had largely been confronted and worked through, what remained were primarily technological-engineering problems. In regard

to race and school change we are very far from the point where a similar prediction can be made. We are not confronted with technological-
engineering problems which in this instance never have been and never
will be such a problem, despite all of the hoopla and hype about the
glories of the information revolution. Today, the complexity and
intractability of racial and school change problems are more complex
than when I wrote that paper. That has not surprised me, I expected that.
Some day, if and when I grow up, I will explain why I have not been surprised, why, for example, there is a growing anti-Semitism in the black
community, especially among its educated members, why the goals of
education and the criteria for judging their appropriateness are under
increasing challenge. All of this goes way beyond race and school
change; they are parts of the social drama and only parts. It's rough stuff
and I remind the reader never to forget Mencken's assertion that for
every problem there is a simple answer that is wrong.

A postscript. What I have said above was written the day before I
flew to Chicago to attend a meeting. (The pilot was commendably brief
in his announcement and there was no smoke in or out of the plane, for
which I thank God for big favors!) The meeting's purpose was to advise
(indirectly) Mr. Walter Annenberg about how his unprecedented gift of a
half a billion dollars to public education might best be used to further
his aim of dealing with, ameliorating, and even preventing the manifestations of violence, social divisiveness, and deterioration of educational
standards and performance, and more. And Mr. Annenberg asked that
the money be directed largely to programs to be established in our large
metropolitan areas, e.g., New York, Chicago, Los Angeles, Philadelphia.
It was also his wish that within four years or so the money should have
been allocated, which is not to say that it will have been spent at the
end of that time. Ted Sizer had, in his typical masochistic style, agreed
to arrange the meeting and to convey the advice of its participants to Mr.
Annenberg through President Gregorian of Brown University. The participants were a very thoughtful, serious, responsible group the majority of
whom had shortened their life expectancy by their hands-on immersion
in school change. I am, to say the least, ambivalent about meetings if
only because of my inability to understand why others do not see the
world precisely as I do. The meeting exceeded my expectations. I
learned a lot.

There was general agreement on one point: coming up with a strategy for action that by the end of four years would have shaped everything
thereafter seemed unrealistic. I considered it egregiously self-defeating,
a complete misreading or miscomprehension or sheer ignorance of what
has been learned by past experience, failure, and research. To believe

that something as complicated as school, school system or school district change can be planned for and initiated by our ordinary conception of calendar time is akin to believing in Santa Claus. You do not have to be the equivalent of rocket scientist in the social-educational disciplines to know that our large metropolitan areas are as wondrously complicated as the atom, and far less harnessable. In the case of the atom it all started with the Greeks, as so much else did. In the case of our metropolitan areas our understanding did not begin to deepen until relatively recently. Our understanding has increased enough to know that a four year time perspective for introducing and sustaining change is self-defeating and the precondition for another disaster.

I hope I am wrong. I write, entreat, and plead that readers who think I am wrong will write to me. Like the rest of humanity I do not change my mind easily, but I know how to listen and I know, at least in the abstract, that I have not cornered the market on truth in regard to the problems about which I have written.

———

Those who have participated in the recent version of the nature–nuture controversy have, for the most part, neglected to confront the derivation of their time perspective in relation to social change in general and historically rooted group attitudes and performance in particular.[1] As in past versions of the controversy, the issues have centered around personal and social values, methodology, the content of the measuring instruments, sampling problems, and genetic theories and laws, and the consequences of these issues for programs of social action. There seems to be recognition by all that social history is an important variable, that inequity and prejudice have been and are rampant, and that it is probably impossible at the present time to discuss the controversy in a dispassionate way. Within scientific circles it is an explosive issue, just as it is in the society at large. I assume that if a study were done asking people if they thought that future versions of controversy (say 20 or 40 years from now) would be conducted in a less explosive climate, almost all would reply in the negative. Indeed, many would probably predict a more explosive climate. If a similar study had been done 50 years ago

---

[1] The text beginning with this sentence and continuing to the end of this chapter is reprinted from the *American Psychologist*, 28 (11), 1973, pp. 962–971. Copyright 1973 by the American Psychological Association. Reprinted by permission of the publisher.

when, after World War I, the nature–nuture controversy was once again peaking, far fewer people would have correctly predicted the present climate of social explosiveness in which the controversy is taking place. (At that time, interestingly enough, blacks were not central to the controversy. The inferiority of blacks was not then a burning issue, presumably because it was uncritically accepted by most people [white and black] as a fact which did not need to be labored. It was the flood of immigrant groups from Europe and Asia that brought together questions of national policy and the status of knowledge about the determinants of intellectual performance.) Today, sides have been taken and with a degree of partisanship that the passage of time will not easily change—a variant of my thesis that changes in attitude and performance of historically rooted groups are relatively immune to change except when viewed from a time perspective in which the basic measuring unit may be a century. When I say a century I do not mean it in a precise or literal way, but rather as a means to emphasize a time perspective far longer than that which we ordinarily adopt.

For a statement and description of my position convincingly to reflect my thinking requires that I be unusually personal and relatively unhindered by considerations of modesty, politeness, and that undefined criterion of "good taste." I shall talk about aspects of myself and my family not only because they are the "data" I know best, but because I assume (phenomenologically I *know*) that I am quite representative of Jews, possessed of all the ingredients that comprise Jewishness. What I have to say has been said, and far better, by other Jews. I justify going over old ground because, as the title of this article suggests, I wish to relate it to an important and fateful social and scientific issue. Here, too, I make no claim to originality, although I believe that I provide an emphasis that has been lacking in the scientific literature.

JEWISHNESS

I begin with my father, a simple, unassuming, relatively inarticulate man who spent a long working life as a cutter of children's dresses. He was not an impressive person. He did not read books, but he went to synagogue and obviously knew the Old Testament (in Hebrew) backward and forward. As he prayed, he kept the books open and turned the pages, but rarely did more than glance at them. He recited the prayers in a most undeviating, ritualistic manner. Beginning at age 8 or 9, having enrolled me in Hebrew school, he expected me to sit and pray with him. Of course, I did not understand what I was reading (or even why), and when from time to time my boredom and anger forced me to ask why the book could not be put into English, he never deemed the question worthy of a response.

He loved children and had a gentleness with them to which they responded, but my memory contains nothing that would support the notion that he had other than a primitive notion of children and learning. The early sources of my anger toward my father were many, but two are particularly relevant here. One concerns a leather-covered Oxford dictionary which I had not the strength to pick up until I was six or seven. I still have the dictionary, and when it comes to its weight I know whereof I speak. I never saw my father use that dictionary, and to me its presence was symbolic of his selfishness: Why did we have *that* around the house when we (I) needed other things? Why didn't we hide it, sell it, or throw it out? Occasionally I would peruse its pages, but the book was so large and heavy that even when I did not have to hold it, I could not comfortably use it. Related to this was our battle about the *New York Times*, which he bought and read every day. Why buy a newspaper that did not have funnies? How more selfish could a father be than to deprive his children of newspaper funnies, particularly on Sundays when all other newspapers contained loads of them? I hated the *New York Times*, which, I need not tell you, I now read every day. I also have an aversion to funnies and truly cannot comprehend why my wife and daughter read them first when the local paper arrives—and sometimes even argue about who will read them first.

And then there were my older male cousins who, when I was in elementary school, were preparing to go to college. At that time I knew as much about college as I did about astronomy. There was a place called college and there were stars in the sky, and that exhausted my knowledge of both. But in the numerous meetings of the extended family that word *college* kept coming up in reverent and awesome tones. Cousin Leo was not going to any college, he was going to a place called Cornell and that showed (not to me) that Leo was smart because not many Jewish boys were *allowed* there. And if Leo did well there, as *of course* he would, he was then going to go to still another kind of college and become a doctor. Cousin Moey was a very smart fellow, too, and wasn't it too bad that he had to work during the day and go to college at night. Go to college at night! What kind of craziness was that? To me that meant he couldn't listen to the radio at night, those being the days when having a radio was still a novelty. It was during those early years that I kept hearing the phrase "He will make something of himself" applied to some of my relatives.

There was Leo's brother, Oscar, who was special. If I had available to me then the words I have now I would have described Oscar to my friends as smart-smart. That's the way the family regarded him. But Oscar posed a real problem because he played football, and extremely well. He was as good in football as he was in the classroom. That Oscar was on the small side was only one reason for family opposition to playing football. It was important because he might get "good and hurt," not be able to go to school, and maybe not even go to college. The more important point was that nice Jewish boys, particularly if they were smart, didn't play football. That was for the gentiles (goys), who were again by nature, crudely physical and aggressive. Football was quintessentially goyish, and it was stupid for Jewish boys to compete in that arena. David may have slain Goliath, thanks to God, but that was in another world. Let's respect David, but let us not go so far as to identify with his actions! One Saturday morning I walked into my cousin's apartment—we lived upstairs, those being the days of extended families in restricted areas, and I use the word "restricted" in its geographical and discriminatory senses—and I heard my aunt yelling and screaming in Oscar's room. There was Oscar curled up womblike being pounded by my aunt at the same time that she was telling him and the world what she thought of a Jewish boy who was going to play football for his high school, *on Saturday.* What had she done to deserve such punishment? What would *they* think? "They" referred to all her Jewish friends and neighbors who, she was sure, would both blame and sympathize with her on one of the worst fates a Jewish mother could experience. How could a mother stand by and watch her child, with such a "good head," go straight to hell? It was an awesome display of physical energy and verbal imagery—my Aunt Jennie was regarded by all as having no equal when it came to using and inventing the Yiddish equivalents of longshoreman language. When her physical energy was spent (the verbal flow never ceased), Oscar got up from the bed, collected his football suit, calmly but sweetly said goodbye, and went off to join the goyim in defense of the glory of Newark's Barringer High School. Needless to say, when he went to Brown, where he was quite a football player during the years when that college had its best teams, my aunt attended a number of games *(on Saturday)* because, I assume she wanted to be on hand when her little boy would be near-fatally injured. He was no more than five feet nine inches tall and probably weighed no more than 170 pounds. Leonard Carmichael, who was then chairman of the Department of Psychology at Brown, once got Oscar aside and expressed concern that he could be injured and was, perhaps, wasting his time playing football when he could start making a career in psychology, in which Professor Carmichael had concluded Oscar had shown considerable aptitude.

Oscar was directly important in my life. Toward the end of the first semester of my first year in junior high school, Oscar, home from college for a few days, visited our family. He interrogated my mother about the courses I was taking and was horrified to learn that I was enrolled in the commercial curriculum, taking such courses as typing, junior business training, etc. He told my mother that if I stayed in the commercial curriculum I would not be admitted to college. My mother was aghast and took action. A few weeks later, at the beginning of the next semester, I found myself taking Latin, ancient history, and algebra.

I do not have to relate more anecdotes to make the point that being Jewish was inextricably interwoven with attitudes toward intellectual accomplishment. To separate the one from the other was impossible. This did not mean that being Jewish meant that one was smart or capable of intellectual accomplishments, but it meant that one had respect for such strivings. Respect is too weak a word to convey the force and role of these attitudes. It is like saying that we have respect for breathing. We did not have to learn these attitudes in any consciously deliberate way. We had no choice in the matter, just as we had no choice in choosing our parents. As children we did not have to verbalize these attitudes to ourselves, we would not have known how. The word *attitudes* is a poor one to describe what and how we absorbed what we did. We learned those attitudes in as "natural" a way as learning to like lox and bagels, gefilte fish, or knishes.

How do we account for the strength and frequency of these aspects of Jewishness? Please note that I am not asking how to account for individuals like myself or my mother and father or my cousins, but rather why these aspects are characteristics of Jews as a group. This is, initially at least, a cultural, not a psychological, question. It is a question which directs us, among other things, to history and tradition and requires the adoption of a time perspective quite different from what we ordinarily use when our focus is on a single individual or generation. Obviously, if these aspects of Jewishness have been manifested for generations and centuries, the outlines of an answer to my question become clear—and I do not confuse clarity of outline with complexity of the substantive answer. These aspects, when looked upon in the context of the sweep of social-cultural history, have always characterized Jewish life. Indeed, when one looks at my question from this time perspective, one ends up by asking another question: So what else is new? Or, one becomes intrigued by individual Jews who do not possess these characteristics, whose mental breathing apparatus inexplicably did not take in ingredients ever present in his social-cultural atmosphere.

The aspects of Jewishness I have thus far discussed are not understandable by looking only at the present or near past. That is an obvious point which needed to be said in order to make a second one: *These aspects have been and will continue to be immune to change in any short peri-*

od of time, by which I mean a minimum of a century. Leaving aside Hitler's "final solutions" as well as other types of world catastrophes, I can think of no set of circumstances in which these aspects of Jewishness would disappear or be noticeably diluted in less than several or scores of generations. These circumstances could not be casual or indirect, they would have to be extremely potent and persistent. More of this later when I question the rationale behind the expectation that certain consequences of some aspects of blackishness can be changed noticeably in a decade or so, or that if blacks and whites differ on test, one can ignore the relation of these differences to differences in the psychological core of blackishness and whiteishness, or that when you have equated a group of blacks and whites on an intelligence test or on a measure of academic achievement you have controlled for the most influential psychological determinants of intellectual performance in real life. (It's like saying that everybody is equal before the law, the person on welfare as well as the millionaire. There *is* a difference between facts and the truth.)

Now to another aspect of Jewishness to which I have alluded: the knowledge (it is not a feeling, it is phenomenologically a fact) that one is in a hostile world. This was crystal clear in my parents' and grandparents' generations. Their thinking went like this: Built into the mental core of every non-Jew is a dislike of and an enmity toward Jews. Yes, there were some nice Gentiles and up to a point you could trust and work with them, but let any conflict or dissension enter into the relationship and you would find that core of hatred asserting itself. It might not be verbalized, but, nonetheless, you could count on it. In the end, and there is always an end, you would get it in the neck—no ifs, ands, or buts. I have long felt that their resistance to mixed marriages—and the word *resistance* does not begin to convey the bitterness and strength of the feelings—was less a consequence of religion or clannishness than it was of the fear of physical injury to or destruction of one's child. To say they mistrusted the non-Jewish world is to reveal a genius for understatement. And if you tried to reason with them it was no contest because they could overwhelm you with history. They could marshall evidence from past centuries, as well as events in their own lives, with a rapidity, force, and cogency that doctoral students in history must fantasize about when they approach their orals. If you get a kick out of unproductive arguments I suggest you specialize in combating history with logic and goodwill—the kicks are endless. (If orthodox Jews are unavailable, try it with blacks, who have more kinship to Jews in this respect than they know.) If an aspect of you is poignantly and consciously rooted in history, you are not a candidate for attitude change. We would have had a more solid and realistic foundation for our efforts at social change if American social psychology had dealt with historically rooted, conscious attitudes of historically rooted groups. At the very least, it might have provided a more realistic time perspective about the attainment of the goals of these efforts.

What about me and my generation who, unlike our parents and grandparents, were born in this country with its traditions of opportunity and freedom? Did we possess the aspect of Jewishness that says this is a hostile world, even though "objectively" we grew up in a social environment radically different from that of previous generations? The very fact that our family had been created in this country and not in a European one meant that it would be different from what went before. You could write for years about the differences and when you were all through and began to list the similarities you would soon be listing the aspect "This is a hostile world for Jews." Some anecdotes from my adult life: When in 1938 I applied for admission to graduate school the knotty question was whether or not I would lie about being Jewish. Those were the days when you were asked for your religion and a photograph. They also wanted to know your father's occupation. So if I told them my father was a cutter of children's dresses, that I was Jewish, plus the fact that I would be graduated from an unrecognized college (Dana College, renamed the University of Newark, housed then in the former Feigenspan Brewery) what would be my chances? The point is not what was objectively true but the strength of my feeling that my application would be read by people hostile to Jews. The strength of my feeling and its automatic and indiscriminate application were not justified, but it is the hallmark of historically rooted attitudes of historically rooted groups that there is a discrepancy between external conditions and subjective impressions. (This is true for blacks in regard to whites, as it is for the Irish in regard to the English, etc.) The fact that these attitudes receive periodic reinforcement is sufficient to maintain their strength and indiscriminateness. For example, why does a colleague of mine still have in his possession a letter written to him in 1939 by a most eminent person who was then chairman of the department of psychology of a prestigious university? I have seen the letter. It is a remarkable but not surprising document because it says that although my colleague had all the paper credentials to be admitted to the doctoral program, he should think hard about coming because, as a Jew, he would not be able to be placed in a teaching job. A list of names is given of Jewish students who finished their doctorates in that department but who could not get jobs. Come, the letter says, but only if you regard it as an "intellectual adventure" and not as preparation for a career. How complicated a theory do we need to understand why my colleague, like myself, generalized our expectation of discrimination indiscriminately?

I lived in a radically different world than my parents and grandparents. I differed from them in countless important ways, but I differed not at all from them in the possession of this aspect of Jewishness. When I was finishing graduate school in 1942, there were two other students, and good friends (Jorma Niven, Harry Older), who were also going into the job market. To avoid competition among us, we did not apply for jobs at the same colleges or universities. Jorma and Harry were not Jewish, but they understood what was at stake when I wondered whether on my vita I should note that I was Jewish and so avoid interviews at places that did not look kindly on Jews. The point of these anecdotes is not to say something about the external world or even my perception of it but rather the pervasiveness and strength of my psychological radar about Jewishness, a constantly tuned instrument that was always at work and always sighting "objects" about which I had to decide whether they were friend or foe. But why do I say was? It is as true of me today as it was then, and with far less justification. My external world has changed dramatically within my lifetime, it has changed even more in relation to my parents' world, and yet that radar continues to work as if the external world has not changed.

A year ago when I was at a social gathering at Yale's Hillel, the Rabbi told me, in confidence and with that all too familiar mixture of pride and fear, that approximately one-third of all students at Yale were Jewish. He did not have to put into words (or even bother to look at me to see if I understood his message) that this information should not be bandied about because it might arouse the envy and enmity of non-Jews. You might expect such an attitude in a rabbi but not in me, but such an expectation simply ignores what fine-tuned, efficient processes and mechanisms cultural transmission consists of, insuring that the most central aspects of our sense of identity are independent of choice and changes in our external world.

I have known scores of Jews of my generation who have visited Israel. They were heterogeneous in many respects so that if you administered to them every psychological test that has ever been standardized, I predict you would find that, intelligence tests and political attitudes aside, the scores would be distributed in a fairly normal fashion. With no exception, every one of them spontaneously described the feeling—compounded of surprise, disbelief, relief, and security—they had in response to the fact that "everyone there is Jewish." As one of them said in deep puzzlement: "Even though I knew everyone was Jewish, I found that I continued to ask myself whether this or that person was Jewish. It was very unsettling at times." There are some attitudinal radars that cannot be turned off, because they have no off-on switch. These visitors shared another reaction, this one compounded of respect, envy, and pride and put by one of them in this way: "They have no fear. They don't care what the rest of the world thinks and does. They are prepared to fight and they have no doubt who will win in the end." To the non-Israeli Jew, "in the end" meant and still means getting it in the neck; to the Israeli it means quite the reverse. It took several generations of Israel sabras, with an assist from Hitler, to effect a change in attitude. Put more correctly: It took all of that for a millennia-old identification to reassert itself. It was all right now to identify with David because one had to, and like David, but unlike those at Masada, the Goliath would be defeated. How strange this is to the American Jew. How strange it would be to the Israeli to learn about my reaction to an item in last week's *Yale Daily* that 50% of this year's Phi Beta Kappas were Jewish. He would have difficulty understanding my reflective fear that this would not sit well in the minds of many non-Jews.

What about the younger generation of Jews in our society? Is this aspect of Jewishness in them or has it been eroded? As best as I can determine, this core of Jewishness is in them despite obvious changes in our society. When I asked a group of Jewish students about this, they looked at me as only smart-smart teenagers can look at dumb-dumb professors, and one of them said: "In high school I read *The Wall*. There *was* the 1967 six-day war. And when I apply to medical school I know the chances of Jews have been decreased because they will take more minority people. How are we supposed to feel when we read that an African leader is sorry that Hitler did not win and that some black groups in our country seem to talk in the same way?" Toward the end of the discussion a young woman said, somewhat hostilely: "Because my parents were like you. What did *you* tell your daughter about going with or marrying a non-Jew?" A bull's-eye! Her comments recalled to me the time our family of three was about to leave our house to begin our first trip abroad. Just as we were ready to leave, my daughter (who then was 10) said she had forgotten something and went upstairs to get it. The "it" turned out to be a chain to which was attached a gold Star of David. No, my wife and I had not given it to her because we are not religious.[2] It had been given to her by a Catholic nun who was head of an agency to which I had been a consultant, but that is another story, albeit a quite relevant one.

Before continuing, let me summarize what I have tried to say:

---

[2] Jewishness, at least for many Jews in our society, is independent of religiousness, a fact which many rabbis keep complaining about, because they believe that when the two are experienced as independent, it will, over time, result in the disappearance of both. That they are experienced as independent was seen during the Israeli–Arab six-day war in 1967, as thousands of American Jews who had no interest in or commitment to Judaism spontaneously gave money for the support of Israel. The generosity of support is perhaps less relevant than the anxiety they felt about the threat to the continuation of Jewishness, not to the religion of their ancestors.

1. There are certain attitudinal characteristics which are part of the core of Jewishness. What is notable is their frequency and strength.

2. These characteristics are a kind of "second nature," learned, absorbed, and inculcated with all the force, subtleness, and efficiency of the processes of cultural transmission.

3. To understand the frequency and strength of these characteristics requires a time perspective of centuries.

4. Similarly, these characteristics could not be extinguished or diluted in strength except over very long periods of time. What centuries have produced will not quickly change even under external pressure.

5. It is impossible to understand and evaluate intellectual performance of groups without taking account of each group's attitudes toward such activity. This is an obvious point to anyone who has engaged in clinical work, and it has received substantial support in the research literature, for example, the test anxiety literature. It is no less valid a point when one deals with the intellectual performance of historically rooted groups and their historically rooted attitudes. (Women's liberation groups, now and in the distant past, understood this point quite well. The original title of this article was "Jewishness, Blackishness, Femaleness, and the Nature-Nurture Controversy.")

I have no difficulty accepting the notion that intelligence has its genetic components, nor do I have difficulty with the idea that different groups may possess different patterns of abilities. It would require mental derangement of a most serious sort to deny that different groups get different scores on various tests of intelligence. But I have the greatest difficulty understanding how anyone can come to a definitive conclusion in these matters based on studies which assume that what culture and history have created can be changed in a matter of years or decades. What combination of ignorance and presumption, what kind of understanding of human history does one have to possess to accept the hypothesis that the central psychological core of *historically* rooted groups can markedly change in a lifetime? It is a fact that Jews as a group score high on intelligence tests, do well on achievement tests, and are disproportionately represented in the professions and academia. It may be true that this is part of a consequence of selective survival and breeding over the centuries. But if one invokes the law of parsimony (not for the purposes of denying a hypothesis or preventing anyone from pursuing a particular line of research) for the purpose of assigning weights to variables on the basis of what we know about culture, one must conclude that the transmission of Jewishness from generation to generation has been fantastically successful—a view of "success" understood but probably not shared by those approaching their deaths in the Nazi holocaust, the Spanish inquisition, and countless other Jew-murdering periods in history. My genes have a long history, an indisputable fact. My Jewishness also has a long history, another indisputable fact. At this point in time we know far more about my Jewishness than about my genes. When as a society we mount programs of social amelioration, I would prefer to act on the basis of the known, recognizing that I will not be alive to know the ultimate outcome.

BLACKISHNESS

What I have to say about "blackishness" has been foreshadowed by my description of certain aspects of Jewishness.[3] Jews and blacks share the characteristic "this is a hostile world." Some would argue that the sensitivity of blacks to anticipated hostility is stronger than it is in Jews. I am not sure this is the case, although some blacks and Jews would consider it self-evidently true. The more I talk to Jews about this, the more I am impressed by two things: how strong this aspect is and how much they want to believe that it isn't strong. Their self-report about its workings is discrepant with its strength. I stick with this point because it is instructive about what happens when two historically rooted attitudes contradict each other: "This is a hostile world" and "this is a society free of prejudice." In any event, this aspect of blackishness (in white society) is historically rooted and will be immune to change except over a long, long period of time. Blacks, of course, are absolutely correct when they say that an equally long period of time will be required for whites to overcome *their* historically rooted attitudes toward blacks.

In our society, at least, blackishness has not had at its core unbounded respect for book learning and the acquisition of academically soaked, cognitive skills. Just as when the Jews in Egypt were slaves, did manual labor, and could only hope for survival and dream of freedom, so in black culture, intellectuality or bookishness (call it what you will) has been far from the top on the priority list. As groups, Jews and blacks could not be more far apart than on the degree to which their cultures

---

[3] Obviously, I cannot talk about blackishness with the affective nuance and depth of knowledge and experience that I can talk about Jewishness, nor is it necessary that I try or important that I cannot do justice to an equally complex cultural-psychological core. Sufficient for my purpose is that I pinpoint certain communalities and differences and their significance for the nature–nuture controversy.

are suffused with "intellectuality." On intelligence tests Jews get higher scores than blacks.[4] *From my perspective, the important question is not how to explain the difference but why the difference is not greater.* This reminds me of Goddard's description of the Kallikak culture and his use of it as proof of Kallikak mental inferiority passed on from generation to generation. From his description of that encapsulated culture, one might conclude that the Kallikaks were a biologically superior group, that is, anyone who could grow up and survive in that culture must have been extremely well endowed constitutionally.

Over the past century, more and more blacks have "made it" in the intellectual arena, but they have represented a very small percentage of all blacks. It is my impression that compared even to three decades ago, more black children experience something akin to what I described of my childhood, but there is no basis at all for concluding that this has become a characteristic experience. What warrant is there in psychological theory and research that would lead to the expectation that the attitudinal core of blackishness could, under the most favorable conditions, be changed in less than scores of generations. And is there a psychologist who would argue that we have even remotely approximated "the most favorable conditions?"

For me, the central question is how theories determine time perspective, that is, how one's conception of what man and society are determines one's time perspective about changing either. I have discussed this in connection with the problem of changing schools and creating new settings (Sarason, 1971/1982, 1972). Two examples of what I mean: What if someone came to us and asked why we cannot teach children to read in 24 hours? Assuming that we knew the person to be sane and we could control the tendency to throw him out of our office, what would we say? It would probably take us 24 hours of uninterrupted talk to explain how children develop physically, mentally, and socially; the inevitable social and interpersonal context in which learning takes place; the complexity

---

[4] There was a time (decades ago) when Jews, like blacks today, were viewed as being mentally inferior because of inferior genetic endowment. I am indebted to my colleague, Edward Zigler (personal communication, 1973), for pointing out to me the anti-Jewish attitudes of the early eugenicists, particularly Galton and Pearson. In a manuscript he is preparing, Zigler states:

Pearson continually employed genetic arguments in his efforts to stem the immigration of Polish and Russian Jews into England, arguing that they were genetically inferior to the earlier settlers of the English nation. He concluded "Taken on the average, and regarding both sexes,

of motivation and its vicissitudes; the knowledge and cognitive skills that are necessary for the productive assimilation and use of symbols; and the problems that can be created when external pressures do not take developmental stages readiness into account. Besides, we might ask this irritating ignoramus, Do you mean why can't we teach a child to read in 24 hours or do you mean a *group* of children in a classroom?

A second example: What if we went to a psychoanalyst friend and asked him really to level with us and explain how he justifies seeing a patient for one hour a day, four or five days a week, perhaps for two, three, four, or more years. "Why does it take that long? Do you really believe," we ask him, "that it takes that long to be helpful to someone? Aren't there quicker ways of giving help?" "Friend (?)," he replies, "there is much you do not understand." He then proceeds to summarize for us what the human organism is at birth, how its cognitive and affective equipment is organized and develops, the ways in which it becomes increasingly psychologically and physically differentiated, how it develops and utilizes a variety of coping mechanisms, the sources of inevitable internal and external conflict, the nature and strength of resistances to change, the relationship of all of this to the interpersonal dynamics of the nuclear family, and on and on depending on whether our psychoanalyst friend is summarizing Freud's *Introductory Lectures* or multivolumed collected works. (If he happens to be a true believer, we would also hear about parricide and the primal horde in the dawning history of mankind.) "Now," he would say, "you can begin to understand why psychoanalytic treatment takes so long. It is not that we desire to prolong it, but rather that our understanding of man requires it if we are to be able meaningfully to help somebody radically change accustomed ways of thinking and acting. Of course," he would admit, "you can help troubled people in a shorter period of time by focusing only on the elimination of symptoms, but that is not our goal, which is to illuminate for our patients their psychological core and its dynamics, and we are not always successful."

---

this alien Jewish population is somewhat inferior physically and mentally to the native population. . . ."

The anti-Jewish attitude of the early eugenicist finally culminated in the complete bastardization of the eugenics movement in Nazi Germany, where the "final solution" of dealing with "races" of inferior genetic stock was to murder them in gas ovens. It is interesting to note that less than 50 years after Pearson's assertion of the genetic inferiority of the Jews, another distinguished Englishman, C.P. Snow, argued that in light of the large number of Jewish Nobel laureates, the Jews must be a superior people. We thus see how tenuous indeed are those assertions that a particular group is inferior or superior.

I do not have to labor the point that one's conception of a problem or process determines one's time perspective about how to influence or change it. The relationship may be grossly invalid either because one's conception is faulty, or one's time perspective poorly deduced, or both, but the fact remains that there is always a relationship. In my opinion, the failure or inability to confront this relationship in a systematic and realistic way is one of the most frequent sources of personal disillusionment and conflict, as it is also one of the central defects in most social science theorizing. Is it not amazing how many social scientists reacted to the Supreme Court desegregation decision in 1954 as if it really meant that desegregation was ended, or would be ended in a matter of a decade or so? Is it not equally amazing how many people really believed that if disadvantaged groups, like the blacks, were provided new and enriched educational experiences they would as a group blossom quickly in terms of conventional educational and intellectual criteria? Is it not pathetic how eager we were to believe that we possessed the knowledge to justify these expectations? What combination of ignorance and arrogance permitted people to proclaim that if we delivered the right kinds of programs and spent the appropriate sums of money we could quickly undo what centuries had built up? When the expectations that powered these efforts were obviously not being fulfilled, what permitted some people to conclude that perhaps the victim was in some ways different from (less endowed than) those in the dominant society? Why were they so ready to "blame the victim" instead of the thinking from which derived such an unrealistic time perspective? And again I must ask: What is there in man's history and in the corpus of social science knowledge which contradicts the statement that few things are as immune to quick changes as the historically rooted, psychological core of ethnic and racial groups? Jewishness and blackishness are products, among other things (and I assume there *are* other things), of social and cultural history, and their psychological cores will successfully resist short-term efforts aimed at changing them.

In one of his syndicated columns, William F. Buckley, Jr. (*New Haven Journal Courier,* March 20, 1969) has provided support of my thesis: needless to say, he does this unknowingly. Buckley quoted approvingly from an article by Ernest van den Haag:

> The heart of Mr. van den Haag's analysis, so critically useful at the present moment, should be committed to memory before the ideologists of racism take the Jensen findings and mount a campaign of I-told-you-soism with truly ugly implications. Van den Haag asked himself:

> Q. Suppose the average native intelligence of Negroes is inferior to that of whites. Would that mean that Negroes are inferior to whites?

A. One may regard others as inferior to oneself, or to one's group, on the basis of any criterion, such as mating, eating, drinking or language habits, religious practices, or competence in sports, business, politics, art or finally, by preferring one's own type, quality or degree of intelligence, skin or hair color and so forth.

By selecting appropriate criteria each group can establish the inferiority of others, and its own superiority. . . . The selection of criteria for superiority or inferiority is arbitrary, of course. . . . I do not believe that intelligence is any more relevant to judgments of inferiority than, say, skin color is.

If Negroes on the average turn out to have a genetically lower learning ability than whites in some respects, e.g., the manipulation of abstract symbols, and if one chooses this ability as the ranking criterion, it would make Negroes on the average inferior to some whites and superior to others. Suppose four-fifths of Negroes fall into the lower half of intelligence distribution. Chances are that, say, one-third of the whites will too. Hence, if intelligence is the criterion, the four-fifths of the Negro group would be no more "inferior" than the one-third of the white group. Judgments of inferiority among whites are rarely based solely on intelligence. There certainly are many people who do not rank high on intelligence tests but are, nonetheless, preferable, and preferred, to others who do. I know of no one who selects his associates—let alone friends—purely in terms of intelligence. God knows, we certainly do not elect to political office those who are most intelligent. I would conclude that whatever we may find out about Negro intelligence would not entail any judgment about general inferiority.

Buckley concluded the column with these words aimed at those who "by their dogmatic insistence on 'equality' at every level succeeded in persuading typical Americans to put far too great an emphasis on 'intelligence'":

Add to these observations the Christian point: namely that all men are equal in the truest sense of the word, and the findings of Dr. Jensen are placed in perspective. But it will take time to undo the damage brought by the ideologization of science during the reign of American liberalism.

It will take time to undo the damage! Mr. Buckley seems to have grasped the principle that historically rooted attitudes do not change quickly with time or evidence. He knows this to be true for political attitudes, that is, the liberal or conservative ideology. He knows this to be true of himself as a historically minded Catholic. If he cannot apply the principle to the nature and consequences of blackishness in our society, we should not be harsh, because it is a principle that unless rooted firmly in self-knowledge *as well as* knowledge of the force and processes of cultural transmission cannot be applied as a general principle.

Mr. Buckley's column was his answer to a study sponsored by the Anti-Defamation League of the B'Nai Brith. It is understandable that he paid attention to the study and not to its sponsor. If he had asked why this Jewish group sponsored such a study, he would have gotten the conventional response: For obvious historical reasons, Jews are not indifferent to any form of religious, racial, or ethnic discrimination; if they do not defend *any* victim of discrimination, their own vulnerability to discrimination is increased; discrimination is a wound-producing act, the effects of which never heal in the lifetime of the victim. Mr. Buckley knows all this and knows it well. But what Mr. Buckley does not know, and what many Jews sense but would have difficulty conceptualizing and articulating, is that historically rooted discrimination (its causes and consequences) is immune to change by efforts based on our accustomed short-time perspective. I suspect that the guilt of whites in relation to blacks has less to do with acts of the past than with the intuitive feeling that black freedom is a long, long way off. I also suspect that the anger of blacks toward whites has the same source. The future is determining the present.

Why say all of this? The answer, which goes back 30 years to when I started work at the Southbury Training School, is suggested in two statements. First, if a neighbor's child had an IQ of 180 and strangled a dog to death, we would not say he did it *because* he had an IQ of 180. Second, if that neighbor's child had an IQ of 60, or prepotent response, *our act of discrimination*, would be to point to the IQ of 60 as the etiological agent without which the strangling would not have taken place.[5] This pernicious double-standard way of thinking, the essence of discrimination, is so ingrained in us that when we recognize our logical error we feel helpless about how we should proceed to think and act. Life is so much easier when we, the experts, like most other people, can "blame the victim" for what he is and "is" means that he has a low IQ,

---

[5] We blame "bad" things on a low IQ, and we explain "good" ones by a high IQ, differences in language which are the hallmark of cultural influence. It is such a part of our thinking, it all appears so self-evident, that we cannot recognize the diverse ways in which these cultural influences work, for example, their self-fulfilling tendencies. For example, 25 years ago, Catherine Cox Miles, a long-time colleague of Lewis Terman, told me that nowhere in his write-up of his studies of "gifted" California boys and girls did Terman indicate the amount of time he spent helping his subjects get into college and graduate school, and obtain jobs. There was absolutely no chicanery involved. It was so self-evident to him that a high IQ was the cause of superior accomplishment that he could not recognize that he was an intervening variable, that is, that he, Lewis Terman, was a reflection and guardian of certain cultural values.

and what more do we need to know to understand him? Why complicate our thinking by confronting the fact that the act of constructing and using tests is both a reflection and a determinant of cultural attitudes and deeply rooted ways of thinking which, as long as they go unrecognized, guarantee that facts will be confused with truth? Why get into these messy issues when you can talk about genetics? Of course, we should study the genetics of intelligence (high, low, black, white) but, unless I misread the history of genetics, productive theorizing about genotypes follows upon clearly described, stable phenotypes. In regard to the genetics of intelligence, we are far from the point at which we can say that we have a well-described, stable phenotype. The one thing we can say with assurance is that our concepts of intelligence are value laden, culture and time bound, and deficient in cross-cultural validity. *It has not even been demonstrated that the level of problem-solving behavior in nontest situations is highly correlated with the level of similar types of problem-solving processes in the standardized test situations* (Sarason & Doris, 1969). And, as I have tried to demonstrate in this article, relatively little attention has been paid either to the different ways in which attitudes toward intellectual activity are absorbed by and inculcated in us, or to how the presence or absence of these group attitudes has behind it the force of decades or centuries.

I began with a story about my father and I shall end with one. He was in the hospital recovering from an operation. I visited him on one day, and my brother visited him on the next. The nurse asked my father what work his sons did. When he told her that they were both professors of psychology, she semifacetiously asked him: "Mr. Sarason, how come *you* have two sons like *that?*" My sister reported that my father, without a moment's hesitation and with the most profound seriousness, replied: "Don't you know that smartness sometimes skips generations?" The nature and force of the processes of cultural transmission never skip generations, particularly when their ways have been finely honed over the centuries. They will not be quickly blunted. I excuse my father for not knowing this (although he may have known it). I cannot excuse this in the participants of the recent nature–nuture controversy. There is a point when one must regard the consequences of ignorance as sinful, and that point was reached for the advocates of nurture when they expected that the core of blackishness would quickly change; and it was reached by the advocates of nature when they concluded that the overall failure of compensatory programs demonstrated the significance of genetic factors on which new programs should be based. With friends like that, the blacks need not waste time worrying about enemies, a lesson Jews learned well over the centuries.

8

Some Observations on the Introduction and Teaching of the New Math

This paper, primarily the initiative and work of Esther, was published in a monograph by the Massachusetts Department of Mental Health, with the title *The Psycho-Educational Clinic: Papers and Research Studies.* It was published in the late sixties. There is no copyright, it is no longer available, and there is no publication date! I still have some copies which I will send to readers on a first come, first served basis.

The paper occupied an important part of the first edition of *The Culture of the School and the Problem of Change.* Indeed, the new math part of the book has been frequently cited by other writers. I have included it here for several reasons. First, and this continues to amaze me, it is the only observational study of the new math that was ever done. Second, our experience with the new math explained much about school change; it was literally an eye opener to me. Third, I have no reason to believe that curriculum reformers have ever taken what we said seriously, despite the frequency with which that study has been cited. Fourth, the observations contained in the paper are as clear an example of teaching subject matter, not children, as you will find. That point was not given the emphasis it deserved in the paper, in part because it was so obvious and in part because our attention was riveted on the substance and logic of the subject matter.

The new math (and the new physics, biology, etc.) has departed from the scene. Unfortunately, the way it was introduced and taught has not. Change should never be equated with progress. Few experiences shaped my developing point of view more than Esther's having to learn the new math and then observing how it was taught in classrooms. Esther was not a researcher but she was a superb observer, which is why she was also a superb clinician. She was always suspicious of theoreticians and abstractions, and never equated what people say with what they do. If what I thought and wrote was convincing to Esther, I knew I was on the right track; at the least, I was not way off base.

——•——

The observations reported herein have to be viewed in terms of two major interests: (1) the culture of the school—the dimensions required for describing and understanding the school as a social system—and (2) the manner in which this system views and adapts to changes stemming from internal or external sources.[1] The history of our interest in the introduction of the new math into the elementary schools requires discussion at this point if only to emphasize how an "obvious" problem was far from obvious to individuals (like ourselves) whose orientation and training tended to preclude recognition of what to others would be a significant problem. For example, if people are brought up to believe that young children have no interest in sexual matters, it is unlikely that they will note those aspects of a child's behavior which would contradict their beliefs, unless experiences lead them to change or reformulate their ideas. The consequences of training and commitment to a theoretical orientation can, like the "beliefs" of individuals, make it extremely difficult for a psychologist to see and state a problem. The history of our experiences with the new math is a good example, at least to us, of how the unavailability of a conceptualization prevented us initially from seeing or understanding a problem.

THE INTRODUCTORY PERIOD

At the same time that the new math was being introduced into a particular school system, we were engaged in a longitudinal study involving all of the elementary schools in that system. Consequently, we spent a good deal of time in all of these schools and had numerous meetings with the teachers and the various levels of supervisors and administrators. We soon became aware that supervisors and administrators were spending a lot of time in meetings trying to decide which new math to adopt, the textbooks

---

[1] The text beginning with this sentence and continuing to the end of this chapter is reprinted from *The Psycho-Educational Clinic: Papers and Research Studies* (pp. 91–107), edited by Frances Kaplan & Seymour B. Sarason. Boston: Department of Mental Health, Commonwealth of Massachusetts. Undated Public Monograph.

to be used, the workshops for teachers that would need to be developed, and the kinds of consultants to be employed. When we say we "became aware" we mean that we were aware of a lot of activity which had no particular significance to us. For example, although our longitudinal study concerned anxiety in elementary school children—a study which would go on for a number of years—it never occurred to us to ask ourselves what the possible relevance might be between what we were interested in and what we observed going on about the introduction of new math.

In reviewing these experiences (and we are aware that recalling experiences is subject to a variety of selective factors) we had several distinct impressions.

1. The decision to change to the new math curriculum did not stem from any longstanding dissatisfaction with the existing curriculum. Rather, the decision seemed to be based on the sincere conviction that the new math would in some undefined way simply be better because it was new and it had the seal of approval of modern science and academically respectable mathematicians. We should emphasize that newness in itself was not crucial; what was crucial was that it was something new developed by respected authorities who had created the impression (or they were viewed as believing) that no self-respecting school system would run the risk of being against virtue and for sin. It is not totally unfair to characterize the situation as one in which the Christian Diors of academe made (or were viewed as making) it very difficult for the public consumer to resist the tides of academic fashion. What would be totally unfair would be to deny that those who were making the decisions were convinced they were "doing good."

2. It was clear from the beginning that the first objects of change would concern the classroom teachers who were minimally, if at all, participating in any of the decision-making. There seemed no recognition that the teachers would be faced not only with a problem in learning but in unlearning as well, with all its attendant consequences.

3. Perhaps the most distinct impression we received was that *the problem of changing the math curriculum was viewed as a relatively simple one in the sense that once the administrative details could be worked through—once the "system" could get the teachers into the learning situation—the process of change would present no particular problem.*[2] That some teachers would not

---

[2] The reader is urged to consult Ausubel's (1967) "Crucial Psychological Issues in the Objectives, Organizations, and Evaluation of Curriculum Reform Movements." Although his critique concerns another subject matter (biology) and is not based on classroom observation, many of his conclusions about the new biology curriculum are similar to those presented in this paper.

look enthusiastically at the new math, that some teachers did not want to devote nonschool time to learning and unlearning, that the amount of time it was expected to take teachers to understand the new math was on the brief side, that the new math would present problems to parents—these and other possibilities were not considered in such a way that the complexity of the process would become apparent. Put in a more general way, there was no awareness of the idea that an important part of a social system was going to be changed and that such a change could have, and indeed would have to have, important ramifications. The process was viewed as involving matters of administration and curriculum, a view that made it impossible to consider that individuals, relationships among individuals, attitudes, and cognitive processes were all inextricably part of a process of change which would inevitably affect what and how children learned.

Although our characterization of what was going on may be incomplete and unfair, we feel that it accurately describes our own level of sophistication, i.e., at that time we were quite unaware of what a fantastically complex means-ends problem was being attacked in a particular social system. We were far from understanding or recognizing two things. First, changing curricula (which operationally can best be defined as that which is contained between covers and has the label curriculum) without changing styles of thinking and teaching is the hallmark of the difference between change and innovation. Second, the school is a distinctive social system that does not respond randomly to contemplated change.

THE TEACHERS

About the same time that our longitudinal subjects reached those grade levels at which the new math was taught, the Psycho-Educational Clinic was started. It was particularly in connection with the activities of the Clinic that we began to be in classrooms and to relate to teachers about classroom problems. These activities involved us in elementary schools in five different school systems. Several things quickly became clear. First, a number of teachers felt that the new math had been imposed or foisted on them, another instance to them of how "they" (the administration) or "downtown" make decisions for and about teachers. Second, a number of teachers did not feel sufficiently secure about their degree of understanding of the new math to feel comfortable in the process of teaching it to children. As one teacher put it, "where the kids tend to get hung up is where I tended to get hung up." Third, there were teachers who gave no indication of discomfort with the new math but who simply could not see that it made much of a difference from the standpoint of children. Fourth, there were teachers who felt strongly that the "idea" of the new math was fine but that it was inappropriate to the capacity of most children in the grades in which it was being taught, i.e., the curriculum was not matched to the capacities of many children. Several teachers stated, "Whoever got up the curriculum obviously does not know children."

We cannot claim that the above views are representative of the views of teachers in general. We do maintain that there is a difference between what teachers will say to a relative stranger and what they do say to individuals (like ourselves) who are not part of the school but with whom a close working relationship has been established. In any event, it became increasingly clear to us that a number of teachers had strong reservations about their relationship to the new math and the teaching of it to children.

But there was one opinion which practically all teachers expressed, independent of all other factors, and that was that the new math was probably most appropriate for, or presented the least difficulties to, the "brightest children." What should be noted here is that in at least two of the school systems the average IQ was significantly above 100.

THE PARENTS

Our observations in regard to parents were more limited and undoubtedly affected by a variety of selective factors. Two major reactions were noted during unplanned contacts with parents who attended seminars in the new math especially designed for them. First, the new math was fine, interesting, and stimulating and they were pleased their children would be exposed to it. It was our opinion that in some instances there was a substantive basis to this view while in others it seemed to suggest the unreflective equating of the new with progress. Second, there were parents who felt that their confusion level had been raised by the seminar and several of them dropped out. As one parent stated, "I have more of an understanding of what a school drop-out must feel."

On various social occasions we managed to steer conversation to the new math. This did not take much managing because a number of parents were encountering a situation in which they had to devote a lot of time helping their child do his math homework because the child was floundering. When the parent comprehended the new math to the point where he could be helpful, he resented the time he was forced to play the role of teacher. When such a comprehension level was not present, the reactions were stronger and tinged with anxiety about or concern for the child. There were, of course, parents who reported no difficulties of any kind. In this connection we have to express the opinion that there is a striking similarity between teachers and parents in that both groups tend to be rather hesitant and defensive about admitting—except in infrequent interpersonal situations—that their children have problems in academic learning for which they feel some responsibility. This undoubtedly says much more about our society than it does about the new math.

Our experience—all informal, selective, limited, and largely subjective—led us to observe six classrooms (two in each of the three school systems) over a period of six weeks during those hours in which math was taught. In each of the three schools there were two sixth grade classrooms, the only classrooms chosen. Each classroom was observed at least three times a week. Principals and teachers rearranged schedules so that the two classrooms in each school could be observed on the same day. In two schools the School Mathematics Study Group (SMSG) program was used while in the third school they were using the Addison-Wesley program. The SMSG program had been used in the previous grades in all schools.

OBSERVATIONS

Multiplication

Let us start with the "old" way in which multiplication was taught. A typical problem is shown below.

$$
\begin{array}{r}
549 \\
\times\ 65 \\
\hline
2{,}745 \\
3{,}294 \\
\hline
35{,}685
\end{array}
$$

For a child to do this problem he must know the multiplication table (e.g., $5 \times 9 = 45$) and then be able to perform certain operations (e.g., put down the 5, multiply 5×4, add to this the 4 from the previous operation, etc.). When taught in this way a child's understanding of multiplication consists of the knowledge that certain facts (the multiplication table) learned in a rote fashion will give answers when combined with certain other operations. It then becomes necessary for a child to learn when multiplication is an appropriate procedure, but here, too, the child tends to learn rules rather than gaining an understanding of general principles.

From the standpoint of new math the old way leaves much to be desired. For example, working with the old math the child is not likely to grasp the idea that there are other ways in which the problem can be solved because a number (e.g., 549) can be renamed, reordered, or composed in a variety of ways. For example, 549 can be thought of or conceptualized other than as 549, i.e., it can be distributed. Some of the ways in which it can be done are as follows.

(a) $(500 + 49) \times 65 = (500 \times 65) + (49 \times 65)$
(b) $549 \times (60 + 5) = (549 \times 60) + (549 \times 5)$
(c) $(500 + 490 + 9) \times 65 = (500 \times 65) + (40 \times 65) + (9 \times 65)$
(d) $[(500 \times 5) + (40 \times 5) + (9 \times 5)] + [(500 \times 60) + (40 \times 60) + (9 \times 60)] = 549 \times 65$

The examples may be written and solved in the manner shown below.

$$
\begin{array}{r}
549 \\
\times\ 65 \\
\hline
\end{array}
$$

45	(5×9)				
200	(5×40)	$=$	$(500 + 40 + 9) \times 5$	$=$	2,745
2,500	(5×500)				
540	(9×60)				
2,400	(40×60)	$=$	$(500 + 40 + 9) \times 60$	$=$	32,940
30,000	(500×60)				
35,685					35,685

It may also be solved in another way.

$$
\begin{array}{r}
549 \\
\times\ 65 \\
\hline
\end{array}
$$

585	(65×9)
2,600	(65×40)
32,500	(65×500)
35,685 $=$	$(500 \times 65) + (40 \times 65) + (9 \times 65)$

When the student understands the distributive principle and the different sets of operations to which it can give rise, he can then understand the traditional or "short-cut" procedure as but another instance of the general principle. Without such a previous understanding the old way consists of rules and operations devoid of generalized principles. The old way, in contrast to the new, tends not to allow the child to see that once certain principles are understood numbers can be "played with," and that one can produce phenotypically different combinations which are, so to speak, genotypically identical. The new math is intended, among other things, to make learning enjoyable by increasing and maintaining intellectual curiosity about the world of numbers.

Division

Let us now illustrate the same idea in division. For example, $1,720 \div 8$ can be renamed and distributed in several ways.

(a) $(400 \div 8) + (800 \div 8) + (480 \div 8) + (40 \div 8) = 1,720 \div 8$

Written in familiar form it looks like:

$$
\begin{array}{r|l}
8)\overline{1,720} & \\
\underline{400} & 50\ (\times 8) \\
1,320 & \\
\underline{800} & 100\ (\times 8) \\
520 & \\
\underline{480} & 60\ (\times 8) \\
40 & \\
\underline{40} & \underline{5\ (\times 8)} \\
0 & 215
\end{array}
$$

(Quotient is the sum of the factors of each component of 1,720)

(b) $(800 \div 8) + (800 \div 8) + (80 \div 8) + (40 \div 8) = 1,720 \div 8$

Written in familiar form it looks like:

$$
\begin{array}{r|l}
8)\overline{1,720} & \\
\underline{800} & 100\ (\times 8) \\
920 & \\
\underline{800} & 100\ (\times 8) \\
120 & \\
\underline{80} & 10\ (\times 8) \\
40 & \\
\underline{40} & \underline{5\ (\times 8)} \\
0 & 215
\end{array}
$$

(Quotient is the sum of the factors of each component of 1,720)

(c) $(1{,}600 \div 8) + (80 \div 8) + (40 \div 8) = 1{,}720 \div 8$

Written in familiar form it looks like:

$$
\begin{array}{r}
8\overline{)1{,}720} \\
1{,}600 \qquad\qquad 200\,(\times 8) \\
\hline
120 \\
80 \qquad\qquad 10\,(\times 8) \\
\hline
40 \\
40 \qquad\qquad 5\,(\times 8) \\
\hline
0 \qquad\qquad 215
\end{array}
$$

(Quotient is the sum of the factors of each component of 1,720)

(d) Finally the quotient is written where it is accustomed to be seen.

$$
\begin{array}{r}
215 \\
\hline
8\overline{)1{,}720} \\
1{,}600 \\
\hline
120 \\
80 \\
\hline
40 \\
40 \\
\hline
0
\end{array}
$$

(e) In time the "short-cut" or traditional way is introduced.

$$
\begin{array}{r}
215 \\
\hline
8\overline{)1{,}720} \\
16 \\
\hline
12 \\
8 \\
\hline
40 \\
40 \\
\hline
0
\end{array}
$$

(f) It then becomes even shorter.

$$
\begin{array}{r}
215 \\
\hline
8\overline{)1{,}720}
\end{array}
$$

As in the case of multiplication the child does not get to the old or short-cut way until he has gone step-by-step as above. What needs to be noted here is that in the particular curriculum used in these schools children are taught multiplication and division in fourth and fifth grades in much the same way (although presumably on a simpler level) as we have illustrated here. That is to say, by the sixth grade the children have already been exposed to the principles and operations. What also needs to be emphasized is that at each grade level the step-by-step sequence is taught over a period of time, the importance of which will become clear later in our discussion.

Now to our observations. We came away with the impression that *enjoyment was one of the last words we would use to characterize our impressions of the children's feelings.* Struggle was certainly one way of characterizing what was going on but it was not the kind of intellectual struggle that generates its own sources of internal reinforcement or elicits such reinforcements from others, in this case the teacher. At no time in our discussion did any of the six teachers say anything which disconfirmed our opinion that neither children nor teachers enjoyed what they were doing, in the sense of feeling intellectual excitement, a desire to persist, and a joy of learning. We had the overwhelming impression of a task being done not because children desired to do it but because that is the way life is. Using the "joy of learning" as a criterion, there appears to be no difference between new and old math.[3]

It will be recalled that one of the important principles which children had to understand was that the same example could be done in several ways. Typically, two or three class hours were devoted to one way (such as steps (a) and (b) in the examples above), a subsequent class hour devoted to another way, until the old or short-cut way was finally reached and its relation to the previous methods demonstrated. It would be more correct to say, actually, that after the first step or method was discussed, the equivalence in principle of all subsequent steps was stressed. The fact is that many children could not state the underlying principle of equivalence and seemed confused by the different methods presented to them. What seemed to be happening was that each explanation or step in the development of a process was experienced by the children as an entity in itself, and practiced as such in rote fashion; the next step was then experienced as different despite attempts by the teachers to

---

[3] We are quite aware that the conclusions about the behavior and feelings of children that we state in this paper do not hold for all the children in the classes we observed. It is, however, our strong conviction that they hold for most children. The nature and origins of individual differences are certainly important questions but we can shed no light on them.

demonstrate an identity of underlying principle. It seemed obvious to us that the children were more interested in "how to do it" rather than "understanding." In one class the teacher was aware that many children were having difficulty grasping the relationship between the old, or short-cut way, of dividing and the "understanding" way. After a particularly frustrating class hour he said, "I know that the understanding way is longer and more difficult than the short-cut way but keep the understanding way in the back of your minds and from now on we will use the short-cut way."

> In one class the distributive method for multiplication was demonstrated briefly but well on the blackboard as an introduction to the traditional method. Despite more lengthy previous exposures to this type of example in the fourth and fifth grades, the children did not grasp the principles involved as quickly as expected. This class happened to be the brightest sixth grade class. Many demonstrations by the teacher were necessary, not only because of many incorrect answers by the children but also by voluntary requests for additional explanations. Following this lesson, on the very next day, the use of the distributive methods was then extended to addition and subtraction. At that time the teacher explicitly stated that the demonstrated methods were too cumbersome for use and were only for understanding purposes. No attempt was really made to assess whether this principle was understood or to relate it to the traditional and still current way of adding, subtracting, and multiplying. From this point on these new arithmetic processes were treated only as examples with the emphasis on practice, the way of years ago.

Without exception the children seemed to have the greatest difficulty with division. This was not helped any by introducing the complication of estimating quotients by rounding off numbers.

> For example, to solve $1,655 \div 450$, the child is instructed to think of 450 as 500 and 1,655 as 1,700, as an aid to locating the correct factor for the quotient. The child is then instructed to proceed with the actual figures ($1,655 \div 450$) on hand. Thus, the child is instructed first to think of 450 as 500 and 1,655 as 1,700 and to ask himself how many sets of 500 there are in 1,700. This figure is used as a starting point in locating the quotient and this form (rounding off of numbers) is followed at each subsequent step of the division process. In each instance the child is referred back to the original

numbers although cautioned that the approximations may not always work, and that they are merely aids to make matters easier.

Children had a lot of difficulty estimating the factors that make up the quotient, especially when the dividends became larger. It seemed that the process of estimating factors did not facilitate matters but instead served only to confuse. The fact that the estimating of factors was introduced at a time when the children did not have a feeling of mastery of the principle and procedure of division made life even more difficult.

It has been noted by many that emphasis in the new math results in a de-emphasis on "facts," e.g., the multiplication table. That is, children taught the new math do not know arithmetical facts as well as those who were brought up on the old math. Our observations confirm such an expectation. We noted numerous times when doing work at the blackboard, children seemed to be taking an inordinate amount of time determining how much 9×7, or 7×8 or 6×7 were.

It could be maintained that a lack of facility in handling the mechanics of arithmetical processes is offset by the advantages gained by an understanding of basic principles. For example, it has been maintained that when a child grasps the meaning of addition, subtraction, multiplication, and division he is better able to handle the verbally formulated type of arithmetic problem. Our observations do not support this premise.

One teacher frankly admitted that his class was completely unprepared to handle arithmetic problems. He threw open to the class a discussion on the difficulties they were experiencing in this area. The discussion centered around the following four points which were summarized on the board as follows:

1. Uncertain about operations
2. Did not understand the problem
3. Long—too many words
4. More than one operation involved

It was apparent that the children experienced a lot of difficulty in connecting mathematical operations with the verbal language that signified their use in a problem.

The discussion aroused a good deal of feeling about math in general. One youngster openly complained that the shift in books from SMSG to the Addison-Wesley series had confused her. She indicated that she no sooner had become accustomed to SMSG when the change was intro-

duced. Other children echoed her feelings. The teacher listened sympa-
thetically and most admirably and openly supported her. It is worthy
to note that this teacher's lesson on relating the verbal language of arithmetic problems to their mathematical operations was superb. He active-
ly involved the children in meaningful searching for such relationships
and insisted that they construct such problems on their own; for example, he gave them problems like: "Johnnie runs 2 yards in 5 seconds.
How many feet will he run in 10 seconds?" Each child in the class had
both a turn to solve a problem and to make one up. Mere answers were
insufficient; the children had to explain the process of solution.

> In still another class, a teacher spontaneously corroborated the
> impression that children found the problems too difficult. He,
> however, felt that the difficulty was experienced because prob-
> lems were unrelated to the units of work that the children fol-
> lowed. This opinion differed from that of the previous teacher
> who felt that the SMSG approach stressed the mechanics of arith-
> metic operations and neglected problem solving.

Our next point concerns the introduction of fractions. The following type of observation was noted in at least two classes.

In one class the children were experiencing considerable difficulty
in accepting the fact that fractions can be renamed like whole numbers,
i.e., $1/2 = 4/8 = 5/10$ and $1/3 = 3/9 = 6/18$. Having presented and illustrated the point, the teacher then demonstrated in passing how fractions
can be added with different denominators, if one is aware that they can
be renamed in equivalent forms. In the example $2/3 + 1/6$, $2/3$ can be
changed to $4/6$ with the $1/6$ being added on to make $5/6$. The teacher
demonstrated this point again and again, giving examples of this type
for seat work and discussion. It might be added that the class had had
no previous exposure to the addition of fractions. During this same sitting two ways of determining if fractions were equivalent were introduced. It was apparent that these ways were introduced spontaneously
in order to elaborate and give fuller meaning to the renaming of fractions.
The explanations showed clear thinking and patience on the teacher's
part. The children, however, were lost and showed this later in the hour
by an inability to rename fractions that were concretely partitioned on
portions of discs. The teacher was aware that his class was not altogeth-
er with him. It was apparent that too much was as bad as too little.

An observation on the teaching of fractions with the SMSG approach
at this point is relevant. In the example given below, the relevancy of
such topics as general factoring, least common multiple, least common
denominator, and work with number lines, among others, was lost by the

highly detailed approach given to each topic. By the time the addition and subtraction of fractions had been reached, the children were rusty in finding a least common denominator that was not immediately apparent by inspection. When the class (a superior one) was tested on the range of topics related to or leading to fractions, more than 75% of the class got marks below 60. With so much detail presented, teacher and children constantly were in danger of losing the overall focus.

The above plethora of detail brings us to our final observation, one which is not peculiar, in our experience, to the new math but may well have a more adverse effect in this area than in other subject matter. We refer here to the unverbalized pressure experienced by the teachers to follow the requirements of the curriculum, i.e., an awareness that certain things had to be taught in a certain period of time because at the end of the year the children were expected to be at a certain point in knowledge, skills, and understanding. At least three of the teachers spontaneously said that the pacing required by the curriculum was unrealistic.

Before discussing our observations we feel it necessary and important to communicate our opinions of the teachers we observed. Without exception they were hard working, motivated individuals who were trying to do their best. Given the difficulties the children were experiencing it is painful to contemplate what might have been the case if these teachers had taken their obligations as teachers less seriously. We were able to observe all the teachers teaching other subject matter, and we can only record our opinion, that as a group, they would be considered competent teachers and in two cases, probably superb ones.

The above opinions are not given with the intention of directing criticism away from the teachers. They probably would agree that they were not accomplishing the goals that they set for themselves or that others had set for them. The intent of these opinions was, rather, to counter the too frequent snobbish tendency to blame the ills of education on the teachers. More specifically, we wish to disagree strongly with university colleagues who, recognizing that the new math is not being taught or learned differently from the old math, maintain their feelings of superiority by derisively blaming the teacher.

IMPLICATIONS

We make no claims about the generality of our observations, although any reader of our national newspapers (e.g., *New York Times,* Jan. 25, 1965) will be aware that over the past several years a number of educators, mathematicians, and others have expressed sentiments and described experiences strikingly similar to our own. Fehr's (1966) recent attack is but a case in point.[4] In connection with the following quotation from Fehr we have to say that his statements about place systems and numerals and numbers are congruent with our observations that these topics and distinctions were associated with much confusion in the minds of the children.

> The teaching of place systems of numeration to other bases than the decimal, and the computational algorisms in these other bases, is nonsense. All over the world, in every nation, bar none, and in every type of communication—social, business, scientific, professional, etc.—the one system that is used is the decimal system. This is the only system that most (at least 95 percent) of the population will ever use the rest of their lives, and they will probably use it every day of their lives.
>
> Of course, other systems are used in digital computers and special scientific studies, but to educate elementary school children as though every one would become a computer programmer is nonsense. That learning place systems in other bases, such as four, five, or seven, will help a child understand the decimal system better is a good hypothesis, but it has never been tested so far as the writer knows. Such generalizations on scales of notation can well be deferred to high school study, where the use of algebra makes them a simple and easy matter to comprehend.
>
> In this connection, also, it is nonsense to stress the distinction between numeral and number. Of course, numbers are abstract, and numerals are names or symbols for the abstract, but, in general, no misconception arises in using the two words synonymously. If a person says he writes a number on a blackboard, all people know to what the person is referring. If one says a two-digit number, there is no doubt in the mind of the hearer about what is meant. Even some of those mathematicians who started this nonsense are now recanting.
>
> There is a story that one experimental group, in writing its elementary books, used a chapter heading: "learning to read and write large numbers." When it was called to their attention that this was impossible, they changed the word "numbers" to "numerals." Then, because the implication was that the numerals were to be large, that is, written in enormous size, they finally changed the title to: "Learning to read and write numerals for large numbers," and by this time no one understood what was meant!

---

[4] The criticisms of the new (or old) math are essentially not new. One of the more reasoned and reasonable discussions of the teaching of mathematics—a discussion strongly recommended to the interested reader—was contained in Alfred North Whitehead's (1929) presidential address to the London Branch of the Mathematical Association in 1913.

Teaching geometric construction by means of a straightedge, a pair of compasses, and the geometrical language of Euclid is utter nonsense in the elementary school. First, many children do not have the motor dexterity needed for such construction. Further, there are other far more desirable and useful forms of motor dexterity that should be developed in the elementary school. To learn to circumscribe a triangle by Euclidean geometric construction is about the height of absurdity in gaining useful knowledge of skill. In fact, all of Euclid's development of geometry safely can be relegated to study by specialists, for there are ways far superior to Euclidean geometry for studying space today.

While there are other minor innovations that are useful but harmless, I mention only one other major piece of nonsense. This is the attempt to formalize the structure of arithmetic—that is, to enunciate formal laws and attempt to build and extend arithmetic through the use of these laws. Now it is essential to understanding that we recognize the principles involved in operations on numbers. How this is accomplished is indicated later. But to enumerate explicitly the commutative, associative, and distributive laws in a formal (algebraic) form, to spell out every algorism into a flow chart in terms of these laws, to stress the identity laws of zero and one, and to use a product set to define multiplication is utter nonsense. The books that are doing this are really substituting a new rote formalism for the old rote learning of so-called facts of arithmetic, and this does not spell progress.

The major reason for making observations resided less in a special interest in the new math than it did in our overall goal of describing and understanding the school culture and processes of change. As we came to understand the school culture better and to observe its response to change we began to see the importance of distinguishing between overt change (e.g., the substitution of one curriculum for another) and the intent to innovate (e.g., to change the quality of the intellectual experience of children). What we also came to see was that the intent to innovate (and its outcome) could only be understood in the context of the history of that intent (that is, its origins in terms of particular groups and events, an example being the reaction to the Russian Sputnik), the presence or absence *on the part of the motivators and administrators* of some kind of conception of the change process, the relation of such conceptions to a knowledge of the distinctive characteristics of the school culture, and the capacity of the system to stimulate and tolerate open discussion. Our understanding of the school culture and processes of change forced us to the conclusion that the aims of the new math—to stimulate the curiosity of children about the world of numbers, to help them "enjoy" the learning process, to enable them to experience the satisfaction of *understanding* instead of the boredom of rote learning—*could not be achieved.* That is to say, it was precisely because those, within and with-

out the school culture, who were pushing the change viewed the problems primarily in terms of a formal curriculum or an "individual psychology," that the social psychological aspects of the entire change process
could not be perceived and, therefore, taken into account.[5] One of the
consequences of our argument is that we would have the same expectation for the new physics, new English, and so on.[6]

We are not prepared to discuss the validity of the psychological assumptions associated with the new math or the justification for the assumption
that most children are capable of understanding in a meaningful way its
principles and logical relationships. These are important issues that obviously have a bearing on how one must view the effects of the new math.
What we have attempted to suggest is that these issues should be viewed
in the context of conceptions of characteristics of the school culture, how
these characteristics relate to the wider society, the implicit or explicit "theory of change" employed, and the significance of the difference (if only
for the purpose of evaluation) between change and innovation.

Our final point makes obvious how necessary it is to view the new
math in social terms. The success of the Russian Sputnik was a deep
wound to the self-perceptions of Americans and markedly accelerated
previous efforts to change the content and goals of the school curriculum.
It is belaboring the obvious to say that one cannot comprehend the present status of the new math in our schools unless one views it in the context of history. In the evaluation of the new math, social history is a variable. The following, from Goodman's book *The Pleasures of Math* (1965),
is one of many such statements that could have been presented here.

---

[5] There is a startling lack of discussion about the psychological assumptions
required to justify the new math curriculum, assumptions bearing both on the
nature of child development and the problem-solving processes. There seems
little reason to doubt that whatever these assumptions are or might be—as well
as those implicit in the manner in which the new math was introduced in our
schools—they reflect a *psychology of the individual*. There is nothing to suggest
that there was recognition of the fact that one was also dealing with a subculture
which was part of a larger social structure, and that the relationship between
the two required conceptualization if only to serve as a guide to the tactics of
change. In short, the initiators of the new math lacked that kind of sophistication in social theory which might have alerted them to the limitations of the theories of individuals. They cannot even be accused of what C.W. Mills (1961, p.
67) calls "psychologism" which "refers to the attempt to explain social phenomena in terms of facts and theories about the make-up of individuals. Historically, as a doctrine, it rests upon an explicit metaphysical denial of the reality of social structure." Since this type of psychologism assumes an interest in social
phenomena and social structure, it is unfortunate that those who introduced the
new math cannot be accused of this level of sophistication!

With the launching of the first Sputnik by the Russians, the American people realized that a society which was regarded as less advanced than ours, was in fact, definitely ahead of ours in at least one field. And of course there was the uneasy feeling that perhaps the Russians were also ahead in many other branches of science and technology. . . .

What can we do? No amount of money and advertising can overnight produce leading scientists. The training must start early and be conducted in an atmosphere that recognizes, appreciates, respects, and rewards the budding scientists. . . .

At present a vast majority of students entering college know a lot of arithmetic, a little manipulative algebra, some Euclidean geometry, and a little trigonometry. But they are totally unaware of the existence of a vast amount of mathematics that is fascinating, challenging, stimulating, and moreover, quite beautiful. The damage inflicted by our present diluted and turtle-paced courses is augmented because the student's mind is allowed to remain dormant during just that period when it should be experiencing maximum growth.

It is fair, we think, to say that one of the major aims of the new math concerned not only schools and children but our entire society—this in the sense that the new math was viewed as one important way of helping to produce more and better mathematicians and scientists since that was what it seemed our society needed. If our observations, and those of others, have validity and generality, one would have to predict that the goal of more and better mathematicians and scientists (relative to the total population)—or the number of college students majoring in math and physics—will not be met. If so, we will have yet another example of how the more things change the more they remain the same.

---

[6] Ausubel (1967) concludes about the new biology: ". . . preoccupation with the recency of subject-matter content, and with the completeness of conceptual, methodological, and historical coverage, can easily lead to the neglect of such basic pedagogic considerations as the educational appropriateness of course approach and objectives, the adequacy of the pupils' existing academic background for learning the content of the course, and the psychological tenability of the chosen ways of presenting, organizing, and sequencing materials. The inevitable outcome, under these circumstances, is the production of instructional materials that are admirably thorough, accurate, and up-to-date, but so ineffectively presented and organized, and so impossibly sophisticated for their intended audience, as to be intrinsically unlearnable on a long-term basis."

THE OVERARCHING PURPOSE
OF SCHOOLING

This is a chapter from my most recent book *Parental Involvement and the Political Principle: Why the Existing Governance Structure of Schools Should Be Abolished,* published by Jossey-Bass in 1995, and reprinted here with their permission.

By the political principle I mean that when you will be affected, directly or indirectly, by a decision, you should stand in some relationship to that decision making process. I discussed the principle in previous books but several things forced me to deal with it and its implications separately.

1. Every argument educators advance, publicly and privately, against meaningful parental-community involvement emphasizes their informational and experiential deficits. By the same token the argument assumes that the political principle is taken seriously within and among educators in the different strata in the pyramidal administrative structure of schools and school systems.

2. The argument and assumption ignore one possibility and one glaring fact. The possibility that parents have assets, or can be aided to obtain assets, relevant to decisions about educational policy and practice is not even discussed. Parents have deficits which are irremediable, period. That, I argue, is a reflection of professional preciousness and arrogance, by no means peculiar to educators. The assumption that the political principle is respected among school personnel is patently invalid. Every argument advanced against parental-community involvement is precisely that advanced by teachers in regard to student participation in classroom governance, by principals against teachers in school

governance, by higher administrators against principal participation, and on and on until you reach the apex of the pyramid. Teachers, of course, are at the bottom of the professional mountain, the voiceless peons possessed only of deficits in regard to the decision making process.

3. The failure of the educational community to take the political principle seriously, within and without its borders, has contributed mammothly to the current situation in which the public's respect for educators is at an all time low and its bewilderment about the intractability of schools to reform efforts is at an all time high. My call for abolishing the existing governance structure and giving serious consideration to alternatives was not lightly made. The existing governance structure is a direct descendant of those times when the purpose of schooling was to tame and socialize waves of immigrant children, when it was never in the heads of anyone to say that the purpose of schooling was to locate and capitalize on individual differences among students, or that these individual differences were differences that made a difference in productive learning.

The above points are spelled out in that book. But, and there is always a but, changing governance and power relationships in no way insures that educational outcomes will discernibly improve. What are the governance changes intended to achieve? Is there an overarching purpose for schooling that should inform such changes? In my opinion, unless you are crystal clear about that overarching purpose, you will change governance structures and nothing else. There are, of course, several important purposes for schooling but there is, in my opinion, one such purpose that is at the top of my list and it is discussed in the next to the last chapter of the book and reprinted here. I expect that most readers will not quarrel with the crucial importance of that purpose, although I also expect that some readers may shrink from pursuing the consequences the acceptance of that purpose requires, not the least of which is abolishing the existing governance structure. Again, I must emphasize that changing governance without clarity about what schooling is for is tinkering. The stakes are too high for more tinkering.

My present point of view is suffused with pessimism if only because for the past thirty years I have seen no signs that reformers (and, therefore, the public) have started with a reexamination of the purposes for schooling. More correctly, they start with the present structure and seek to make it do what it patently cannot do and never has done. There are a few people who know the game and score but they, like me, are politely listened to, patted on the back, given brownie points for the afterlife, and then business goes on as usual. I do not say this out of pique or frustration but rather with sadness.

A man said to his friend, "This is the best of all possible worlds." To which his friend replied, "I am afraid you are right." The friend's reply implies that things will remain as they are. I fear they will get worse. In no way am I suggesting that if schools change in ways I have indicated, everything else will, so to speak, fall into place. If schools change in desirable ways it will be because our society will have been forced to realize that schools cannot continue as they are and that alternatives to what is have to be tried. But for that to happen requires that there be articulate leadership within and beyond the educational community. Within that community there is no such leadership. Beyond it is a leadership whose hearts are in the right place but their heads are not; in their calls for this or that change (e.g., vouchers, technology, privatization) they expose their inability either to comprehend why past reform efforts have failed or to state and take seriously the overarching purpose of schooling.

Let us start with the first physical-psychological-educational site we "attend," namely the unit we call a family.[1] And let us ask this question: Why do parents have children? The answers are many, ranging from religious reasons to "they just came along." But whatever the reason, once the child is born parents begin to think and fantasize about what that child may, could, might, or should be. Parents, of course, want the child to be healthy and happy but they also want the child to be a distinctive "something," e.g., rich business person, celebrated actor, great writer, doctor, lawyer, or scientist. Parents are used to saying that they want the child to be whatever he or she chooses to be, implying that it is morally wrong to foist their desires and goals on the child. I say "morally wrong" because they are implying that it is an unjust exercise of their powers to mold the child in accordance with parental dreams, that to do so would be a source of guilt. I have never talked with parents who, when pressed, would not admit that they would feel fulfilled if the child became the "something" of their fantasies. But why fear the guilt, why is it so important that the something a child becomes should come from

---

[1] The text beginning with this sentence and continuing to the end of this chapter is reprinted from *Parent Involvement and the Political Principle: Why the Existing Governance Structure of Schools Should Be Abolished*, 1995. San Francisco: Jossey-Bass. Copyright 1995 by Jossey-Bass Inc., Publishers. Reprinted by permission.

his or her experience, interests, and talents? Such importance was very rare in earlier centuries and there are literally billions of parents and children today in different parts of this earth where choosing to be a something does not exist as a problem; survival is the problem. It is a western, especially American, problem. Why this is so, how it came about, is a long, complicated story far beyond the purposes of this book even to sketch. Let me just say that if the something a child is to become or be shaped into increasingly became *psychologically* an issue for parents, and therefore, for children over the past couple of centuries, it erupted like a volcano into national consciousness as a consequence of the mammoth upheavals which were consequences of World War II. Few people, if any, were exempt from these consequences. Lives, attitudes, outlooks, time perspectives, definitions of self, identifications with the past—all these and more underwent sea-swell changes. And one of those changes was implied in the very frequent parental declaration, "We made a mess of this world, our children should have the opportunity to shape a better world." And that change was also reflected in the labels applied to the decades after World War II, "The Age of Psychology," "The Age of Mental Health." It was a change about parental responsibility in regard to respecting and reinforcing a child's individuality, expanding and not restricting the child's options for new experience, and fostering independence of, not dependence on, parent dreams. Contained in that change is the answer to my earlier question "But why fear the guilt, why is it so important that the something a child becomes should come from his or her experience, interests and talents?" There was good reason why Dr. Spock's book about child health and rearing became the bible for millions of parents anxious (not only concerned, but anxious) to know what children are and how one comes to understand where they are psychologically coming from and going, a coming and going which if ignored or misunderstood would have untoward effects. Someone said that the children born in the "Age of Permissiveness" were those who became the "Me too" generation. That is an oversimplification and a very misleading one because it completely ignores perhaps the most obvious feature of the post World War II years. I refer to the fact that as never before children and adults could literally *see* the world and because of speedier modes of transportation (e.g., jets, cross country interstate highways) could experience it other than vicariously. It was not only that children were taught to expect more and to experience more of this world than had been true for their parents, the expectations of and for children were more possible than ever before in human history. You *could* be what you wanted to be, you *should* be what you want to be, there is a world to conquer and you should try to conquer it. Those are not new themes in the

American psyche but they mightily increased in strength in the post World War II era. If for circumstances not of their making many children would not have their expectations realized, they nevertheless heard and absorbed those themes, even those parents who knew that there was a difference between the rhetoric and realities of those expectations.

I started this chapter by asking why parents have children, and I have answered (all too briefly) the question by saying that, however varied the answers, the goal of parents in the post World War II years was to capitalize on the child's natural curiosity to explore and experience, to want to be competent, to feel their interests have not been ignored.

In the musical *Carousel,* the setting of which is in bygone days in New England, the roguish male central character sings "My Boy Bill," the longest soliloquy in the musical theater. In the first half of the song he expresses in the most macho fashion his expectations-fantasies about the boy he will father, a replica of himself. The music is appropriately stirringly macho. And then he suddenly stops as he realizes that the child he will father may be a girl. He is stunned, but only momentarily. And then to music that is delicate, soft, and poignant he describes his girl as one who will meet all of his conceptions of what a girl should be. Billy Bigelow knew what that child would be, *he* would make sure of that. In recent decades that parental stance is less than rare, replaced by one that (publicly at least) gave top priority to the individuality-uniqueness of the child. Permissiveness conjures up the wrong imagery, as if parents were indiscriminate about the child's interests and desires. It would be more correct to say that parents felt between a rock and a hard place; on the one hand, fearful that they may not be sufficiently aware of or sensitive to or providing sufficient stimulation to the child and, on the other hand, conscious of the importance of not foisting their dreams and hopes on the young child. It is no wonder that parents sought help and reassurance from Dr. Spock and many other Dr. Spocks. The message that parents heard and bought was "you could harm a child by shaping him or her in your image, or you could support a child to find his or her developmental path." And that message did not come only from the Dr. Spocks but also from a body of research indicating that from its earliest days the child is on a developmental course characterized by stages in which cognitive characteristics (e.g., exploration, curiosity, memory, perception) become increasingly differentiated in the context of an emerging picture of self, others, and the surrounding world; and the productive consequences of that development depended on how well parents understood, respected, and supported that complicated development. The child was not passive human clay to be molded in an image, waiting, so to speak, to become a something in accord with parental dreams. It was an active, purposeful, quizzical, experience devouring, competence-seeking human clay with the potential to become more than the one parentally inspired "image." If any label captures what I have been describing it is "The Age of the Child Centered Parent."

The above, I should hasten to add, is intended only to convey the change in many people (by no means all!) in their view of their children and their parental obligations. Historically speaking, it was a momentous change, if only because it recognized to a greater degree than before the importance of taking account of what young, developing children are, psychologically speaking, i.e., they literally are not mindless, they come into this world with the potentials derived from a developmental "code" that can be blunted or nurtured, they are a complicated something long before they become an adult something—ignore all that and you have short-changed the child.

There was a problem, however, a very predictable one that parents encountered: You can read the Spocks of this world, you can articulate and agree with everything they say, you can try to act consistently with what you "know" and "learned," but, as one parent put it, "When I have to deal with *my* unique, *concrete* child in *concrete* situations which are never simple, which do not tell me with textbook clarity what I should do or think, situations not of my making and too frequently not under my control, I often find myself reacting unreflectively, really instinctively, and then I feel guilty that I may have screwed up" (emphasis mine). That is the kind of statement I have heard from eminent colleagues in child development when they describe, both with humor and chagrin, their departures (with their children) from what they believe to be the "right" way of thinking and acting. The real world of children, mothers, fathers, sibs, and a lot more, is not organized to allow consistency between theory and practice to be other than a sometime thing. There were (and still are) parents who pinpointed their guilt on this or that departure that had untoward effects on the child, and that guilt increased for those parents aware that the number of departures was not small. Have I been too harsh, too constricting, too insensitive, too permissive, too indulgent, too blind, too inconsistent, too undecisive?—these and other questions plagued parents who accepted the responsibility to identify and nurture the individuality of their offspring, to respect that individuality, not to confuse *this* child with the category of "children in general." No parent operates without some conception of what is good and bad, right or wrong, problem producing or problem avoiding in regard to child rearing. When that conception is based on the belief (which I regard as a fact) that each child is unique in terms of his or her combination of temperament, cognitive characteristics, reactivity, curiosity, interests—

a combination we try to signify by the abstraction personality—consistency between theory and practice, conception and action, will inevitably fall short of our mark. That is obvious and predictable and my purpose here is not to labor the obvious but rather to emphasize that in the post World War II era more people than ever before came to regard it as self-evident what the Spocks of this world were saying: *this* child is like all other children at the same time he or she is different from all other children and it is the parental responsibility to identify, exploit, and support that individuality in ways that are productive of the potentials that individuality suggests. The emphasis on individuality is not new in American history or psyche, but that emphasis until relatively recently was primarily in regard to adult individuality and adult self-responsibility for accomplishment, i.e., "making something of yourself." Beginning in the latter part of the nineteenth century, and accelerating in this century, was the view that adult individuality depended on many things not the least of which was the fostering of that individuality in the pre-school years.

That change in emphasis suffused the rhetoric of educators from whom hopeful parents heard that the goal of schooling was to help each child "realize his or her potential." I say rhetoric because the implications of that statement totally ignored the chasm between those implications and the history and structure of the public schools. The Spockian messages were read by parents with one, two, or several children. Schools as they are were developed for classrooms with many more children. In the development of our schools features were obvious which, although many historians have written about, most (otherwise knowledgeable) people have forgotten or never knew:

1. Because of wave after wave of massive immigrations public school classrooms contained forty or fifty or more students. The concept or value placed on individuality was not a luxury, it was simply not in the picture.

2. The goal of schooling was not to explore or "get out of" students their individual interests and talents but rather to "put into them" knowledge-facts considered essential to citizenship and work. Students were trained, not educated; they were passive, not active learners; they were judged by how well they could memorize and recall, not how well they could think for themselves; they were not question askers, they were question answerers; they were there to be molded regardless of individual variations.

3. Pedagogical theory was concerned with classroom organization, the authoritative and didactic role of the teacher, maintenance of discipline, techniques that made for efficiency of coverage of a totally pre-

determined curriculum, instilling proper "work or mental skills," and upholding American values. It was pedagogical theory tailor made to teach masses, not individuals. The practical realities determined theory as much as theory determined practice. It was these kinds of theories and practices against which John Dewey rebelled at the end of the nineteenth century. Dewey started with the question: what are the psychological characteristics of the developing child? The conventional theory and practice started with the question: what do *we* want *them* to become? Dewey saw teachers of the time as "commanders," and his use of that word referred to the military-like role of teachers and the soldier-like obedient, conforming obligations of students.

4. The administrative-bureaucratic structure of schools and school systems, the pressures to segregate poor learners, and the initiation of age-graded classes were primary consequences of the attempt to make schools more efficient, in principle similar to the ways in which the manufacturing industries were increasing their productivity and efficiency. When Henry Ford said that you could purchase any color Ford you desired as long as it was black, he was conveying the message that what consumers wanted would not interfere with an efficient mode of production the products of which were indistinguishable from each other. If you can imagine Ford cars having "minds," you can also imagine how the bulk of students felt, not counting, of course, that large number who dropped out. Dropping out, now and then, included an undetermined number of consumers who wanted to be other than a black Ford. (Not so incidentally, that was and is the case for some students who drop out of college.)

The above is by way of description and not criticism. If there is a note of criticism, it refers to the fact that as the decades passed, as the Deweyan perspective gained currency, as researchers demonstrated the individualities and communalities of psychological development, as the clash between the cultural backgrounds of multicultural America became plain to see, and as schools remained monolithically organized and incapable of "flexing" to individual variations—schools remained pretty much as they had been at the same time that the rhetoric of individuality became more shrill. The insights, the evidence, and the rhetoric changed; practice and organization did not. No one denied that "teachers should teach children, not subject matter." That maxim was intended as a criticism of what was obvious in the classroom. Even though today the number of students in a classroom is much less than earlier decades in this century, "teaching students, not subject matter" is the rule, not the exception, despite the fact that, unless my experience is atypical, teachers know in their heart of hearts that neither by their preparation nor by the ways schools are organized can they give other than lip service to individuality. And if the reader has any question about that observation, I hope it does not extend to what to me (and many others) is an indisputable conclusion: the bulk of students experience classrooms as boring, stultifying places where they are compelled to be in order to learn facts for reasons not at all clear to them, not related to their interests and concerns, incomparably less stimulating than the world they see and their experience outside of school.

Let me ask why in the post World War II era did the public become dissatisfied with our schools? The answer was that test scores steadily decreased. That is like saying that if your child has a high fever and it gets higher then you should be worried. Decreasing test scores like an increasing high fever tells us we have a problem, it does not tell us what the answer is; they tell us we should seek answers. However unsophisticated we may be about matters of health we know that an increasing high fever means that something is *systemically* wrong with us, i.e., something is awry with our bodily physiology-chemistry. In the case of decreasing test scores the answers were many but they did not call into question the system qua system, its usual way of doing and justifying its business, so to speak. That is to say, the system was basically appropriate and its outcomes would be improved if, for example, curricula were changed, new pedagogical techniques employed, preparing educators more steeped in subject matter, giving more time to the "basics," insisting on and maintaining performance standards students should meet, involving parents more in matters educational, instituting preschool programs that made it more likely that children would be able to benefit more from formal schooling—these and other "answers" had in common the unverbalized acceptance of schools as they have been and are: Their governance structure, their decision making processes, their encapsulated classrooms, their relation to preparatory program, their curriculum-calendar driven time perspective, their classrooms in which teacher questioning swamps student questioning, their classrooms in which imparting knowledge-facts makes eliciting student motivation a rarity, where the pressures to conform inhibit any tendency to express personal opinion, pressures no less effective in regard to teachers in their relationships with their administrative superiors.

Some readers will say that what I have said is overdrawn. To say that it is overdrawn is not to say it is wrong. It may be overdrawn but it is not wrong, and I am by no means the first person to come to these conclusions. A foreign visiting friend said to me, "It makes no difference where in America you see and go into a Wendy's, a McDonald's, or a

Burger King, they not only look alike but you can predict the behavior of everyone in them." In principle that is what John Goodlad concluded in *A Place Called School* (1984) based on a heroic study of many schools representative of schools in general. And that is what the initiators of the eight-year study concluded over sixty years ago. And that was a major theme in Cuban's classic *How Teachers Taught* (1984).

I am reminded here of John Gunther's 1936 book *Inside Europe*. In his chapter on Nazi Germany he says that the situation there is serious but not hopeless. In the next chapter on Austria he says that the situation there is hopeless but not serious. As a system for education our schools, *as they are now organized and governed,* are both hopeless and serious. They are and will be intractable to improvement. That brings me to the second question.

How did it come about that educators and the general public used test scores as *the* criterion, the overarching criterion, for judging the effectiveness of schooling? Why is it that when test scores began their decline, blame assignment became a cottage industry; almost any "reasonable" suggestion that gave promise of elevating test scores was tried, and the number of those suggestions was legion, including changing or constructing new tests so that they better measured what students had or should have learned. It was regarded as self-evident that there had to be a measuring rod for evaluation. After all, how can you evaluate without a measuring rod? You just could not hand a student a high school diploma unless he or she had gotten test scores indicating that the student met an agreed upon measured standard. Tests were means for measuring knowledge learned in school. Learning that knowledge was the purpose of formal schooling; tests were *the* form of quality control about knowledge learned and academic skills acquired.

Before going on I feel compelled to assure the reader that I am no mindless critic of tests. Given their purposes and awesome responsibilities, schools must use some reliable and valid means for evaluation. The issue for me is not whether the decline in test scores is to be accepted or believed. I accept and believe them as measures of knowledge learned and academic skills acquired. I also accept them as valid indicators of the failure of reform efforts to improve the amount of knowledge learned and skills acquired. And that is the point: Are the failures of the reform efforts attributable to the failure to question whether knowledge learned and academic skills acquired is *the* most important purpose of schooling? Is it possible that there is another purpose which if ignored sets drastic limits to achieving other purposes? If so, should we not reexamine why we are so wedded to tests that rather well measure knowledge learned and skills acquired? Should we not stop taking pot shots at tests and test makers who are giving us what we ask of them? This is not to say that what we ask of them is unimportant. Knowledge learned and skills acquired are important. But what if what we ask of them ignores a purpose which if not achieved guarantees that our present purposes are unattainable? Yes, I am saying that we have met the enemy and it is not the tests but us, our inability to take seriously a purpose we know is the most important of all over the course of our lives.

In recent years I have met with a variety of parent, teacher and school administrator groups. With each of them I asked the following question: "If at the point of a gun you were forced to state the one characteristic you want your child to have when he or she is graduated from high school what would it be? I know that there is more than one important characteristic you want your child to possess, but is there one overarching one?" That, it turns out, was a difficult question, not because anyone said it was not an important one but because they had not, as one person said, "ever had to prioritize purposes of schooling. Before you asked the question I could have listed three or four major goals I want my children to reach but I never had to choose among them. I do not feel I can choose one as more important than the others. I trust you will not pull the trigger." (I felt sympathy for that person because it took me years before I could ask that question of myself, let alone answer it to my satisfaction.) Because these meetings had agendas and time was limited I would break the silences by giving my answer: "If when a child is graduated from high school that child is motivated to learn more about self and the world, then I would say that schooling has achieved its overarching purpose. Put in another way, the student knows that the more you know the more you need to know. When I say `motivated to learn' I refer to that individual's curiosity about his or her interests and talents and where and how they can be tested and exploited in a world not of their making but a world they know they have to comprehend. And that should be as true for the student who is not college bound as it is for those who are. To want to continue to explore, to find answers to personally meaningful questions, issues, and possibilities is the most important purpose of schooling. When that kind of motivation is absent, then knowledge learned and academic skills acquired are not only empty of meaning but devoid of motivational power. To learn because you *have* to is one thing; to learn because you *want* to is quite another thing. And that is my overarching criterion: school is a place a very young child enters with awe, curiosities, expectations, questions, and the desire to feel competent and recognized, and that young child should have those personal characteristics when he or she finishes formal schooling. For those characteristics to be extinguished, to go underground, to get expressed primarily in fantasy is to impoverish a lifetime."

That is both an answer and a mini-speech. What I have found so encouraging is that no member of any of the groups who heard my answer disagreed with me, and I do not think I am deluding myself when I say that their agreement was not a way of pleasing a visitor, a Yale professor, a passionate old man. I shall assume that most readers will also be in agreement with my overarching criterion, keeping in mind that there are other important purposes we expect schools to accomplish. So, if you accept what I say is the most important purpose, what follows, what does it mean for action and change? Is that purpose as I have stated it so laudable, so unobjectionable, as to compel assent without requiring us to confront the chasm between what we believe and the way things are? Let me reconstruct an interchange which took place on one of these occasions between me and a middle school history teacher. (It really was between me, the history teacher, and a high school math teacher, but since the two teachers asked and said essentially the same things, it makes the reconstruction easier if I report it as a dyadic interchange.)

> Teacher: I get the feeling that you are implying more than you are saying. For example, are you implying that if a student is learning what we expect him or her to learn but you don't get the feeling that the student is all that interested in learning, then we haven't done our job?
>
> SBS: That's a fair question and I will answer it. But may I first ask you this question: as a middle school teacher you probably have five or six different groups in the course of a day, that is, you teach a lot of kids; how many of them are there about whom you could say they are truly interested in your subject matter?
>
> Teacher: That's why I am asking the question. There is only a handful about whom I can truly say, really, obviously like history; the others are there, with few exceptions they do acceptable work, but I cannot say they are interested. In fact, I've given up expecting them to be interested. Does that mean I'm short changing them? If you say that then you would have to say that about almost all teachers in my school because they feel exactly the way I do.
>
> SBS: Let's leave blame aside for a moment. Are you aware that there have been studies clearly indicating that, generally speaking, students do not find schools to be interesting places and that you and your colleagues are by no means alone in wishing that students would be more interested in what they are being taught?

Teacher: No, although from what I have read in magazines and Sunday supplement articles, I would say that you are accurate. And, to be completely honest, my own two children in high school complain about being bored in school.

SBS: Would you say they are bored at home?

Teacher: Definitely not. If we did not insist that they do their homework before they do anything else, they would be into this or that, spend hours on the telephone, go here or there, or watch TV. In fact, about the only thing they find boring is going to family gatherings.

SBS: How do you account for the difference between how they experience school and home?

Teacher: I'd really have to think about that.

SBS: I've been thinking about it a long time. May I try out my formulation on you and others in this room? In their activities outside of school they are initiators; those activities express in some way their interests, needs, curiosities; they feel in control; they feel competent; they are exploring themselves, others and their world. Put it this way, psychologically speaking they *own* those experiences because they make concrete sense to them. They don't own their school experiences in those ways. In school they are passive not active learners, reactors not initiators, impersonal not personal, question answerers not question askers, conformers not individualists, not individuals but part of a category called students, not individuals with assets but individuals with the deficits of ignorance, regurgitators not articulators, reproducers not producers.

Teacher: Wow! You are really down on schools!

SBS: No. I am not down on schools the way I am down on crime, pornography, and racial, religious, or gender discrimination, i.e., people who know well that what they are doing is judged wrong by society. Our schools are not uninteresting places because people will that they should be that way. There is no malicious intent. What I am down on is our—and I use that pronoun to mean people generally—inability to recognize that we have an asset we do not exploit. And that asset is that we know damned well when and why we have had a productive learning experience which is followed by the feeling that we know more about ourselves and our world. That is an asset but you would never know it from the way our schools are structured, organized, and run.

Teacher: So what do we do? What do you recommend?

> SBS: (with a feeble attempt at a smile) *Tonight* the issue is not what do we do but do we agree that our schools are based on a conception of learning that guarantees that that learning will be unproductive. Once there is that agreement, once we believe it in a truly gut sense, we will be able to begin to use the asset we all have. And then, and only then, will you be able to answer *for yourself* the question you asked earlier: If students pass "normally" through the grades but with little or no indication that they are interested in learning—they learn because they have to not because they want to—does that mean we haven't done our job? My answer is not that you haven't done your job but that *we*, in and out of schools, have not done our job.

Unless my memory is completely out of whack, or my capacity to fool myself is greater than I think it is, I would like to offer conclusions derived from hundreds of responses of adults to questions I asked about their experiences in schools. More specifically, they were responses to the open-ended question: How would you describe your experience in schools? It was rare for anyone to describe their experience as enjoyable, interesting, or recalled with nostalgia. What was very frequent, indeed near universal, was that these adults could name one, but no more than two, teachers who influenced them in positive ways. Those ways were of two sorts. The first, very small in number, was hearing a teacher say something that sparked the person's interests or curiosity, either because what the teacher said was so strikingly novel or because it contradicted what the student believed. Here is an example that stands out in my mind:

> It was during the civil rights upheavals in the sixties and, of course, I heard a lot about it at home and on TV. Needless to say, I was all for civil rights and against discrimination, and against everything slavery had produced. But very little of what was going on ever really got discussed in our classes even though my high school then had about 25% black students. One day in history class Mr. Merriam said that the civil war did *not* start over the issue of freeing the slaves but rather over whether states had the right to secede from the union (emphasis his). That floored me, really floored me, and I thought Mr. Merriam, who was an old man, had gone off his rocker. How could he say something so palpably wrong? I told it to my parents that night as an example of why going to school was a waste of time. They told me I probably heard wrong. So the next day I uncharacteristically screwed up

my courage and asked Mr. Merriam if he meant what he had said. Mr. Merriam, a gentleman WASP if ever there was one, politely told me that what he had said was a historical and legal fact, the civil war did not start because the south would not free the slaves. We talked for about ten minutes. Although I have no memory for what he said, I knew he was right. I don't think I ever again felt so humble and stupid. I even went to the library and read about the civil war in the *Encyclopedia Britannica*. That is when I became interested in the law and that was the experience that started me thinking about becoming a lawyer, a civil rights lawyer of course. For about a week I asked all of my friends why the civil war started and when they gave me the answer I had always given, I paraded my newfound knowledge before them with the appropriate professional certainty.

The second category of response, the most frequent by far, is also easier to summarize in this way: "That teacher took a special interest in *me*, I knew she was aware of *me*, she would go out of her way to talk to *me*, to encourage, or to help, or to support *me*. In her class I did not feel I was *anyone*, I was a *me* she wanted and liked to know. I felt *special*. I could trust *myself* to be *me* with her." It is obvious that the words I italicized were to emphasize that what these people were saying was that they felt their *individuality* was recognized; that teacher not only recognized their individuality but encouraged and supported it, it was not a sometime thing.

Why could these adults recall only one or two such teachers? When I have presented these "data" and conclusions to educators I have gotten one reaction and one explanation. The reaction is a combination of defensiveness and guilt, as if what I presented was in the spirit of criticism. My denial would not get very far. I could then count on someone to ask what did I think my "data" meant? Before answering that question I would confront them—and it was a confrontation—that *no one seemed to be denying that they did not treat each child in their class as a unique individual different from all others in that classroom.* I was absolutely certain, I would say, that they knew *some* children the way my adult interviewees had described one or two of their teachers. And that was my point: they did not know the bulk of their students in that "special" way. And, I would continue, that is blatantly the case with middle and high school teachers who in the course of a day may have several scores of students.

What explanation did teachers proffer? In each group, and aside from the occasional teacher who regarded me as an ivy league, arm chair, professorial spoilsport (or worse), the explanation was quite simple:

"Given the different subject matter grounds we have to cover, there is no *time* to get to know each child's interests, curiosities, needs, and problems. Sure, it would be nice *really* to get to know each student in a personal way, to get from them what turns them on and off, to *really* teach children and not subject matter, but that takes *time* which we simply don't have. Maybe in an ideal school, but we do not teach in ideal schools."

No, schools as they are do not approach the ideal, they are demonstrably counterproductive in regard to what I called the overarching purpose of schooling: to give expression to, to capitalize on, to nurture individuality in learning, to exploit that individuality for its motivational, propelling, cognitive properties. Unless, of course, you do not accept that purpose as the overarching one, in which case you will go along with the tinkering of the present and past, inspired by this or that new educational medicine, disillusioned by its inevitable, paltry consequences, directing blame now to this group and then that group, and, if fortunate, still capable of hoping that there must be a way that schools as we know them can be discernibly improved. The actuarial odds are all against you, and it is unlikely that there will be divine intervention.

Is it not possible, some might argue, that if we *dramatically* reduced class size, teachers would have the time to act more consistently and appropriately in accord with the overarching criterion? Maybe yes, maybe no, but I tend to the maybe no because the question erroneously assumes (or implies) that the preparation of teachers adequately provides them with a basis for how to think about and act in accord with the overarching purpose. And if anything is clear it is that preparatory programs are utterly inappropriate in regard to that purpose. I devoted an entire book *The Case for Change: Rethinking the Preparation of Educators* (1993) to why that is the case. What these programs do well is prepare teachers for schools as they are now, not as they should be if they were in accord with the overarching purpose. As I indicate in my book, teachers teach the way they have been taught, which is why I would not have high expectations of a dramatic decrease in class size, although I would be heartedly in favor of such a decrease (just as I was in favor of Headstart when it was initiated even though I publicly said that its impact and consequences would not be great).

When we say that we want children to learn we imply more than our words denote. What we imply is that we want that learning to be productive, to reinforce the desire to learn more. For learning to be productive it has to be in a context alert to and supportive of manifestations of the individual's desire to explore, to master, to incorporate, psychologically to "own" the fruits of his or her efforts. We see this most clearly in the very young child fascinated, puzzled, and drawn to people and the world around him or her. Indeed, we sometimes wish that child would not want to explore, to be into, to do and to "own" everything. As parents we hear ourselves saying that "we can't keep up with the child" for whom the world is busting out all over. We "follow" the child, which is not to say that we do not "lead" the child. We lead the child but only *after* we pay heed to where the child is taking himself or herself. We are not mindlessly permissive—not everything goes—we are unconditionally supportive. We have moral sensibilities and values but we do not *dictate* them because we know that dictating can win you the battle and lose you the war. We know that our task is to help the child to incorporate those values because he wants to and not because he is forced to. We want the child to regard those sensibilities as his or hers, not only as our sensibilities, not as alien to his or her self-regard.

The fact is that as parents we inevitably fall short of the mark either because of our imperfections or because we live in contexts that have unpredictable and uncontrollable features. (So what else is new?) But at the least we hope that parents know the importance of respecting a child's individuality, of knowing the obligations of following and leading, of "bringing out" and not "pouring in." There are, of course, parents who are insensitive to the child's individuality, whose conception of productive learning is virtually non-existent, who in principle regard the child as they do their pet animal: something to be "tamed" or "housebroken." Of course they love their child but, as the saying goes, love is not enough.

What I have been saying about parents and the preschool child holds for schools and students. Parents and educators are in agreement, on the level of rhetoric, about respecting individuality. I say on the level of rhetoric because educators, generally speaking, well know that the governance, structure, and traditions of schools, plus the inadequacies of preparatory programs, make respecting individuality impossible. We are not in the mess we are in because of the laws of chance but because pedagogy for respecting individuality *never* has been an overarching purpose of schools. If it had been, we would have schools (and preparatory programs) dramatically different than they became and are. If we understand why, given our national history in the nineteenth century (immigration), schools became what they still are, and we can even be sympathetic to those who had to deal with the realities of those times, let us have the courage and candor to say out loud that we can no longer afford to accept schools where the overarching purpose is not and *cannot* be realized. Today we are dealing with social realities no less thorny and no less potentially destabilizing than those the society faced when schooling became compulsory. What will it take for educators and the general public to realize that, in the case of schools, we "inherited" an institution the features of which doom us to disillusionment and worse? When will we own up to the most obvious feature of schools and preparatory programs in the post-World War II era: their intractability to change in accord with what we say should be their overarching purpose?

As I have in previous books, I must remind the reader that at the beginning of this century the inadequacies of medical education were probably greater than those of our schools today. You may find that hard to believe in which case I urge you to read Abraham Flexner's 1910 report on *Medical Education in the United States and Canada* (Flexner, 1910/1960). The significance and impact of that report is hard to exaggerate. If I had to sum up (in my words) in several sentences what Flexner said, it would go like this: "Musicians say that the Beethoven Violin Concerto is not for the violin, it is against it. Medical schools are not and cannot be for the development of physicians who can think but are against it. Given how they are organized and run they are incapable of improvement. We cannot afford to tinker, to work within their present structures and purposes. If we really want physicians who are knowledgeable and thoughtful, a very different kind of medical school will have to be envisioned and developed, and I [Flexner] will outline what that medical school should look like and in reality be." Medical education was transformed, bearing little similarity to the deplorable, semi-scandalous state of affairs it had been.

Dr. Emory Cowen, whose research in schools is like an oasis in the desert, found the following in his mailbox at the University of Rochester. The unknown author summarizes almost all of the major points I have made in several books; it obviously says a good deal about professorial longwindedness.

Horse Story

Common advice from knowledgeable horse trainers includes the adage, "*If the horse you're riding dies, get off.*" Seems simple enough, yet, in the education business we don't always follow that advice. Instead, we often choose from an array of alternatives which include:

1. Buying a stronger whip.
2. Trying a new bit or bridle.
3. Switching riders.
4. Moving the horse to a new location.
5. Riding the horse for longer periods of time.
6. Saying things like, "*This is the way we've always ridden this horse.*"
7. Appointing a committee to study the horse.

8. Arranging to visit other sites where they ride dead horses more efficiently.
9. Increasing the standards for riding dead horses.
10. Creating a test for measuring our riding ability.
11. Comparing how we're riding now with how we did ten or twenty years ago.
12. Complaining about the state of horses these days.
13. Coming up with new styles of riding.
14. Blaming the horse's parents. The problem is often in the breeding.
15. Tightening the cinch.

As I was writing this chapter the *Hartford Courant* carried news articles about the serious consideration the city's board of education was giving to contracting out the *entire* school system to a private corporation, the same (I think) company that had been entrusted to run several Baltimore schools. There are other examples around the country, and there is no reason to believe that only a few boards are giving thought to such proposals. Basic to such proposals are three assumptions. Schools and school systems are inefficiently and counterproductively run, i.e., the structure of schools is O.K., they are simply not being correctly administered. The problem is not money; indeed, the private company expects to earn a profit. From my standpoint those two assumptions in no way disconfirm the wisdom in the Horse Story. But there is a third assumption, and that is that schools have not exploited modern technology so as to increase student interest and performance. That assumption has the virtue of recognizing that student interest in school learning is alarmingly low. And by modern technology is meant, of course, putting computers in classrooms. Computers are the new panaceas, the silver bullet that will engage and propel the student not only to learn what society wants students to learn but (presumably) also to allow them to get answers to questions meaningful to *them,* not only questions teachers pose to them. That assumption, especially the part that suggests "individuality," would appear to disconfirm the Horse Story.

It so happens that back in the fifties I had the opportunity systematically to observe the introduction of *talking* computers in the early grades in a private school. I had no doubt then (as I do not have now) that computers are fascinating to students, not all but almost all students. Why? Was it because it literally told them when they were right or wrong and if they were wrong it did not engender a feeling of stupidity as frequently happens when you give a wrong answer in front of a teacher and a class? Was it that they could proceed at their own pace? Was it the satisfaction associated with the sense of learning what needed to be learned? Was the content of that learning a stimulus to want to learn more? The answer to each question was, in my opinion, in the affirmative. But, there is always a but, it seemed obvious to me that far more important than anything these questions suggested was the child's sense of control over, mastery of, the machine. I did not get the feeling that the content being learned was fascinating or gripping in any intrinsic sense, although it would be unjustified to say that sense was absent. The imagery that comes to mind when I replay my observations is that of the child who successfully takes his or her first steps: The "look, Ma, I'm dancing" facial expression, although it really was as if the child is saying, "Holy cow, I, I, I am finally doing it," the sense of competence as a result of *self*-initiated action. I watched several children once a week over a period of several weeks. They did learn what the technology had been programmed to help them learn. But there was also no doubt that once they had mastered the technology they did not approach the talking machine with anything resembling the curiosity-eagerness I observed in my initial visits. And the reason, I had to conclude, was that they were not learning what they wanted to learn but what they had to learn, and whatever sense of mastery they experienced, and I assume that sense was not totally absent, was not much in evidence. I in no way derogate learning what one has to learn. I do thank God for big favors. But let us not forget for a moment that the number of students who do not want to learn what they have to learn is somewhat staggering, and foremost among the reasons is that what they have to learn may have little or no meaning for their interests, curiosities, desires, life context, criteria for utility; in short their individual selves. Do not confuse the surface appearance of a passive, uninvolved, even somnolent student in the classroom—the student who appears unable or unwilling to think—with what is going on in his or her head. How many times have you sat through a lecture in college with your mind elsewhere? For most students in our schools the times are many, and for some it is continuous, not just now and then.

Despite the fact that the talking computer was heralded as a breakthrough it was more a fall down. It went nowhere and I do not fully understand why, unless because it required that each child have his or her own soundproof cubicle and that kind of respect for individuality was considered economically unfeasible. We have had a surfeit in education of breakthroughs that fell down, but, to me at least, the talking machine seemed to have promise, despite the limitations I observed.

But that was in the fifties when computers were in their infancy although there was no doubt in the minds of their proponents that computers would revolutionize the world, and not least our schools. I have friends and colleagues—and I do read—who assure me that today's computers are to the earlier ones as a jet plane is to the contraption the Wright

Brothers flew. As one of my knowledgeable friends said, "The information highway is being paved, part of it is already done, you have seen
nothing yet." If I did not respond with enthusiasm, it was for two reasons. For one thing, the word information suggests to me a concept of
learning—pouring facts into students—quite congenial to the way most
students are taught, *the* way that has contributed to the poor performance of students. But there was another reason for my lack of enthusiasm. In the past several years I have had opportunity to observe the use
of computers in classrooms, not a lot of classrooms but several in each
of four schools in different parts of the country. With that limitation in
mind, I have to report that what I observed I consider a charade and a
disaster. To say that the computer programs were stimulating, captivat-
ing, or even mildly interesting to students would be totally unjustified.
Yes, they liked the computer but there was no basis for saying that what
was on the computer screen in any way "hooked" them. What the computer programs reminded me of was the "Oh, oh, Puff Puff" first grade
books of earlier decades. And if I was unenthusiastic, so were most of the
teachers one of whom said (in a whisper), "I do not know what the shout-
ing is all about in regard to the wonders of these computers. *Besides, we
were told that we would have and have to use computers. We did not ask for
them.*" Perhaps with one or two exceptions these teachers were not what
is called "computer literate." When the computers were to be introduced
the teachers went to workshops varying in length from three days to a
week. Apparently, those workshops were as helpful as those given in
the sixties when the new math disaster took place.

Thou shalt use computers! That commandment, like the ones in the
sixties, typifies how change in school is introduced. It is the top down,
fall down theory of change. A decision is made on the Mt. Sinai of the
school structure by the board of education and the Moses-Superintendent
and the golden calf will be destroyed! It is as simple, obvious and utterly self-defeating as that.

Computer technology does have enormous, positive possibilities for
education. For what purposes? Are all purposes coequally important?
On what basis do we decide where on a priority list a purpose should
be, which is not to suggest that you downplay, let alone ignore, purposes
not at the top of your list. In this chapter I have argued that at the top of
my list of purposes of schooling is to recognize, respect, nurture, and
exploit what children are before they enter school: curious, questing,
question asking, competence seeking *individuals* in search of an identity that propels them to want to learn more about themselves, others, and
their world, to want to experience that sense of growth or change, that
sense of self worth without which daily living is literally unproductive,

it is routinized, aimless existence, a prelude to a similar future, to an unexamined life. To some ears that will sound flowery, lofty, idealistic, utopian, soupy, and sentimental. If I were capable of stating that purpose in language that students in our schools would understand, I would get unanimous assent just as I would get a thundering no to the question: "Is that a purpose you feel your schooling helps you realize?"

Ideals *are* ideas about what *should* be, at the same time we know and regret that we will fall short of the mark. It is one thing to aim and fall short of the mark, it is inexcusable if knowing you will inevitably fall short of the mark, you do not even take aim. In regard to the overarching purpose I have stated, we have hardly taken aim even though we know that in our individual lives that is the purpose we want to experience and realize. Even if what I have said is taken seriously, schools will fall short of the mark, if only because too many parents fall short of the mark either out of ignorance or life circumstances antithetical to the recognition and support of a child's individual perspectives and needs. I am quite aware that we live in a real world where there are no magic wands or perfect solutions. In the realm of social-institutional living we are never dealing with problems that have a once-and-for-all solution. They are problems we have to deal with again and again and again. That is all the more reason that we have to become clear about our purposes and direct our aim to an overarching purpose we know will make realizing other purposes more likely.

There are people in and out of the educational arena who proclaim the necessity of "returning to the basics" by which they mean reading, writing, arithmetic and the world of factual knowledge. To argue against learning the "basics" is truly to be for sin and against virtue and motherhood, leaving patriotism aside. These people are very well intentioned. They are also ignorant of what the public schools have always been: a place where drill in the basics takes precedence over everything else including the interests, motivations, curiosities of students who would rather be elsewhere. By advocating more time for the basics—or lengthening the school year—they will make a bad situation worse. They are in principle kin to the parent who wakes up one morning and decides that her child is going to be toilet trained, proceeds determined to succeed by next week or the week thereafter, and then does not understand why she has a battle on her hands. In the classroom it has been called "the page 72 syndrome": "by November 1 we *must* be on page 72 in the book." With advocates like that education need never fear for the lack of enemies.

I sound harsh. I do not intend to sound that way but if it does sound that way it stems from a feeling of desperation derived from the perception of numerous outcroppings suggesting that people are beginning to accommodate to the possibility that the demise of the public schools may not be such a bad idea. They feel that since reform efforts have failed, that schools as they are have been intractable to change, we should seriously consider alternatives, such as privatization or vouchers, alternatives we think we know how to handle. And that is the point: we define the problem in ways that allow us to think we know what should be done, and glossing over the possibility that we are avoiding doing what needs to be done. What I am trying to say is captured in the joke about the man who is ill, it is midwinter, and he goes to his physician. He receives a thorough examination and then is told to go home, take off all of his clothes, open all windows, stand in front of a window and breathe deeply for a half hour. To which the aghast man says, "but if I do that I will get pneumonia." To which the physician replies, "*that* is something about which I know what to do."

I should remind the reader why I wrote this chapter. Earlier in this book I argued that the existing governance structure of our schools should be abolished and replaced with one less likely to be as productive of problems or as effective an obstacle to much needed change. In several places in that argument I emphasized that however important and necessary those changes in structure, organization, and power relationships were, the benefits from those changes would be drastically limited unless they were based on and powered by the overarching purpose I have elaborated on in this chapter. We are used to hearing that form follows function, which is to say that form should reflect purpose. How many buildings are there whose form seems reasonable and even attractive, but to those who live and work in them the structures meet the criterion of semi-unliveability? So, if I have convinced some readers that the governance structure of our schools should be changed (that is, abolished and replaced), I hope they will also agree that unless that change reflects the overarching purpose of schooling, our expectations should not be high. It is obvious, and I do mean obvious, if that purpose powers the change, schools will look and be very different places than they are, which is why some will shrink from examining the consequences and some will say they have no time to fantasize, they are too busy trying to deal with the educational equivalent of pneumonia, the lethal, viral strain.

10

LETTERS TO A SERIOUS
EDUCATION PRESIDENT

To understand an important aspect of my current point of view, and why in 1993 I wrote the book bearing this chapter's title, I have to begin with my favorite Jewish joke.

> It is about the journalist assigned to the Jerusalem bureau of his newspaper. He got an apartment overlooking the wailing wall. After several weeks he became aware that regardless of time of day, there was this old Jew praying vigorously before the wall. There must be a story there, he concluded. So he went to the wall, introduced himself, and asked, "What are you praying for every day before the wall?" The old Jew looked at him somewhat puzzled and said, "What am I praying for? In the morning I pray for world peace. Then I pray for the eradication of illness and disease from the earth. I go home for lunch and then I come back and pray for the brotherhood of man." The journalist was taken in by what the old Jew said. "You mean that *every* day you come to the wall and pray for these things?" "Yes," said the old Jew. "How long have you been coming to the wall to pray for these things?" the amazed journalist asked. The old Jew became reflective and replied, "How long? Maybe twenty, maybe twenty-five years." The journalist was stunned. Finally he blurted, "How does it feel to be praying all those years before the wall?" To which the old Jew replied, "How does it feel? It's like talking to a wall."

For all practical purposes, I have been talking to a wall. Yes, my writings on school change have been well received, but as I surveyed the scene I had to conclude that nothing had changed and that the situation may be getting worse, especially in our urban areas. Those who by law or custom (local, state, federal) make and are responsible for educational policy either are unaware of or ignore or reject the import of what I have written (and predicted) over the years. Although I have never been without hope that my concerns would be taken seriously sometime, somewhere by some of the people, I believed that for my ideas to be generally discussed, let alone acted on, would only occur after the policy makers had been, so to speak, hit over the head by social realities and disasters, forcing them to give up their self-defeating, unverbalized assumptions about school change. That is, the situation has to be seen as desperate and pressures external to schools far stronger and demanding than they now are. We are moving to such a situation but I venture no prediction about when the upheaval will occur. There are today, as there will be in the foreseeable future, isolated instances here and there where the necessary changes are being discussed and in part implemented. You can always find exceptions but they only make more glaring how in general nothing is changing.

I write these words after a four hour meeting with Kenneth Wilson, Professor of Physics at Ohio State University, the second such meeting I have had with him this year. For the past several years he has devoted himself to as thoroughgoing a review of the school change literature as I have ever known. He knows that literature. As a result, he has begun to develop a point of view that, in addition to being conceptually comprehensive and sophisticated, has led him to a plan of action which he has begun to implement, i.e., he has begun to seek support, by no means astronomical, for what I consider a bold, promising, and practical series of actions. Let us suppose that he gets the support he deserves. In that case the pace of the changes he advocates will depend on, among other things, whether his ideas and program gain general currency, i.e., whether his ideas and program get the kind of discussion and recognition that will make ignoring him very difficult for the educational community, although it has been easy in the present and past for that community to adopt a file-and-forget stance. Professor Wilson is aware of this. That is not the point here. The point is that unless and until his point of view gains general currency his efforts will have "local" not general impact.

Like Professor Wilson—who I learned from other sources months after our first meeting was a Nobel Laureate in Physics—I have struggled with how my ideas, which have a history antedating my birth (I am a latecomer on the scene), might gain general currency. So one day it dawned on me that I should write *Letters to a Serious Education President* and make sure that he and his advisors got copies. In those letters I tell the president a lot of things but two are emphasized. First, the president has to become more knowledgeable about why reform has failed, what the basic issues are, and, perhaps most important, how he has to use his own school experience and get clear in his head why so much of that experience was uninteresting, boring, and personally meaningless. I say to the president precisely what I say in Chapter 2, "You know more than you think and more than they give you credit for," i.e., my message to those entering a teacher preparatory program. The second part I emphasize is that only the president can convey to the citizenry a vision, a moral vision, of what classrooms and schools should be; only the president stands a chance of giving general currency to and gaining public support for the changes that vision requires. Tell the public: no more cliches, no more empty rhetoric, no more bromides. And I make some concrete suggestions, involving relatively little money, about some beginning steps.

Several months after the book came out I got a call from a colleague who was at LaGuardia Airport having just returned from a one hour, one-on-one meeting with the Secretary of Education. On the secretary's large coffee table, he told me, was one obviously much handled, marked up book: mine. For a moment I was joyous, I was "getting through" to those in a position to move in new directions. But only for a moment. I said to my friend, I would like to believe that they will take the book seriously, but if I had to bet I would give odds that day they will go on doing the same damned things they have done before." Two years after that call I have every reason to believe that the book is somewhere on a shelf gathering dust at the same time that the gathering storm is more ominous than two years ago. Unlike the old Jew at the wailing wall, I cannot even pray.

What follows are the first three letters to a president in the year 2000.[1]

━━◦━━

I

November, 2000

Dear Mr. President:

Yesterday's results make you the first president elected in the twenty-first century. Given my very advanced age, I am delighted to be alive to wish you well. But, again because of my age, I feel compelled to do

---

[1] The text following this sentence and continuing to the end of this chapter is reprinted from *Letters to a Serious Education President* (pp. 1–21), 1993. Newbury Park, CA: Corwin Press. Copyright ©1993 by Corwin Press, Inc., Newbury Park, CA. Reprinted by permission of Corwin Press, Inc.

more than to convey my sincere wishes for a productive presidency. During the recent campaign you eloquently expressed two things: your frustration—frankly, bewilderment would be a more appropriate term—that past efforts to improve our schools have, generally speaking, failed, and, second, your explicit resolve and hope that you will truly be a more successful "education president" than any of your predecessors, save Thomas Jefferson. In one of your campaign speeches you said,

> Improving our schools is not an important problem, it is *the* problem because the survival of our ideals is at stake. In his inaugural address Franklin Roosevelt, faced as he and the nation was with the catastrophe called the Great Depression, said that we have nothing to fear but fear itself. I must tell you that today, as well as for the past half century, we have not been as fearful as we should be about the deterioration of our educational system. We have been concerned but not fearful, certainly not fearful to the point where we have been willing to say that we must have the courage to admit that we have identified the enemy and it is us: our past ways of thinking, our temporizing, our resort to quick fixes, our belief that somehow the nightmare will end and we will wake up to see a better day. My predecessors were well-meaning people, but it is obvious that good intentions, like love, are not enough. And neither is money. If money is the answer, should not the billions we have poured into our schools have had some discernible positive effects? If instead of billions we had expended trillions, would our educational problems have disappeared or dramatically lessened? I wish I could say that the answer is yes or even maybe. Money was not the answer to the Great Depression, World War II was. As president I will not wait for the equivalent of a war to forge a new, more effective educational system. The moment of truth has arrived. Let us greet the moment honestly, courageously, inventively, in full awareness of the failures of our past ways of thinking and acting.

Those were stirring words, even to someone like me who long ago gave up hoping that our political leaders knew (or even wanted to know) what the educational game and score were. More correctly, that even if they *knew* the game and score, would they have the will to lead the nation in truly new directions . . . even though they, like Franklin Roosevelt and Harry Truman, will be called, in certain quarters, blind radicals, or bleeding heart liberals, or betrayers of national values, or utopian fools?

May I be so bold as to say that you may not be aware of the full extent of your kinship to Franklin Roosevelt. In his campaign for the presidency in 1932—the Great Depression was in its early stages—he ran on a platform that had two major policies: to reduce and to balance the federal budget. In short, his diagnosis of the causes of the economic breakdown was monumentally in error. It was not that he was a fool but rather that he, like everyone else, simply underestimated the dimensions and complexity of what was happening. It was not until he assumed the presidency that he began to comprehend how wrong his diagnosis and policies had been. Like you, he then gave us stirring words that heralded the New Deal era. And, again like you, he told the nation that past ways of thinking and acting were no longer adequate. He had the will, and he engendered that will in the nation, to take bold actions. What is the relevance of this for your presidency? Let me put it bluntly: Nothing in what you have said about our educational problems contains your diagnosis of what we are faced with. You have said all of the right things about past failures and our head-in-the-sands stance. It is to your credit that you have put education at the top of your agenda. Given all that has happened in the past decade, you clearly have convinced most people to support the priority you have given to education. But a priority is not a diagnosis. In this instance what I mean by a diagnosis begins with the recognition that we are not dealing with a problem and a diagnosis but a truly bewildering array of problems. If you do not know that now, your overwhelming moment of truth is not far off. What you should fear is not fear itself but the sense of being so overwhelmed by complexity that you substitute action for thinking. How will you decide what is a primary or "basic" problem? How prepared are you to resist the pressures to adapt this or that "solution," especially from quarters that, however well intentioned, have been part of the problem? Are you prepared to say loud and clear that you, we, are not faced with problems that have "solutions" in the way that four divided by two is a solution?

I confess that there is one absolutely crucial point about which you have said nothing and, therefore, that warns me not to be taken in by your inspiring words. Let me put my reservation in the form of a question. How clear is it in your head that you should have two overarching *moral* obligations: *to repair and to prevent?* It is only a slight exaggeration to say that up until now the emphasis and funding have been on repair, not prevention. Inevitably, they are interrelated, but the thinking that informs the repair effort is very different from that which informs efforts at primary prevention. You were correct to say that it was World War II that got us out of the Depression, i.e., that the repair efforts of the New Deal were inadequate. What I hoped you would go on to say is that the one piece of New Deal legislation that not only was a radical departure from our past but also the most successful was the Social Security Act. Undergirding that landmark legislation was the primary prevention way of thinking, i.e., to prevent the personal and social catastrophes of undue dependency in one's later years or in unemployment. I am sure you agree with me on that point. But have you thought through what that means for how you will approach educational problems? What balance will you try to maintain between repair and prevention?

Friends tell me that there are more productive ways I can spend my remaining days than writing to you. For one thing, they tell me, it is wildly unrealistic to expect that a president can have other than a superficial knowledge of education in general and schools in particular. Instead of writing to the president I should find out who are his educational advisors and write to or meet with them. Better yet, they say, I should try telling the president from whom he should *not* seek advice and give him a list of people he *should* consult. Obviously, I have not heeded their counsel, and for a reason I shall get to in a moment after I have expressed the major doubt I had about writing you.

Presidents, I have concluded, are not readers. That may sound strange because a good deal of a president's time is spent reading more memoranda and reports than there are hours in the day. Indeed, a president depends on his staff to give him summary reports about reports, ending with options to consider for the purposes of action. Whatever a president reads has gone through a filtering or screening process. He assumes that what he reads contains the "guts" of a problem and the alternatives for action available to him. So why say that presidents are not readers? I say it for several reasons. First, reading summaries of summaries is no substitute for grasping the complexities of problems. Problems, *important* problems, are not only horribly complex but they have a history of errors of omission and commission that, if you are ignorant of them, makes it likely you will repeat those errors. No one, least of all me, expects you to bone up on the history of all important problems. But I do expect that that is precisely what you should feel obliged to do about a problem, in this case education, that you have put at the top of your agenda. To the extent that you depend on summaries of summaries, to the extent that you do not feel *compelled* to familiarize yourself with this problem, to the extent that you do not have the *curiosity* truly to read, to sample, in the literature on education, you are very likely to pursue courses of action that end up proving that the more things change the more they remain the same. Or, as with education, the more they get worse.

Franklin Roosevelt, Harry Truman, and John Kennedy were readers. They had a sense of history, better yet, a respect for history. They did not view history as a museum of relics to which you go on a rainy Sunday. I confess that nothing I have read about you suggests that you are a reader, that you will not be satisfied to "see" education only in terms of summaries of summaries. I hope you prove me wrong. Why anyone would want to be president of the United States has long mystified me. In many ways it is an impossible job. We are used to hearing that the presidency is the most powerful office in the world. I assume you have read enough to know that by the time a president leaves office he (someday it will be a she) is the world's expert on the constraints on the office. In regard to education you will find many constraints: constitutional, political, economical, and institutional. Those constraints are real, strong, and trying. But there is no constraint on articulating a vision, and by that I do not mean the mouthing of cliches, pious generalizations, and empty rhetoric. In fact, one of your major obstacles in improving our schools is that many people believe the situation is hopeless. No one has given them reason to hope, once again, that we are moving in new, challenging ways. No one has given them a compelling basis for believing that someone is, finally, getting at the heart of the problem. Far from being hopeful, people are resigned to a hostile apathy. No one has made them think. No one has clearly posed for them the hard choices they must think about. No one has reinvigorated, or even articulated, a sense of national mission. The people are wise, not jaded. Their stance is: We have heard it all before, why should we listen again? They know something is wrong. They are waiting for a new vision that will have the ring of truth, the ring that says: Yes, *that* is what we have forgotten, *that* is what we have to take seriously, *that* we must act on come what may.

So what should you read? I attach a small list of books. I hope that you will not view it as a display of hubris on my part that a couple of my books are included. They are there not because I have ever said anything new but because they contain the ideas of several writers you should take most seriously. Indeed, if the pressures on your time permit you to read only one book on that list, it would be the one by Alfred North Whitehead. He was no bleeding heart liberal or mindless reactionary. He was a philosopher, a stellar logician-mathematician who understood two related things: the nature and force of children's curiosity, and the ways that curiosity is too often blunted or extinguished in classrooms. That is to say, he understood the differences between productive and unproductive contexts for learning. What Whitehead understood gets to the heart of the matter: how to sustain the boundless curiosity of very young children who leave their "wonder years" for years in the classroom. Many other writers have said the same things. And that is the point you must not allow yourself to forget: The core problem has long been identified. There is no great mystery here. Our past failures inhere in the inability or unwillingness to take it seriously. Inability or unwillingness may be inappropriate characterizations. It may be more correct to say that there has been a lack of leadership to give people a vision of what we would have to do if we took these things seriously. What you have thus far said publicly is not a vision but an expression of your resolve, your concerns, your hopes. In times of threats to our national security a president has no difficulty rallying people around our flag. The threat is concretely there, the people know it, they are willing to do whatever is necessary to repulse the threat. The people know *it* and the recognition of *it* does not follow a Madison Avenue campaign of persuasion. In the case of education—which, as you have said, is as serious a threat as a foreign enemy to our security—no one has defined the central problem, the *it*. If people know anything, it is that in response to the educational crisis there have been many "its" and many failures. The American people are neither niggardly nor stupid. In the case of education today it is as if everyone is from Missouri. They want to be convinced and so they ask: Where is the beef? Why should we get our hopes up again?

This letter is much longer than I expected. I initially thought I would convince you that you know far more about the important problems in education than you realize. Indeed, I was going to urge you to refrain from undue dependency on experts. You will have need for experts, but their value to you will be determined by how conscientiously you first look into your experiences as a student. You do not regard yourself as an expert, but I will try in my next letter to convince you that in an important way you *are* an expert.

I have not introduced myself to you and that was deliberate. Who I am, what I have done, what I have written should be of no importance to you. I know that sounds strange, if not ridiculous. My plea to you is to read this and subsequent letters with one question in mind: Do these letters have the ring of truth? I shall not, I assure you, present you with "data": statistics, graphs, research data, commission reports, etc. If sheer volume of *valid* knowledge were necessary and sufficient, we would not be in the morass we are. I have read that your favorite musical is *Guys and Dolls*. You will recall that delightful song "Adelaide's Lament" wherein she concludes that medical explanations of her psychosomatic upper respiratory colds are for the birds because they do not get "where the problem is": her single, unmarried status. What I shall endeavor to demonstrate in these letters is that in the case of our educational problems we have not dealt with where the problem is.

Between now and your inaugural you will be quite busy. But I do hope that you will find it in your self-interest to read my letter. It will certainly brighten my remaining days if you were to respond, however briefly, to anything I write. I confess I entertain the thought (fantasy?) that what I will say to you is very important for you and our country. It may be a delusion of grandeur on my part to believe that if you take what I say seriously, you will not end up as a footnote in future history books but with pages describing your courage to give the American people a basis for *re*-educating themselves about the purposes of American schools. Our country has two kinds of history. One celebrates our traditions, values, and accomplishments. The other catalogues our departures from what we have stood for and should have done. You have the opportunity to lead this country in ways that will justify celebration and not add to the litany of our failures.

Respectfully

Seymour B. Sarason
Professor of Psychology Emeritus
Yale University

P.S. Before writing this letter I assumed that I would not write a second one until I received a reply from you. I have changed my mind for two reasons. The first is that it is unrealistic to expect you to reply "promptly." You are swamped with the details of planning, selecting staff and cabinet, and ordering your priorities. The second is more personal but no less realistic: I am understandably aware that my days are numbered and that I should devote what energies I have to doing what I enjoy most, which is thinking and writing. So at varying intervals I will be sending you letters. But I do hope that at some not-too-distant week I will hear from you.

II

Dear Mr. President:

I assume that you do not consider yourself an expert on education but that you are expert in choosing and listening to people with new ideas. Put in another way, you have confidence in your ability to distinguish between those who are giving you old wine in relabeled bottles and those who are giving you a new, bracing brew. In this letter I shall try to convince you that you have more than a little expert knowledge about a fundamental educational problem.

A Greek philosopher said, "The fox knows many things, but the hedgehog knows one big thing." One of our best observers of the human scene, Isaiah Berlin, put it this way in his book *The Hedgehog and the Fox:*

> . . . there exists a great chasm between those, on one side, who relate
> everything to a single central vision, one system less or more coherent or
> articulate, in terms of which they understand, think and feel—a single,
> universal, organizing principle in terms of which alone all that they are
> and say has significance—and, on the other side, those who pursue
> many ends, often unrelated and even contradictory, connected, if at all,
> only in some *de facto* way, for some psychological or physiological cause,
> related by no moral or aesthetic principle; these last lead lives, perform
> acts, and entertain ideas that are centrifugal rather than centripetal, their
> thought is scattered or diffused, moving on many levels, seizing upon
> the essence of a vast variety of experiences and objects for what they are
> in themselves, without, consciously or unconsciously, seeking to fit them
> into, or exclude them from, any one unchanging, all-embracing, some-
> times self-contradictory and incomplete, at times fanatical, unitary inner
> vision. The first kind of intellectual and artistic personality belongs to
> the hedgehogs, the second to the foxes.

That, you will agree, is a helluva long sentence, but it serves the purpose, my purpose, of defining what I mean by a vision: a central idea, a
big idea, that radiates out and magnetically attracts and interconnects a
lot of other ideas. When I say that I am a hedgehog, or that someone else
is, it does not automatically confer validity on their big idea, even though
hedgehogs have no doubt that their big idea is right on target. Like it or
not, you are hoist by your own petard. By virtue of the fact that you have
put education at the very top of the national agenda, you will ultimately be judged by how good a hedgehog you were, how clearly you articulated a central idea, the flag around which you rallied the people. Your
predecessors were foxes, they had no big idea. I do not say that to dis-
parage them—some of history's important people have been foxes—but
rather to indicate that they did many things to improve education which
were basically unrelated to each other. Parts remained parts. Some called
it a crazy quilt approach. That's wrong because a crazy quilt has *one* purpose: to keep you warm in bed.

Lyndon Johnson was a partial exception. If you go back, as you
should, and read his justification for Head Start, you will find his one
big idea, his vision: Disadvantaged, impoverished preschoolers had the
intellectual and personal capabilities to exploit and benefit from schooling if appropriately stimulating contexts were made available to them.
They had all the marbles, so to speak, but no context in which to use and
develop them. Provide them with that context and they will stay in the
race. It was a morally inspired idea informed by a belief in the potential
of these children *and* in the superiority of preventive over repair efforts.
Why do I say that President Johnson was a "partial" exception? Because

his vision of what children were and needed focussed on the preschool years and wrongly assumed that when these preschoolers entered "real" school the context of learning would be no less stimulating, enriching, and productive. If the results of Head Start are encouraging but by no means dramatic, it is because his big idea was not big enough to alert him to the characteristics of most classrooms, to lead him to say: "What preschoolers want and need are what *all* students want and need but our classrooms are not providing because they are intellectually and personally frustrating and uninteresting places. What we owe these youngsters before they come to school, we owe to them *and everyone else* once they are in school."

Enough of this academic-professional preface! Professorial habits are not easily overcome. So forgive. I promise you no more quotations.

You and I grew up in very different worlds, and we come from very different socioeconomic, religious backgrounds. Despite all of the obvious ways we differ, I shall make the assumption that in one crucial respect we are very similar. Frankly, I would say we are, were, identical. Therefore, let me pose a question I shall answer in terms of my preschool experience, an answer I have no doubt you will find true for your early life. The question is: What stands out in your mind when you recollect what your preschool years were like?

What comes to my mind is that I was agonizingly aware that I did not understand most of what was happening in my circumscribed world. That is putting it negatively. The fact is that I had more questions about things, people, and happenings than anyone in my family could answer, even if they had been aware of the extent of my questions. It was not that my parents would not respond to my questions but rather that I rarely felt satisfied by their answers. Please do not conclude that I was a frustrated little kid whose parents did not "understand" him or, worse yet, were not interested in "stimulating" my mind. On the contrary, my Jewish parents (and grandparents) never let me forget that I had a "head" I was obligated to use and develop so that when I entered school I would do well. More correctly, even better than well! And that meant that I would not have to struggle as they did in an America in which they were fearful, very unsophisticated immigrants. If asked how they instilled in me a need to achieve, I truly cannot tell you. It's like my learning to like the ocean and to swim in it: It was before I entered school, and it had to be under the tutelage of my father who was quite a swimmer.

If my parents could not satisfy my curiosity, or were unaware of all the questions I had that went unasked and unanswered, they at least did nothing to cause me to give up the myriads of internal questions I had about myself, people, and their relationships. Why is the sky blue?

What makes an automobile move? Why is my sister's body not the same as mine? Why does my grandfather have a beard and my father does not? Why do my grandparents talk in a language (Yiddish) I do not understand? What is Yiddish? Why do my parents argue with and even holler at each other? Why should I be afraid of "goyim": Italians, Irish? Where is Manhattan? What is Manhattan? Who is Babe Ruth? Why is money so important and why doesn't my father have more of it, much less than my aunts and uncles? What happens when a person dies? Where is heaven? Who is God? What is a school? What is a dream? How does steam come up from the cellar to our apartment on the sixth floor? How is rain made? Snow? How come a telephone rings, you put the receiver to your ears, and you hear a voice? Why don't we have a telephone? Why does an aeroplane stay in the sky? Why does heat make water boil? How does a clock work?

The fact is, Mr. President, that those early years are truly years of wonder, awe, fascination, and bewilderment. That was true for me, for you, and for every biologically intact preschooler. Even if you believe that newborns vary in their genetic-intellectual endowment, that belief in no way invalidates the fact that they are quintessentially question-asking organisms who, if their questions are ignored or not answered, come up with their own answers. You can no more stop this internal or external question asking than you can stop the ocean tides. You can restrict, inhibit, and even punish this question asking when it is articulated, but you cannot extinguish it. It may go "underground," it may impoverish the desire to explore. It may have all kinds of consequences that negatively affect the pursuit of learning, but question asking is too built into the human organism to be extinguished.

There is no doubt that parents of very young children vary dramatically in their comprehension of the significance of question asking. It is far beyond the purposes of these letters to suggest how we can productively improve that comprehension. But it is my purpose to tell you that too many of our educators do not grasp the big idea that what fuels productive intellectual development are question asking and answers which then engender new questions.

I have observed scores of preschool programs (Head Start and others) and I have found very few that have taken that idea seriously. They are very well intentioned in that they seek to give children opportunities to work with interesting and stimulating materials, to learn how to be with other children, and to experience a personal sense of competence. These are laudable goals that some programs, by no means all, achieve. But with very few exceptions these programs view these youngsters as if they come with no burning desire to understand themselves, others, and the world. These children are asked to conform—and it is a requirement—to what adults consider interesting and important. What they, the youngsters, have experienced and are experiencing in their lives—the questions they have, the puzzles that stimulate or plague them—are rarely a focus. They are supposed to think and do what others say they should think or do. That is why I consider these programs adult and not child centered. To be child centered means, to me at least, that you start where children are: what they bring, what they think, what they want to know and learn. They have what is called an "inner life" and that is what you start with. Yes, they seek new experience, but they also seek answers about themselves, others, and the world.

You don't ask a president to spend a few mornings observing preschoolers. But that is what I do ask you to do so that you can determine for yourself whether what I have said—what you and I can recall about our preschool days—is true: That however interesting these programs are to children, they are not geared to the concrete questions children have. Unlike me, you were in a preschool program. To what extent did your preschool program provide a forum that allowed *your* questions, *your* concerns to surface? Your children were in preschool programs, as my daughter was. Were you as struck as I was about how much that was on her mind, and on the minds of all children, rarely surfaced in her preschool program? Some, perhaps you, might ask: Is a preschool program supposed to be a substitute for the parental role of comprehending, eliciting, discussing what are to children puzzles, questions, concerns? Of course not. But it does not follow that these programs should produce a gulf in the minds of children between what they are asked to think and do in the program and what they think and do when they are "alone with their thoughts." That gulf, Mr. President, not only mammothly increases when children start "real" school, but for many children, rich and poor, that gulf becomes unbridgeable. Two unconnected worlds.

Am I making too much of the centrality of question asking in human development? Is it a big idea that can be carried too far? Perhaps, but I doubt it. What cannot be doubted, what research has conclusively demonstrated, is that the preschool child possesses all of the intellectual characteristics of the budding scientist and artist: the capacity to ask questions, to seek answers, to doubt, and to explore. Yes, children need a lot of things from those who care for them. They do not need to be taught to ask questions. That is built into the human organism and is quite obvious in children long before they have acquired language. Humans are curious from their earliest days. Nurturing that curiosity is our most important obligation and task. We discharge that obligation very poorly as parents and educators.

I have been in the game too long to expect that you will not have *questions* about the big idea. I do expect that on reflection you will agree with much that I have said. Your questions, if I am right, will be about more practical matters. You are a man of action. You will want to know what you should *do* consistent with the big idea. But before you think in terms of action, you will have to ask *and* answer a question: Why has the big idea not been taken seriously? I shall answer that question, albeit too briefly, in my next letter. Needless to say, my self-appointed task would be more easy and certainly interesting if I knew what was going on in your mind. I do not like being in the position of too many teachers who follow a curriculum that their students find uninteresting and irrelevant to what concerns them, i.e., their "other" world.

Our greatest presidents were not simply men of action in the narrow sense. They were individuals possessed by a vision they sought to convey to the people. Putting, as you have, education at the top of your agenda is a decision, not a vision. What is the big idea you want the American people to accept and, therefore, to be willing to support? That is why I ask you to ask why the big idea has not been taken seriously. How you answer that question will determine whether what you convey to our citizenry is an assemblage of cliches or a galvanizing vision.

Respectfully,

Seymour B. Sarason

P.S. I hope that you do not take my remarks about preschool programs as being unduly critical. In no way did I mean to suggest that they are without merit. Candor requires that I say that a fair number of those programs perform a baby-sitting role competently, and that is about all they do. It will only be when you have, as I have, observed programs informed by the big idea that you will understand why I say what I do. And you will understand why I would despair if you defined action primarily in terms of increasing the number of programs, personnel, and budgets. Doing that is the easy way out, the quick-fix approach. It's like depending on sand bags to contain a roaring, swollen, ever rising river. Just as money cannot buy you happiness (the usual exceptions aside), it cannot buy the goal of capitalizing on and exploiting the productive, creative, self-motivating capacities of children.

III

Dear Mr. President:

I await patiently a reply to my letters. I have become quite knowledgeable about the physical frailties associated with advanced age but I am grateful that I can still think and write. Therefore, I shall continue to write to you. It adds meaning to my (few) remaining days. I find it amusing that I regard you as my wife, Esther, regards me: someone who needs to be protected from himself. My hope is that you will come to see that much of what I write has the ring of truth and that it will not take you years to hear it. It took me years—after much kicking, screaming, resisting—to admit that my Esther was right far more often than not. So, if I have reached an advanced age, it is because I finally allowed myself to hear that ring of truth. Yes, Mr. President, I am a hedgehog who thinks he is right on target. And, yes, you have to become a hedgehog in regard to what you have put on the very top of the national agenda. America today needs a hedgehog, not a fox. Now to the question I asked you to ponder: Why has the big idea not been taken seriously?

There are many perspectives from which human history has been written. It is not surprising that the one that fascinates me describes how difficult it has been for people to change their conceptions about human capacities. It is not happenstance, of course, that there has been an intimate relationship between the struggle for human freedom and changes in conception about what people are capable of becoming. Over the millennia the most frequent situation was one in which rulers viewed the ruled akin to cattle who needed and wanted to be told what to think and do. To the rulers their people were an undifferentiated mass each human atom of which had an undifferentiated "mind." I speak as if all that is in the past. As you well know, Mr. President, there are many places in the world today where that situation is all too obvious.

Why do we continue to be astounded by the early Greeks? How do we explain them? Thousands of books have tried to answer that question and thousands more will be written. If our explanations still leave us with mystery, there are things about which we are certain. One is that these early Greeks asked questions—about the world and the human mind—never asked before. It is as if the shackles on the human mind disappeared and the questions poured out, questions for which answers gave rise to new questions in the tradition of science where the more you know the more you need and want to know. No society, *then or now,* had such *respect* for the human mind, *all* minds. Not only the minds of rulers but the ruled as well. The other thing we know is that they took seriously the idea that everyone had the obligation and capability to participate in ruling. For me the Greek "lesson" is that how you regard the human mind is never logically separable from how you nurture that mind. And that, Mr. President, is as true for what happens in a classroom as it is in the society at large.

The history that fascinates me is a history of the struggle against the underestimation of the capabilities of the people. I trust you are aware that in our national history there has never been an immigrant group that was regarded as other than intellectually stupid, culturally barbaric, and a source of pollution in the body politic. And what about the capabilities of women? Of Blacks? Of old people? Of handicapped people? We have a national history of which we should be proud, but that pride should not blind us to how we have been victims of underestimating the capabilities of people. We like to believe that we are no longer victims of that tendency. If that is true, how then do you explain why you have been forced to put education at the top of the national agenda? Clearly, I assume, you did not do that because you believe that school children are incapable of learning and thinking better than they do. You believe that they *are* more capable than educational outcomes indicate. You *know* that they are not being "reached." You *know* that too many of them have not been turned on but rather turned off by schooling. And there is one other thing a moment's reflection will tell you you know: When you observe these turned-off youngsters—both in our inner cities and suburbia—*outside* of schools, they are active, motivated youngsters seeking to understand themselves, others, and their world. They have curiosity, questions, and creativity in regard to matters or goals you and I may not like. We would want them to be more interested in ideas, history, literature, and science, but they are not. Why not?

One reason is that in our well-intentioned but misguided efforts to pour information into the minds of children we are rendered insensitive to what *their* interests, concerns, and questions are. Let me put it this way: Although we know that much is in their heads—they do think, feel, fantasize, and strive—we regard what is in their minds as unimportant, or irrelevant, or (worse yet) as an obstacle to what *we* want *them* to know, feel, and strive for. We do not *respect* what is in their heads, i.e., they are not thinkers, they have unformed minds that are up to us to form. It is as if our job is to clean out their Augean mental stables. How can you take seriously people whose minds you regard as unformed and chaotic? What is there to get out of them? Empty heads need to be filled! The fact is—and it is a fact, Mr. President—that children, even very young children, have minds that are organized, stamped with purpose and curiosity.

There is a second reason that is no less fateful. *In practice* we regard children as incapable of self-regulation, unconcerned about or ignorant of the rules of social behavior, as organisms one step above (if that) animals or cannibals. Give them an inch and they will demand a mile. Trust them to be responsible and you will regret it. Open up the sluice gates of "permissiveness" and you will drown. Give them their "head" and they will take your body. My words may strike you as caricature, but please remember that caricature is a way of emphasizing a truth. In this instance the truth is that we regard children as in need of taming.

When you put the two reasons together we have a situation characteristic of our classrooms: *"Where* students are" is ignored and *"what* students are" is something we should fear and, therefore, tame or extinguish. As a result, we have classrooms in which students are passive, uninterested, resigned, or going through the motions, or unruly, or all of the above. It is a classic case of the self-fulfilling prophecy, i.e., we begin with invalid assumptions and then act in a way that "proves" their validity.

I have to ask you this question: Do you react to what I have said as if I was an advocate of a mindless permissiveness which assumes that if you let children be "where and what they are" they will find their own ways to values and goals you and I cherish? That if we get out of their way, they will do the right thing in the right way, as if they possess a kind of wisdom we who teach them do not? If you, like many people, react in these ways, it is because you have not had the opportunity to test your assumptions, thereby confusing assumption with empirical fact. *Sit in classrooms, Mr. President.* Make your own observations. Fairness requires that I tell you that there are classrooms in our public schools where teachers have taken the big idea seriously. Far from being chaotic or devoid of law or order, or a struggle between a well-intentioned teacher and passively aggressive, bored students, they are lively places where learning is pursued, where minds are active, searching, challenged. Please note that I did not say happy minds because true learning is and should be experienced as challenging, at times frustrating and puzzling but always energizing. Unfortunately, these classrooms are, relatively speaking, minuscule in number. The modal classroom is a boring, uninteresting place unconnected to the interests and questions of students. Forgive me for being repetitive. For these students there are two worlds: the isolated world of school and the "real world" of passions, personal needs, strivings, personal and social identity, and, yes, questions about what is, what should be, and what will be.

Back in the legendary sixties it became fashionable for college students to take a year off and go abroad. A wag quipped about one such student, "He went to Europe to find himself except he wasn't there."

Well, Mr. President, young children begin school expecting to find themselves but they end up disappointed.

If you take the big idea seriously, the educational task is quite clear: How do you capitalize on, exploit, direct, and interconnect "where and what children are" to bodies of knowledge and concerns that contribute to an examined life in which horizons broaden and a sense of historical identity is forged? In short, how do you bring the two worlds together? If we do not seek to enter their worlds, they will not seek to enter ours.

One of the books I suggested you read was *The Teacher* by Sylvia Ashton Warner, an account of how she went about teaching the native Maoris of New Zealand to (among other things) read. More correctly, how she *thought* about how to get these children to *want* to read. She did not regard these native children the way too many Americans view the capabilities of our natives, or Blacks, or Hispanics, or our poor, rural "hillbillies." Mrs. Warner had no doubt whatsoever that these Maori youngsters had active, curious minds. So what did Mrs. Warner do? She asked each child what words he or she wanted to learn, *not* what a predetermined "curriculum" said children should learn. It made no difference if the words concerned the body, sexual matters, or whatever. If they wanted to learn a word—which was then written on a card for them—that is what she helped them learn. And they learned! And at a pace and with a level of motivation she did not find at all surprising. She did have problems with the educational authorities! The important point, Mr. President, is that Mrs. Warner was a hedgehog whose central, big idea was that if you start with "where and what children are"—if you intellectually engage and hook them—you can then, and only then, help them want to acquire knowledge and skills that expand their horizons and options.

Mrs. Warner's book had, I think, the status of a best seller. Obviously, for many people, it had the ring of personal truth. Unfortunately, for all practical purposes it had no impact on our educational practices. The perception of a truth does not necessarily make you "free."

In, I suppose, typical professional-academic style I have not given you a direct, persuasive answer to why we have not taken the obvious seriously. That was not evasion on my part, because I wished first to persuade you that you have to come to grips with where you stand in regard to "what and where children are." So in my next letter I shall try to be more direct and, I hope, persuasive. If I am persuasive, I predict that there will be a part of you that will regret it.

Respectfully,

Seymour B. Sarason, Ph.D.

GOVERNANCE, POWER, AND THE
DEFINITION OF RESOURCES

What gives me kicks is when I see relationships among issues, problems, and arenas of action ordinarily seen as dissimilar. I am suspicious of "differences," I am set to see communalities. For example, early on I came to see that existing, traditional power relationships among personnel in a school or school system was a violation of the political principle: If you are going to be affected, directly or indirectly, by a policy, you should stand in some relationship to the decision-making process. That is hardly the case today, although the rhetoric of the political principle is more frequently heard today than ever before. We hear much about site-based management but in my experience site-based management makes token gestures to the political principle; it too frequently has the features of a charade. No one who has sought and obtained power is willing to share it in a meaningful way, especially if they are in a pyramidal organizational structure as schools and school systems are. And yet, I had to conclude, unless power relationships in schools changed, one of the necessary but not sufficient conditions for school change was absent. I say "not sufficient" because changing power relationships begs the question: For what benefits or purposes are these changes intended? How you answer those questions are the justifications for seeking to change power relationships. Unless there is a compelling, overarching goal for centering power relationships, what is the point? (I answer that in later pages of this book.)

At the same time that I had argued for changing existing power relationships among school personnel, I had also been arguing for changing power relationships between teachers and students. How are the rules of the classroom developed? How is the "constitution" of the classroom forged? The answer is that the teacher is the legislature, the executive, and the judiciary. Students need to be socialized and tamed, they are incapable of participating in any way in classroom governance. John Dewey said that school is not preparation for life, it is life, and what students experience is that in regard to classroom governance their opinions, perceptions, and conceptions of what is morally right and wrong will not be respected or listened to and that it is best to be and remain voiceless. Students do know the game and score, appearances to the contrary notwithstanding.

I find it fascinating and humbling that I had made no connection between power relationships between teachers and students, on the one hand, and those between teachers and their "higher ups," on the other hand. In principle they are not similar, they are identical. In both instances every argument advanced for why power relationships should remain as they are is truly identical. But once I saw the connections I understood as never before the ubiquity, significances, and wisdom of the political principle in all relationships in the school culture. More correctly, I understood why the blatant violations of the political principle in the school culture were such a source of conflict and other untoward consequences.

Other connections got forged in my head. One had to do with the preventive orientation. Efforts at school change were predominantly of the repair variety, i.e., trying to fix rather than prevent problems, akin to closing the barn door after the horses have escaped. So, for example, preservice programs are unconscionably deficient in helping would-be teachers grasp the history and significances of power relationships in schools. What adds insult to injury is that these students are prepared unreflectively to accept existing power relationships, a fact that is problem producing for them and their students in the "real life" lived in schools, and guarantees that efforts at repair will be necessary and costly, and, more often than not, minimally effective.

Another connection had to do with the political principle and the way resources are defined. Once you think through and in a gut sense accept the political principle, your perception and definition of people as resources are radically transformed.

The political principle, prevention, and the definition of resources—it was the connections I made among them that stimulated me to write *The Case for Change: Rethinking the Preparation of Educators,* published in 1993 by Jossey-Bass. Those connections were semi-explicit in *The Predictable Failure of Educational Reform,* published in 1990 by Jossey-Bass, as well as in my 1983 book *Schooling in America: Scapegoat and Salvation,* published by the Free Press. It was not until the 1993 book that I understood (or thought I did) why the political principle, prevention, and definition of resources were organically intertwined, i.e., dealing with one required that you deal with the other two. I would argue that *The Case for Change* is the most mature book I have written about education in the sense that it represented a broadening of my point of view, a bringing together more clearly of ideas of which I had been aware but had not adequately interrelated.

The maturing process is not explained by the mere passage of time. In my case that process was facilitated by Elizabeth Lorentz, a colleague with whom I wrote two books about the resource exchange rationale and resource exchange networks. Elizabeth has no customary professional credentials and has never held a salaried position in schools or the human services. However, over a long life she has made it her business to observe and to become connected with a variety of non-profit organizations, including schools. In the course of these experiences, plus having a fantastic inquisitive and acquisitive mind, plus having a mind of her own—characteristics which some status-concerned and status-preserving professionals have found annoying—Elizabeth developed the conceptual relationships between prevention and the definition of resources. Long before I did, she articulated those relationships, and when our collaboration began twenty five years ago she was the teacher and I was the student, although she mistakenly did then as now see our collaboration in the reverse. I have given up arguing the point. I said she has a mind of her own and nothing I can say will cause her to change her mind. All of this is by way of saying that my point of view about school change developed in my head but it was and is a head shaped by her ideas and experiences. If I credit myself with anything, it is that I am a very good listener and that I do not take myself or my ideas so seriously as to render me insensitive to or rejecting of the points of view of others, even those who like Elizabeth have no professional credentials. Professionalism has its virtues but it too frequently has the drawback of causing you to view so-called lay people as having no right to opinions about professional perspectives and practices. In my experience, wisdom and maturity among so-called lay people are distributed in a bell-shaped fashion just as they are among professionals, which is to say that in both groups you will find stupid, opinionated, arrogant people for whom their truths are the only truths, the whole truths, so help us and God forgive them. Elizabeth may not be one of a kind, but she is on the high, positive end of the bell-shaped curve with a few others.

What follows below is the last half of a chapter "Governance and

Issues of Power" and the whole of the chapter "Governance and the Definition of Resources" from *The Case for Change: Rethinking the Preparation of Educators.* I had great difficulty deciding what to reprint from that book precisely because it brings together several strands of ideas each of which is separately treated before interconnecting them.

GOVERNANCE AND ISSUES OF POWER

Whenever I have talked to teachers, regardless of topic, at some point in the discussion the subject of the status of teachers would come up: how they were perceived by their administrative superiors, parents, the general public, and frequently their students.[1] They saw themselves as misperceived, misunderstood, misled, and powerless. There were exceptions, of course; there always are. But even these exceptions seemed to agree that given the constant stream of criticism directed to schools in general and teachers in particular, it was understandable if so many teachers saw themselves as convenient scapegoats.

On several of these occasions I put the following prologue and question to the group:

> You regard yourselves as the objects of a policy, not as formulators of a policy. You are low person on the totem pole. Directives flow from others to you. It is a one-way street. You do not see light at the end of the tunnel. There is no real collegiality, no forum where your needs and ideas can be *safely* presented and discussed, no sense that life in the school will become more interesting, more stimulating, more challenging. What you fear is that it will become more challenging but in ways you prefer not to think about. I understand and sympathize with what you say and feel. But now I want to put a question to you, the intent of which I hope you will not misunderstand and/or take as criticism. Rather than put it in the form of a question, I will put it as an assertion:

---

[1] The text beginning with this sentence and continuing to the end of this chapter is reprinted from *The Case for Change: Rethinking the Preparation of Educators* (pp. 175–202), 1993. San Francisco: Jossey-Bass. Copyright 1993 by Jossey-Bass Inc., Publishers. Reprinted by permission.

The basis of your criticism of your powerless role in regard to school governance is similar to the basis of the criticism many students make of their lives in the classroom.

Generally speaking, students are given no role—either in discussion or formulation—in regard to classroom governance. They do what they are told to do, learn what they are told to learn, regardless of what they think or are interested in. They are expected to conform to what others require of them. They are *individual* learners, responsible only to themselves. There is no collegiality among students in regard to learning. There is no "forum" which allows them to learn with and from others. Indeed, learning with and from others, learning to help others learn, too frequently is verboten because it makes evaluation of individual accomplishment difficult. If my assertion is only 50 percent right, it helps explain why so many students find classrooms and subject matter uninteresting and see the light at the end of the tunnel as coming from some place other than school.

There have been two major reactions to my assertion. The first is one of surprise at the thought that teachers and students experience governance in similar ways. Some teachers quickly see and agree with the assertion; some think it wrong or unwarranted. It may be that I am too partisan to my own assertions, but no teacher who disagreed with me could make anything resembling a case for their disagreement. The teacher's case was quite simple: the way things are is the way they should be. So speak those in the castle on the top of the mountain!

The second reaction is in the form of a question: am I advocating a cooperative-learning style of governance, the new panacea? My initial answer is definitely not. Before you latch on to the technology of cooperative learning, you have to work through your political-moral rationale for how people in a classroom should live with each other in regard to needs, responsibilities, obligations, decision making, and capabilities. Do you believe that children are "naturally" irresponsible, immoral, subversive, uncomprehending of the need for law and order, unformed organisms that need to be shaped, directed, and indoctrinated only by an adult, organisms possessing far more deficits than assets? My assertion is powered by the Deweyan maxim that the classroom is not a preparation for life; it is life itself. How should we live it? That question is precisely the one that is engendered in teachers by the ways they see themselves as being treated by their superiors.

My assertion *does* lead to the methodologies of cooperative learning in the classroom, just as it leads to alterations in governance in our schools. But let us not make the mistake of confusing a methodology with its political-moral-social rationale. Once you become clear about how life should be lived in classrooms and schools, the methodology you employ should be informed by that clarity. Methodology is a servant to our values and goals. There is no one correct way to employ that servant. Life, in classrooms, schools, or elsewhere, is not organized so as to permit us to assume that if you do A then B and C will inevitably follow. Values and goals are not maps; they are beliefs, imperatives, and stimulants on the basis of which we plan our actions. Between values, on the one hand, and actions, on the other, is a series of booby traps, testimony either to our imperfections and inconsistencies, or an inhospitable social-institutional surround, or both. Methodologies are, in the abstract, morally neutral and useless. They become otherwise when we choose them to reflect our values and goals. And when we are unclear about our values and goals, and when our identification with and commitment to them are at best superficial and at worst mindless—they have not become part of our "guts" and what we call mind—we choose a methodology to which, when it fails as it must, we assign blame. Methodologies, no less than people, suffer the dynamics of blaming the victim.

Preparatory programs have been criticized for their emphasis on the methodologies of pedagogy. In the post-World War II era those criticisms have resulted in fewer such courses being required. To appease the critics, there has been an increase in subject matter requirements. That is what I would call shadow boxing, or window dressing, or the blind leading the blind. The point is wrapped up in the joke [from Chapter 9] about the man who in dead winter became ill and went to his doctor who after a "thorough" examination said: "Go home, take off all of your clothes, open up all your windows, stand in front of them and breathe deeply for fifteen minutes eight times a day." The aghast patient replied, "But if I do that I'll get pneumonia." To which the healer said, "*That* I know how to treat." Our preparatory programs deemphasized pedagogy, emphasized subject matter, and neither prevented educational pneumonia. I take no satisfaction whatsoever from having predicted the pneumonia. But I do have a lot of anger at all of those people who *today* cannot face up to their egregiously mistaken diagnosis and prescriptions. And by people I mean both the critics and those who appeased them.

What the participants in this cyclical controversy seem unable to comprehend is that pedagogy and subject matter are experienced in a social context the features of which are reflections of governance. Pedagogy, subject matter, and curriculum are not independent variables like height, weight, or age. Their significances take on meaning only in the social actions and transactions of people governed by implicit and explicit rules about mutuality, obligations, power, and capabilities. You can substitute one curriculum for another because one is supposed to be more interesting or stimulating than the other, but if that alteration changes nothing else in the social crucible of the classroom, we end up confirming that the more things change the more they remain the same. For the teacher, a new curriculum poses two tasks: grasping the rationale for the new curriculum—not only its contents and sequences but its underlying logic and structure—and then, fatefully, setting the stage for students to grasp what the teacher grasped. If that "stage" is one that has all of the political-moral-social psychological characteristics that make living and thinking in the classroom uninteresting, why expect that the new curriculum will make a difference? Have we learned nothing from the history of curriculum reform?

Readers of my previous books will know that I regard the constitutional convention of 1787 to be one of the most important and instructive events in human history. I shall not repeat here the justifications for such a judgment. Suffice it to say that that convention agonizingly wrestled with these questions: How do you protect the rights of individuals from the arbitrary exercise of power? How do you square those rights with the requirements of collective living? Can we devise a form of governance that gives citizens a voice, a role, a force in decision making? How can we ensure that those who govern will be responsive to and respectful of the ideas and needs of the governed? How should we distribute power so as to check and balance man's imperfections in handling power?

What went on in that amazing convention over several months in Philadelphia is no different than what Pauly describes in the crucible of the classroom. With one crucial difference: the founding fathers were excruciatingly aware of the important issues wrapped up in the question of how people should live with each other. They did not oversimplify the issues. They knew that questions of who should govern, in which ways, and for which purposes were complicated questions that had to be raised, thought through, and resolved, with full awareness that experience would require "amendments." That convention was an exercise, a most practical one, in philosophy, psychology, history, and politics.

Preparatory programs are most inadequate in how and how much they expose the would-be educator to the subject matter of governance. For the students in these programs governance is a method with the most shallow political-moral-psychological underpinnings. This is true not only for the teacher in the classroom but the teacher in regard to administrators and parents.

What do we mean when we say we should *respect* each other? That a teacher should respect his or her students? That parents should respect their children, and vice versa? What we mean is that we should realize that others, like ourselves, have needs, rights, ideas, and feelings we should not ignore or derogate. "To refrain from interfering with" is one of the meanings of *respect* in my dictionary, the implication being that we should not do unto others what we would not want done to ourselves. But, as our founding fathers knew, respect for the integrity of the individual had to be seen in relation to the purposes of and respect for the collectivity. Governance is the way we seek to align those two objects of respect. In brief, governance is about respect for what you think the rights, obligations, and capabilities of people are as individuals and as members of a collectivity.

It has not been my purpose to present a blueprint for governance in a classroom or school. Before you start making a blueprint you have to be clear about what you want it to reflect. A blueprint has a prior history. Our national constitution is a written document reflective of two things: recognition that an earlier written document (the Articles of Confederation) was dangerously inadequate, and agreement on the major considerations that should be reflected in a new document, discussed at the constitutional convention. Our written constitution was possible only after consensus was reached about the rights and responsibilities of individuals, states, and the federal government.

In matters of *school* governance a discussion of sorts has started, albeit with a conceptual and philosophical shallowness that does not bode well for the future. In matters of *classroom* governance there has been little or no discussion. What I have attempted to do in this chapter is to indicate that the issues of classroom and school governance are in theory and practice identical, and to view them as different has two unfortunate consequences. The first is that it directs our attention away from how the conventional style of classroom governance contributes to a passive, conforming, disinterested stance in students. The second, a derivative of the first, is that this conventional style adversely affects how subject matter will be experienced and assimilated by the learners. Governance and subject matter are, in a phenomenological sense, never experienced as separate variables. The effort to change attitudes toward subject matter and make its acquisition more personally meaningful and productive is a doomed effort if it is not accompanied by a change in power relationships in the classroom. The idea—I hesitate to dignify it by calling it a conception—that for *schools* to improve there will have to be changes in their governance, appears to be garnering support, albeit largely on the level of rhetoric. The idea that governance of *classrooms* will have to change if educational outcomes are to improve has yet to attain anything resembling currency.

There is another source for my reluctance to offer a blueprint: the empirical fact that when clarity about values and purposes have been achieved, there is not a single blueprint that alone will reflect that clarity and agreement. Our country has a written constitution. There are countries that have no written constitution, whose legal system differs in many respects from ours, whose culture is not ours, but who are no less wedded to the basic values and purposes which gave rise to our written constitution. And, let us not forget, there are countries that modeled their written constitution after ours, but that is where their resemblance to our society ends.

More important at this time than working on blueprints for school and classroom governance is gaining clarity about the values and purposes of governance, the challenge they present to the way things are, and what is personally required to act consistently in accord with an altered way of thinking. Put it this way: in relation to the governance of classrooms and schools, are we able to own up to the educational equivalent of the Articles of Confederation and, having done that, can we agree on a set of principles, values, and purposes whose meanings and force derive from personal experience? *That kind of question should occupy everyone at every point in a preparatory program.*

It would be grossly unfair to say that the literature on preparatory programs is without value. At the very least, it recognizes that preparatory programs are part of the problem and not of the solution. But it would not be unfair to say that the literature hardly alludes to the importance and complexity of issues—their political, philosophical, psychological facets—of classroom and school governance. And where there are allusions, they are no more than that.

When and how should these issues be raised? How can and should the previous experience of would-be educators be mined? What is the relation between governance issues in the classroom and school? How does governance influence attitudes toward, the assimilation of, and the productive use of subject matter? What similarities exist between the needs, rights, and obligations of teachers and their students? These and kindred questions remain on the level of allusion, not confrontation. You can advocate for the selection of "brighter" candidates for preparatory programs, you can require more psychology courses, you can require a better grasp of subject matter, you can insist that preparatory programs be on the graduate level, you can require a longer practice teaching experience, you can require more and closer supervision. You can require any or all of these, as has been done, but they will not (have not) to any discernible degree prepare teachers productively to cope with those governance issues in class-rooms and schools that will influence and shape their lives.

If the conditions that make for productive growth and learning do not exist for teachers, the teachers will be unable to help create and sustain those conditions for their students. When preparatory programs begin to take that seriously, they will be serving the purposes of primary prevention. What happens to teachers is no less important than what happens to their students. When the juices stop flowing in teachers, and Farber (1991) has noted that this happens too frequently, the juices will not flow in students. Blaming teachers for this or that on this or that basis is too easy. They are sitting ducks for those who are prone to blame the victim. Teachers, like the rest of us, are a product of how they have been taught. So, instead of taking aim at teachers, should we not focus on how they have been prepared for the complex, challenging, frustrating, demanding, energy depleting, satisfying role so inadequately reflected in the title "teacher"?

GOVERNANCE AND THE DEFINITION OF RESOURCES

In the previous chapter I stated that the rationale for governance in large measure determines how subject matter will be experienced and assimilated. In this chapter I attempt to show that that rationale also determines the resources available to a teacher and a school.

Let me start with the universal complaint of educators: they do not have the resources to deal adequately with the problems they face. In general it is difficult for people to accept the fact that resources are always limited and finite. That difficulty in large part derives from the "habit" of defining a resource as that which you pay for and, therefore, control. The less money you have, the fewer your resources will be. That, of course, is true; nothing I shall say should be interpreted as suggesting that money is not a problem. But it is also true that preparatory programs do not confront their would-be teachers with two questions. How do we explain why so many people (educators and the general public) are dissatisfied with our schools, even though in the post World War II era billions of dollars have been poured into public education? Even if you believe that those billions were insufficient, is it unreasonable to expect that there would have been some discernible positive, general consequences? Does not the absence of those consequences suggest that money is not the panacea we like to believe it is? The failure of preparatory programs to deal with this question reinforces in people the belief that money is the universal solvent. They think that the major problems in education are the result of a niggardly public's derogation of education, a belief that robs educators of the ability to consider ways of thinking and acting of which they are potentially capable and which would productively compensate (again in part) for a perceived lack of money—ways of thinking and acting that expose the fallacy that without money is to be without resources. Someone once defined money as a necessary means of exchange among strangers. Schools are governed in ways that, for all practical purposes, make the people within them strangers to each other. They not only do not have money as a means of exchange, they are, by virtue of being strangers to each other, unable to exchange resources.

There is a second and related question: what are the resources potentially available to educators that do not require money? How do we, should we, define people as resources? And by people, I mean not only those with a direct interest in schools (for example, educators, students, parents) but others beyond the encapsulated schools. Is it possible so to redefine people as resources so that we capitalize on their assets and in the process prevent that poignant feeling in teachers that they are alone and lonely in a densely populated setting? I continue to be disheartened and surprised at the number of young teachers who are disheartened and surprised by their feelings of loneliness, social isolation, and alienation. If walls do not good neighbors make, neither do encapsulated classrooms in encapsulated schools. Not only were they not "warned" about this, but in no way were they provided with ways of thinking and acting to cope with such a situation.

My colleague, Murray Levine, once wrote a chapter (Sarason et al., 1966) entitled "Teaching is a Lonely Profession." It was a chapter in a very thick book, but his was the chapter about which we received the most unsolicited letters from teachers around the country. Their message was simple and clear: "Thank God you understand what loneliness means and does to teachers." And that is the point: the dynamics of loneliness— the feeling that "it will always be this way"—over time have adverse personal and professional effects. Those effects have not gone unnoticed. They are one of the factors powering some reform efforts, and those efforts are to be applauded. But as their proponents well know, it is difficult to overcome experience from which teachers conclude that it is safer to stay lonely than to participate in an altered governance requiring altered relationships which are unfamiliar and potentially dangerous. If educators had better preparation to think and act in regard to these issues, it would prevent or dilute the obstacles the reform efforts encounter. Is it asking too much of preparatory programs to prepare their students for a "real world" which they must understand and seek to change if as persons and professionals they are to grow, not only to survive?

Let us start with two examples that concern the definition and *rede*-finition of resources. The first example is a plan I devised whereby Yale University faculty and graduate and undergraduate students would set up, without cost, a department of psychology in a high school. And by department I meant one that spanned the traditional areas in the field.

> Several school systems were quite eager for us to use their high schools. Although we monotonously repeated that there was a fair chance that we would fall on our faces, that we did not view ourselves as experts in high school teaching, that graduate and even (highly selected) under-graduates would be involved in addition to faculty, that we did not want to be viewed as in any way impinging on any one else's territory—the response was uniformly enthusiastic and for two reasons. First, in each school system there were some personnel who asserted that I was a responsible individual who knew something about schools. Second, they said they had so many unmotivated students, and since psychology was intrinsically fascinating to everybody (they obviously never sampled undergraduate opinion!), they could only see our involvement as help-ful. In essence, we had no "port of entry problem" to speak of. The fact that we posed no credentialing issues was also a plus. The project last-ed one year and could not be continued because of a variety of serious illnesses in my family that made planning and commitment an exercise in futility. The school was eager for us to continue. Not only was the teaching perceived as successful, but in diverse ways our group became involved with different individuals, groups, and departments in ways that we had hoped for and that were regarded by school personnel as extremely helpful in achieving desired changes.
>
> And now for the major point: We came to the schools. We offered certain services and a long range plan which the schools saw as a pos-sible help to a serious problem. It never occurred to them to come to us. Given their accustomed way of viewing the community, it could not occur to them that perhaps they had a "right" to request and even to demand help. They viewed the problems with which they were faced as their responsibility, solvable either by existing resources or additional ones they could buy (knowing full well that they would never be able to buy resources adequate to their needs as they defined them). They can-not take the stance that one of their major tasks is to refuse to assume exclusive responsibility for or to be seen as having the expertise to deal adequately with all the problems existing in schools. They cannot say aloud what they say privately: We will never have financial resources to cope effectively with our problems; unless we call on community resources—unless we make the community share responsibility—the disparity between what we can do and what needs to be done will con-tinue, and perhaps become greater. (Sarason, 1976, pp. 20–21)

What deserves emphasis in this example is that it could never occur to school people that there could be people in the community whose professional self-interests might lead them to provide services to schools on a quid pro quo basis: "if you do this for us, we will do that for you." No one has to tell educators that they have problems for which they need help. And no one needs to tell educators that there are people in the community who can be of help to them with those problems. But it is almost axiomatic in the stance of educators that these community people cannot be approached without the carrot of compensation. "They are busy people. They probably do not have enough time in a day to do all they want and need to do. How can we ask them to give us time free for nothing?"—that is the usual view of educators of the availability of community resources. It is, obviously, a realistic view but only if your approach is: "We have a problem. You can be of help to us. Are you willing to give us that help for which we cannot pay?" In other words, you appeal to their altruism, not to their self-interests, i.e., to the possibility that providing the help will in some way have a significant pay-off for them.

I have no objections to appealing to people's altruism. Indeed, as I stated in the example, educators have a "right" to request and even demand that community people and agencies give of their time and skills to schools insisting they have an obligation to do so. But as long as educators see themselves, and therefore are seen by others, as solely responsible for what happens in schools—a stance that keeps private inadequacies that should be made public—they tend neither to request nor demand. Instead, they devote their energies internally to getting increases in school budgets that would permit them either to add personnel or to pay for externally situated services. When, as is usually the case, those increases are not forthcoming, educators feel rejected and derogated and resign themselves to making do with what internal resources they possess. Their feeling of rejection when the political system fails to give them what they perceive they need is precisely the feeling they expect to have if they approached community individuals and agencies hat-in-hand, that is, as beggars. Educators have never been able to say out loud, "We have never had, will not have, and perhaps should not have, sufficient resources internally to accomplish our tasks the way we want and the public expects. Unless and until we call on community resources we will be unable to compensate *to any extent* for the brute fact of limited resources."

If I have no objections to appealing to people's altruism, neither do I expect such appeals to be very fruitful. It is not that I think people generally are without altruistic feelings but rather that the appeal to self-interest (which is not to be confused with selfishness) is far more likely to be fruitful. If that is true, as my experience clearly suggests, the task of the educator is to be as knowledgeable as possible about the self-interests of community individuals and agencies so as to be able to determine when the self-interests of educators and others can result in an exchange of resources.

No money, no resources. When educators begin to see that this is not as true as it needs to be or should be, that what they have may be seen by others (in terms of their self-interests) as assets, that bartering for and exchanging resources can engender and sustain satisfying and productive relationships, that the failure to accept the fact that resources are always limited constrains creativity in thinking and acting—in short, when educators can begin to alter their way of defining resources, the concept of community participation will become more than what it now is: empty, unproductive rhetoric.

On any one day hundreds (perhaps thousands) of academics are carrying out research in schools. Their expectation is that schools have an *obligation* to permit research because the findings will add to the cumulative knowledge about how to improve schooling. I italicize obligation to emphasize that the appeal is to the altruism that schools should act on, that is, their permission will not bring them resources they can utilize to deal with the concrete problems of their concrete schools but rather it will discharge the moral obligation to contribute to knowledge. As generations of researchers can testify, schools have rarely enthusiastically rolled out the welcome mat. Schools perceived, and rightly so, that they were entering a one-way street relationship. The researcher was crystal clear about his or her self-interests, the schools felt they were being exploited, that whatever satisfaction they might experience from allowing the researcher to do his or her thing was small recompense for what they were giving. (But it does say something positive about the appeal to altruism that many schools have given permission.)

Why is it that I have never known school people to say to a researcher: "We know what your needs are. Let us tell you what our needs are and see what you can do for us. Perhaps we can work out an exchange which would be mutually productive?" In order to adopt that approach several things have to be clear. The first, of course, is that you know what additional resources you would like to obtain for the school. The second is that you have determined the skills and interests of the researcher, neither of which may be fully (or at all) reflected in the research proposal. The third is that that determination suggests a possible match between a school need and a researcher's skills and interests. In other words, you do not look upon the researcher qua researcher but as a person with diverse skills and interests you can exploit for your self-interest, some-

one who can do something you would like done but for which you have
neither the personnel nor the funds. As long as you see a researcher *only*
as a researcher, you have blinded yourself to and enormously narrowed
your perception of the diverse "resources" the researcher may have that
can be of use to you. "What do you have that I need, and what do I have
that you need"—that is a stance which facilitates *redefining* people as
resources, permitting you to go beyond stereotypes and categorical thinking. That point brings me to my second example.

> A colleague, Richard Sussman, visited a professor he had had in
> child development in Teachers College, Columbia University. He
> met with her and her graduate assistants to find out what research
> they were planning and carrying out in regard to schools. They
> outlined a series of researches they wished to do with elementary
> school children, research that would require several schools. How-
> ever, they said, they had been unsuccessful in getting permission
> from schools to carry out the studies. At one point Dr. Sussman
> asked: "If I could make available to you a dozen highly selected
> high school seniors, would you and your assistants be willing to
> explain your study to them and train them to collect your data?
> (Asking that question reflected the fact that a high school with
> which he was associated had a "problem" keeping bright, college-
> bound seniors from goofing off in their final semester.) Also,
> would you be willing to give them a mini course in organizing
> and analyzing data?" Needless to say, Sussman had determined
> that the high school students were adequate to the tasks. Also,
> again needless to say, the professor and her assistants did not look
> kindly at his offer. Use high school students to collect data? Teach
> them to organize and analyze data? Their reservations were dis-
> pelled when he played his trump card: "If you are willing to use
> these students, I am quite sure I can make available to you as
> many elementary schools as you need." The project went so well
> that at its completion the students were invited to give a colloqui-
> um at Teachers College and later made a presentation to their
> Board of Education. Money was never in the picture.

To the college professor, high school students were high school students, period. That is not unusual because when we say that someone
is a student, whether in the first grade or in high school, we tend to be
more impressed with what they do not know and cannot do than with
what they do know and are interested in. It is only slightly unfair to say
that our stereotype of student emphasizes deficits and not assets. But it

is not unfair to say that our tendency to categorize people—to attribute to them all of the characteristics of the abstract category—gets in our way of redefining them, of seeing them as multi-faceted individuals.

The above examples and discussion had several purposes. The first was to show that the usual way educators (and people generally) define people as resources adds, so to speak, insult to the injury of limited resources. The second purpose was to indicate that the usual way educators view the availability of community resources limits using those resources in a quid pro quo way. The third was to suggest that there are resources within schools which are not exploited because they are seen (if not as deficits) as without educationally exploitable assets. The fourth, and most general, purpose was to alert the reader to the mischievous fallacy that there is nothing wrong with schools that increased funding will not correct. It was *not* among my purposes to deny in any way that there are many schools that lack the *minimal* (however defined) physical conditions, educational materials, and personnel required by considerations of equity and morality. Having said that, I have to say that a few of these truly deplorable-looking schools seemed to have been forced to creatively redefine and exploit resources within and without the schools. These instances should not be used to buttress the argument that poverty is a good thing, but they do buttress the argument that there is a way of redefining resources that to a certain extent ameliorates the consequences of limited resources.[2]

Any form of governance justifies itself on assumptions about differences in the capabilities and knowledge of the governors and the governed. That is a glimpse of the obvious, but what is somewhat less obvious is that those assumptions lead the governors, far more often than not, to define the governed in unwarranted and narrow ways. The assumption that if you have no money you have no resources is a universal truth; so is the assumption that the governed lack all of the resources possessed by the governed—if not all, then those that are perceived as crucial by the governors. You can put it this way: if an individual in an

---

[2]A number of years ago, in the process of collaborating on two books (1977, 1979) concerned with resource exchange networks, I became aware of the obvious: between schools in the same system and between adjoining or nearby school systems, there was no exchange of resources, even though it was easy to demonstrate that an "asset" possessed by one school (usually a particular teacher of a particular subject matter) was a perceived "deficit" in another school, and that the latter school had an asset the other school lacked. That schools and school systems could or should exchange resources in mutually beneficial ways (to any degree for any length of time in any respect) is apparently unthinkable. I am indebted to my friend, Bruce Thomas, for bringing to my attention *The Network*

organization has title A and his "superior" has title B, it is assumed that there is little or no overlap in the capabilities and skills between the two; there may be overlapping in sheer knowledge but not in skills, professional maturity, conceptual vision, and the ability to make appropriate decisions. Governors govern, the governed are followers—instruments of the governed.

More concretely, what has been the response of school administrators to the proposal that teachers have a more direct involvement in educational policy formulation and decisions? That proposal has been justified by its proponents on two grounds. The first is that because teachers are affected by policies and decisions they should have a voice in them. That is a moral-political argument. The second is that teachers have knowledge and capabilities which, if recognized and exploited, will contribute to more effective policies and decisions. That is the "resource" argument—that teachers are not simply teachers whose knowledge, skills, and capabilities are applicable only in encapsulated classrooms, but by virtue of their experience in classrooms they have much to contribute to educational policy and decisions. In brief, as long as you define teachers in the customary way, you cannot recognize and exploit the resources, actual or potential, that teachers possess. If you redefine what you mean by teachers, you increase the resources available to you.

The definition or redefinition of teachers as resources is barely alluded to in preparatory programs, even though the definition of self, both in the personal and professional sense, will predictably be a source of conflict and frustration. Almost every aspect of these programs focuses on the teacher in the classroom, that is, how he or she should govern students, ignoring how the teacher will experience and cope with the governors. It is not surprising, therefore, that only when teachers begin their careers do they experience what it means essentially to have no voice in school governance. Not only are they not prepared for that kind of experience; they do not possess a rationale for justifying redefining themselves as resources.

---

of Complementary Schools which is a group of schools around the country, public and private, joined together to serve their students in a unique way by sharing their specialized programs. "These schools, realizing that the number and range of options which they can individually provide their students is limited, saw that by pooling their offerings they could present their students a wider range of quality programs." I mention this network far less as a practical model for action but rather as an unusually clear instance of the principle of resource exchange. The interested reader should read the brochure of the network (79 Main Street, Dover, Massachusetts, 02030).

This glaring omission has had the unfortunate consequences of engendering in teachers a reluctance, even a fear, to assume responsibility for anything beyond the confines of their encapsulated classroom. That is bad enough, but in many instances—my experience, albeit obviously limited, leads me to say all instances—where teachers have gained more voice and responsibility, they find that nothing in their training prepared them for how to cope with an enlarged role. No preparatory program can do more than to alert its students to what they predictably will encounter and to provide them technical, moral, and political principles with which to cope with these predictable problems. No preparatory program can and should be a complete substitute for learning by the seat of your pants. But it is inexcusable for a preparatory program to fail to expose its students to the predictable problems they will have to cope with in matters of school governance, matters that directly or indirectly influence what goes on in the classroom. This omission in preparatory programs can be justified only by those who believe that the phenomenology of teachers in regard to school and school system governance has no bearing on what happens in a classroom. That belief makes as much sense as one that states how you conduct yourself at work is in no way influenced by what is happening in your family.

How have school administrators responded to the proposal to redefine teachers as resources in regard to school governance? It should occasion no surprise that their response has been, to indulge understatement, very negative. From what I have said above, one has to conclude that their objections are not wholly without merit. But when you examine their objections, they reduce to one major assertion: teachers lack the formal training (and the knowledge that goes with it) to appreciate and effectively contribute to the administrative complexities that accompany policy formulation and decision making. This assertion assumes that the resources necessary as a basis for effective policy and decision making can be only learned, comprehended and utilized by those who have completed a preparatory program for administrators. Absent such formal training, what does a teacher have to contribute to policy and decisions? This stance implies that the teacher has seen and experienced nothing that would justify a role in policy and decision making. In such matters the teacher is without assets and with deficits. The governed should leave important educational matters to the governors whose superior training has equipped them for responsibility.

I am reminded here of a professional controversy that raged after World War II, a controversy that has lost steam and point. Who should be allowed to do psychotherapy? Psychiatrists-physicians said that *of course* only they had the training to discharge the responsibilities that come with the practice of psychotherapy. Over the next couple of decades that position was challenged by clinical psychologists, social workers, school psychologists, and others. They had no trouble pointing out non-medical people who were incontrovertibly successful psychotherapists. They were able to demonstrate that by its nature, medical training contained features inimical to the practice of effective psychotherapy, and that the special training psychiatrists obtained was largely psychological and not medical. What the medical community was in effect contending was that the training and experience of the challengers, however valuable in other respects, did not give them the resources required to practice psychotherapy. The response of the challengers was: "We will no longer permit you to define us as resources in your terms. We will no longer define ourselves in terms of the limitations within which you want us to stay. We have the knowledge, skills, and capabilities to contribute to the unmet personal needs of many people." There was, in the two decades after the war, a kernel of truth to the psychiatrists' position that the formal training and experience of the challengers was not all it should be. But it was *not* the psychiatrists' position that there was any basis on which one should be allowed to practice psychotherapy short of four years of medical school, internship, and special residencies. Absent that background, psychotherapy was off limits for you; you lacked the appropriate resources. Their stance, like that of school administrators, was: "If you want to do what I do, get the formal training I did." That is defining resources only in terms of formal training, the kind of defining that all too often contributes to the most narrow, unwarranted perception of the resources possessed by those who lack that formal training— a way of defining that undergirds professional preciousness and imperialism. Today, the "psychotherapy wars" are over, a relic in the museum of fallacious assumptions behind conceptions of resources, human or otherwise, actual or potential. A fascinating feature of the post-World War II era is the number of groups who refused to accept any longer the way they had been defined by custom and tradition, and who then redefined themselves as possessing far more assets that their previous "governors" had conceded to them (Sarason, 1977).

I am not opposed to formal, preparatory programs, whether for teachers or administrators. I do not argue the assumption that anyone who has not been certified by a formal program has nothing to contribute to those who have been certified. When that assumption, rarely verbalized and even more rarely discussed, becomes in the most subtle ways part of one's outlook, it contributes to a devaluing perception of the assets of those in other roles and to an unreflective rejection and resentment of proposals in opposition to the assumption. To the extent that each type of professional within an organization defines resources only or even largely in terms of formally attained credentials, two things are guaranteed: limited resources will be more limited than they need be, and there will be interprofessional struggle and conflict. In order to redefine one's conception and definition of resources one has to be willing to alter power relationships, that is, the nature and direction of power relationships. That, apparently, is a type of change few people are voluntarily able to contemplate and implement. It takes the symbolic equivalent of a loaded gun to get most people to accept such a change.

Where I fault preparatory programs is their failure to deal with the psychological, political, moral, and economic aspects of the relationship between resources and governance—how governance style and structure affect and are affected by how resources are defined. My criticism is not that they don't (or may not) see that relationship the way I do but that it is handled in an egregiously superficial way. As I said earlier, when I have asked proponents of the status quo to spell out their rationale, what they offer cannot be labeled as a rationale but as rhetoric that has little depth or breadth; it is defensively reactive and raises visions of catastrophe if the status quo is changed, concluding that the problem is a need by the governors for more unfettered power. At the very least, I would expect that preparatory programs would enable students to understand the differences among competing views of the relationships between governances and resources. And by *understand*, I mean the ability to see these differences in a historical context in which issues of power and governance have been given salience and urgency, which, in light of public dissatisfaction, will not go away and, indeed, will give rise to nostrums that bespeak more of desperation than of reasoned conviction. There are times when defense of the status quo is justified. Are these times, in regard to matters educational, to defend the status quo? If you so believe, it is in your self-interest to come up with a defense that is intellectually, philosophically, and empirically respectable. I have yet to hear such a defense.

What I have been saying has been in regard to how administrators see teachers as resources in the formulation of educational policy and in decision making. *In principle, the issues I have raised are identical to those in the case of teachers as governors and students as the governed.* The usual exceptions aside, teachers have been taught to view students as having few resources relevant to the attainment of educational goals. Their preparation has not enabled them to unlearn the attitude that students are, for all practical purposes, without resources. And by practical I mean in relation to having a voice (which is not to be equated with a vote) in classroom governance and in taking individual and group responsibility for learning. It is an attitude that says: "Students *need* to be governed, to be *given* the rules of governance, *to set aside* their diverse interests and curiosities, to learn what *we* know they need to learn, to conform *now* in order *later* in life to give expression to their interests and curiosities, to *respect* and *accept* the superior wisdom of their governors." It is an attitude based on the fact (and it is a fact) that students are inexperienced, unsophisticated, and in need of guidance and direction. But it is not a fact that students are uninterested in governance, that they are indifferent to it, that they neither want nor need a voice in governance, that they do not relish a role of responsibility, that how they experience governance does not color their experience of subject matter, that their interests and curiosities are antithetical (or at least not relevant) to subject matter. It is the failure of most teachers to recognize these truths. A glaring omission in their preparatory programs allows them to view students as without resources to partake in matters of governance or to assume significant responsibility for individual and small group learning of subject matter. In point of fact, students have the crucial resources of interests, curiosities, and a potent desire to feel worthy and "grown up."

Let us not overlook one other resource: however young the school child, that child has had experience in being governed. Being governed is not a new experience for the child. So when we say that students are inexperienced and unsophisticated, it does not mean they are without resources that can be capitalized on to begin to enlarge both their experience and their sophistication. The idea that "some day" far in the future they will be experienced, sophisticated, and responsible and until then we should regard them otherwise, is worse than nonsense. It is self-defeating of the purposes both of the governors and the governed.

Classrooms are, generally speaking, uninteresting places. They do not engender in students a commitment to and satisfaction from the pursuit of learning. This lack of personal commitment is kin to the lack of commitment that gets stronger in teachers in regard to their schools as the years go by. As teachers resign themselves to being perceived as having competencies only in their encapsulated classrooms—that what they know and have experienced is unwanted by their governors—why should one expect that they can sustain commitment? Similarly, indeed identically, as students with each passing year resign themselves to the role of passive, resourceless, powerless objects of the purposes of their governors, why should one expect them to feel worthy and grown up?

How you are governed is determined by, among other things, how you are being defined—what resources, actual or potential, you are perceived as possessing. Governance and resources are not separate variables. *They are indissolubly related and very much determine how subject matter will be presented and experienced.* Far from being an "independent" variable, subject matter is enmeshed in the relationship between governance and the definition of resources.

Some school reformers who will agree with everything I have said will also know that it is a 1992 summary of what John Dewey said early in this century, what Alfred North Whitehead said in the twenties and thirties, and what John Goodlad has said (with data) in recent decades.[3] I lay no claim to originality. I do lay claim to the predictions I began to make in the sixties that if we do not take seriously the words of these and similar thinkers, the fruits of schooling will become increasingly unpalatable.

School reformers know one other thing: changing the attitudes and practices of school personnel is as difficult as it is necessary. I have never met a school reformer who did not struggle against the perception that he or she was trying to level a mountain with a teaspoon. I speak from a fair amount of experience with schools as they are. It took me years to begin to see clearly how the reform movement was one of repair, not primary prevention. It should not have taken years because the prevention theme was both implicit and explicit in *The Preparation of Teachers, An Unstudied Problem in Education,* written by Kenneth Davidson, Burton Blatt, and me in 1962, and reprinted in 1986. The question we posed three decades ago is what informs the present book: how can we prepare school personnel so that they are more sensitive to the realities of schools and less likely to need reformers to help them cope with problems which today suffuse the ambience of schools and the lives of their inhabitants? Just as we view Headstart as a deliberate preventive effort to inoculate children against the viruses of low achievement and disinterest, so must we view the preparation of school personnel. And, I must remind the reader, that preventive stance was what undergirded Abraham Flexner's (1910/1960) recommendations about the preparation of medical personnel.

In an earlier chapter I discussed parents as educational resources, but only in regard to providing information about their child to the teacher and forging a collaborative relationship with the teacher. By col-

---

[3] Misinterpreting, indeed misreading and misquoting, John Dewey has long been a cottage industry. So, for example, there are people today—some who have read snatches of Dewey, and many more who have read nothing—who identify "permissiveness" with Dewey. Dewey was not the most felicitous writer but to identify him with permissiveness betrays either motivated ignorance or dyslexia. I urge the interested reader to read R.B. Westbrook's *John Dewey and American Democracy* (1991), especially the chapters on education.

laboration I do not mean cooperation, which far more often than not in practice conveys a one-way street message: "Let me tell you what you can do for me." There is nothing inherently wrong with that message except when the conveyor implicitly conveys the additional message: "This is my turf so please do not intrude." The best example of this territoriality in the nature of PTA-school relationships in which parents are expected to be supportive in ways defined by school personnel; needless to say, that definition does not include meaningful participation in classroom practices and school policy. That stance, of course, is justified on the basis that parents do not possess resources relevant to either arena.

It is a stance by no means peculiar to professional educators. It long was a stance characteristic of the doctor-patient relationship. The doctor decided what needed to be done, frequently not telling the patient the universe of alternatives which the doctor had considered and the difference in consequences associated with each alternative. Doctor knew best. The obligation of the patient was to cooperate dutifully with the doctor's decision. Since when do you give patients the responsibility to decide what is the best course of action for their condition? Give patients that responsibility and God only knows what the untoward consequences will be! Until recent decades that stance was accepted by patients, no questions asked. It was accepted to the point where only the rare patient requested more information, let alone a second opinion. And it was very infrequent that a patient would sue the physician for malpractice. The patient was perceived as having no resources relevant to courses of action, and patients so perceived themselves. The patient's task was to cooperate with the physician, *not* collaborate because collaboration means, at least to me, that each of the parties has rights and resources which should be reflected by their explicit presence in decision making, and for two reasons. The first is, obviously, moral: if what my doctor is recommending will have significant effects on me, I have a right to decide whether I will go along. I do not want to feel that I am powerless to participate in decisions significant for my body and life. I do not want to feel that I am being "governed" in ways that assume I am an ignoramus incapable of seeking and contributing information, questioning opinions and practices, and making decisions. If this first reason is moral, it is also political because I do not want to feel or be powerless. I find it hard to label the second reason but it goes this way: "Of course my physician has much more medical knowledge and experience than I do. In this regard, we are not equals. But we are equals in our capacity to be wrong, to choose unwisely among alternatives, to ignore or overlook important factors. In addition, I am well aware that possessing as he does superior experience and knowledge, my physician, *like all other professionals*, may not take kindly to my need to understand what is at stake, to make decisions, and will view me as challenging his professional competency. He prefers that I cooperate, not collaborate with him."

I assume that the reader is aware that in recent decades the moral and political nature of doctor-patient relationship has undergone change. This is reflected in the exponential increase in malpractice suits but that in turn is a reflection of a more widespread change in the attitude of people generally about having a voice in regard to policies (for example, environmental) that will affect them. Hospitals now have posted a "declaration of patient rights" and an increasing number of physicians—by no means a staggering number—are far more informative to their patients than in earlier decades. Indeed, in some states there is legislation which mandates "full disclosure."

A similar change has been occurring in education. The first and most dramatic example of the change is the "civil rights" section of the 1975 Public Law 94-142 for the Education of Handicapped Children. That section spells out in detail the rights of parents to be informed about and meaningfully to participate in decisions about their handicapped children. One of the people who helped draft that law told me that its aim was to make it difficult, legally impermissible, for educators to make unilateral decisions as they were accustomed to do. More recently, several states have mandated a role for parents in school governance undreamed of two or three decades ago.

Again I have to say that nothing in my recent experiences with new teachers alters my conclusion that preparatory programs are unconscionably deficient in helping their students understand the historical social context from which these changes have emerged, the political-moral-philosophical issues involved, the rationales for differing views, the predictable problems educators have and will confront, and the different ways these predictable problems might be coped with. These new teachers were simply unprepared to think about the issues except in terms of a power struggle. None of them saw kinship with parents redefining themselves as resources as *a reaction to the perceived inadequacies of schools and to the insensitivities of educators.* These teachers have no trouble accepting the rhetoric of cooperation. Collaboration is another dangerous, power altering, governance changing affair. If these teachers see no similarity between how they react to how they are governed and how students react to their governors, they also do not feel kinship with how parents feel about how educators prefer to govern them.

I am not partisan to the view that lay people (including students) have a kind and degree of folk wisdom that professionals lack. That you are a parent (or a patient) does not mean that you have a corner on truth or wisdom. What it does mean is that you have a vested interest in what schools are and do and that you see schools differently from the professionals. You are a stakeholder with two obligations: to represent your interests and to seek to understand the nature and complexity of *educational* issues. Those obligations hold no less for the professional educator. But, as has been too frequently the case in recent days, when parents and educators have been *required* to collaborate we have gotten power struggles, direct and indirect, that have had the unintended consequences of not coming to grips with *educational* issues. If schools are not what we would like them to be, it is not *only* because of who had power to decide what, but also because of failure on the part of those with power to question the validity of their views about the social contexts that make for productive learning for everyone in the school: students, teachers, and administrators.

Let us also acknowledge that almost all of the changes designed to make life in the classroom and school more intellectually and socially stimulating, to forge collaborative relationships between educators and parents, could have been recognized, accepted, and implemented before there was legislation, pressure, and exploding adversarial conflicts. It was not that power was an obstacle but that it was undergirded by conceptions of learning that were both invalid and self-defeating. Altering power relationships has no value if those alterations do not achieve the end of nurturing the needs of everyone in the school to experience a sense of intellectual and personal growth. The American colonists did not go to war with their English governors *only* to gain power but rather to attain that power to attain and protect articulated values.

CHAPTER

12

EXPERIENCE IN AND
OUTSIDE OF SCHOOL

In the course of my career I unlearned and learned a lot about schools and school change. Of all I have learned and experienced, one insight stands out. The experience was in the course of writing the second edition of *The Culture of the School and the Problem of Change*. I was having trouble avoiding conveying the impression that reform efforts in the future would be as disappointing as in past decades. I did not want to be seen as a wet blanket and I certainly did not want to convey the impression that I believed that nothing could be done. But I saw nothing on the scene to suggest that anyone was taking seriously what I had previously written. That, I know, will sound mammothly egocentric and grandiose but that is how I felt. So I found myself trying not to appear nihilistic or intellectually self-serving, and having a hard time. In some inchoate way I sensed there was "something" I was not allowing myself to think about, a something that was part of the problem and contained part of the answer to how we should think and act in regard to school change. As I was finishing the book it hit me like the proverbial ton of bricks.

I have always been intrigued by the fact that our thinking and actions are undergirded by what I call axioms—those unreflectively assimilated attitudes or beliefs that seem so right, natural, and proper that we rarely if ever put them into words. It never occurs to us to question these axioms because if we did our outlooks would require drastic, unsettling revision. The processes by which we are socialized into our society have as their goal that we assimilate those axioms. What we call social change is a consequence of having some of these axioms flushed out and challenged. Well, the axiom that hit me, that came, so to speak, from nowhere was: education best takes place in encapsulated classrooms in encapsulated schools. I had accepted that axiom and so did everyone else I knew. What I immediately recognized was that the axiom was in part or even wholly invalid. That, I can assure you, was both unsettling and humbling because everything I have ever written about school change, and everything anybody else was doing about school change, assumed the validity of the axiom when its status as a God-given fact was patently unwarranted. That line of thinking forever changed how I thought about school change in that I saw that any reform effort riveting on the encapsulated classroom in the encapsulated school had two strikes against it from the outset.

I have to assume that one source for this new line of thinking was my perception (and that of many others) that the gulf between what students experienced and thought in school and in "real life" was not only wide but approaching unbridgeability. That gulf always existed but it was never as wide as it became after World War II and because of factors and forces that war unleashed. Nowhere were these effects more pronounced than in our cities. I have written about this in some of my books. The crucial point is that the school change movement made only token gestures to the widening of the gulf; the focus was on classrooms and schools, not on how one might use community sites for the purposes of education, for making it possible for students to see that traditional subject matter was not only something on pages between two covers but had concrete, personal, intellectual, and social meaning.

I finished that second edition and immediately started to write *Schooling in America: Scapegoat and Salvation* (1983) where that axiom is analyzed and challenged and new directions indicated. If I had to choose the one book I wrote about schools from which I learned the most and in which I believe I made my most distinctive contribution, it is that book which despite a favorable critical reception has been read by few people and taken seriously by none. That was no surprise to me. After all, it took me years to reach the point where I could allow myself to articulate and challenge the axiom, to see how it helped me see my past experiences in a new way, and to confront the practical, upsetting consequences of that challenge. Why should I expect others warmly to embrace a point of view that undercut what always seemed right, natural, and proper? Someone once said that one of the preconditions for individual or social change is to have been hit over the head, so to speak, with the reality that things cannot go on as they have, that the stakes are too high, that we have met the enemy and it is us: our unreflective, unexamined acceptance of undergirding beliefs.

In what follows are Chapter 1 of that book (The Argument in Summary) and Chapter 4 (Experience Inside and Outside of Schools).

THE ARGUMENT IN SUMMARY

This book marshalls considerations about schools leading to conclusions that some readers will find strange; others, unpalatable; and others, impractical.[1] A few may find them liberating and helpful. And yet it is safe to assume that every reader is dissatisfied with schools, albeit in varying degrees, ranging from mild disapproval to vitriolic disdain to a call for their demise. Perhaps the most frequent reactions are puzzlement and frustration about the failure of efforts to improve schools, i.e., we conclude that something is wrong somewhere when, instead of getting better, schools appear to be impervious to improvement and may, in fact, be worse than they were. The explanations have been many, as have been recommendations for new efforts, but no one seems at all confident that what is proposed will be effective. Following the 1960s, when the substance, structure, and goals of schooling were center stage in our society, educational debates noticeably subsided, except in relation to certain civil rights issues that got reflected in legislation or were consequences of court decisions. I refer specifically to issues concerning racial segregation and the rights of handicapped children to an education in the least restrictive environment.

Today there are signs that schooling may be returning to the societal agenda because of the perception that "scientific illiteracy" has reached proportions endangering our economic stability and military security. The scientists are upset, the Department of Defense is worried, and presidential speeches written by advisors in the Department of Education predict a gloomy future if remedial action is not taken. A large part of the problem is seen as deriving from errors of omission and commission by the schools. Our society has always looked upon schools as a vehicle for secular salvation, which, when this goal is obviously not being reached by our youth, leads people to scapegoat schools. The current conversations (they are hardly discussions, let alone debates) reflect this ambivalence. One facet of these conversations I find truly astounding: the failure to realize that everything being said and proposed was said, proposed, and acted upon earlier as a reaction to the narcissistic wound experienced by our society when the Soviet Union orbited the first sputnik in 1957. I am forced to the conclusion that as a societal problem scientific illiteracy is far less serious than the ahistorical stance.

The arguments I advance in this book cast past and present discussions of schooling in a distinctive light. By using the adjective "distinctive" I do not wish to appear blithely to arrogate merit to my conclu-

---

[1] The text beginning with this sentence and continuing to the end of this chapter is reprinted from *Schooling in America: Scapegoat and Salvation* (pp. 1–9, 57–84), 1983, New York: Free Press. Copyright by Seymour Sarason.

sions; rather, I am signaling that my perspective is remarkable for its absence in matters educational. I am not the first to offer this perspective, but I do think I have marshalled the arguments in a new way. Let me very briefly summarize the major points I raise:

1. Schools as we have traditionally known them have been, are, and will be uninteresting places.

2. Responding to the changes wrought or reinforced by World War II, the generations born after the war assimilated a world view that made the world of classroom and school frustratingly unrelated to the "real world." For these generations, curious and interested in that real world, exposed to that world through new mass media and new means for quick travel, and prompted by their elders to explore that world, the chasm that has always existed between the inside and the outside of schools became wider and, from the standpoint of students, unbridgeable.

3. As the post-World War II decades succeeded each other, the ability of schools to engender and sustain student interest, especially in junior high and high schools, steadily decreased. "Let's make schools interesting" became the basis for a new industry stimulated and subsidized by federal, state, and local policies and monies.

4. The efforts, by no means minuscule in scope and budget, to improve schools were based on an axiom as potent as it was unverbalized: *education best takes place in classrooms in school buildings.* That axiom, embedded in a world view that is millennia old, could be neither formulated nor challenged. It so riveted attention on the physically and socially isolated school building as to preclude recognition that the axiom was both unfounded and self-defeating.

5. More than ever before, schools in the post-World War II era sought ways to give young people experience outside schools that spoke directly to student curiosity and needs. These programs, varying considerably in their intellectual-educational thrust, justification, and quality, were "add-ons" to the curriculum and were hardly related, if at all, to core subject matter. In the main, these were programs for students for whom core subject matter seemed inappropriate or too difficult. Nobody worried that those for whom core subjects were considered appropriate continued to experience the classroom as a boring place and to regard the learning of subject matter as labor and not work.

6. Can traditional subject matter be assimilated more quickly and have more sustained and productive consequences outside schools in contexts in which the substance and structure of subject matter are manifest in their need and meaningful in their employment? What if it were illegal to teach math or science of biology in a classroom in a school? Where and how would you teach these subjects? If you start with such

questions, unimprisoned by the imagery of a classroom and a school; unhampered by the artificial, arbitrary separations between theory and practice, on the one hand, and between them and the contexts from which they are derived, on the other hand; if you take seriously what anecdote after anecdote describe when students are exposed to subject matter in contexts in which it is both necessary and practical—once you begin to be liberated from a world view in which is embedded a picture of where and how schooling "should" take place, you begin to understand why efforts to improve schools are doomed.

7. If education can better take place outside the traditional classroom in the traditional school, what do we *do*? How do we *do* it? Isn't this notion wildly impractical? These are productive and fair questions *only* if you have concluded that schools cannot be interesting, intellectually stimulating places and that alternative educational settings must be seriously considered. The millennia-old view has such a hold in our minds that when it is challenged we retreat to what is familiar to us. The fact is that there are many ways to answer these questions.

That is the skeleton outline of my argument. It is not one that stems from a particular social, political, or economic orientation and it is not one that assigns blame to any special group. As I make clear in the following chapters, however much various groups of critics differ from each other and however much they collectively differ from professional educators (who are not unanimous either in their views or in their responses to critics), they all agree that education best takes place in bounded classrooms and schools. Whether challenges to this axiom will gain currency I cannot say. When you consider how long it took for world views about men and women, races, old people, and handicapped people to begin to change—for new views to gain currency to the point that new actions and roles were first imaginable and then possible—you cannot expect that my proposals will have a different fate.

This book is about an axiom in a world view. It is not a call for action, not because I am opposed to action but because in this instance I would define action as appropriate only if those to be affected by it had worked through the turmoil associated with giving up an old stance and adopting a new one. It is a turmoil that I experienced when, after decades of thinking and writing about schools and of being involved in undertakings related to them, I came to realize that like everybody else I had not flushed out and confronted certain axioms in my world view. After I took this step, I began to ask specialists (especially in the sciences) how their subject matters could be taught outside the classroom. I was encouraged by the ease with which they generated possibilities and, in a number of instances, by their accounts of how they had done just that with middle or high school students. And yet the significance of what they had done, the contrast between what they described and what bothered them about the traditional classroom, had not propelled them to challenge in any way the millennia-old axiom about where schooling should take place.

This book is an attempt to state and examine a particular axiom. It is not my purpose to look into how and why our schools came to have the structural, organizational, and physical features they do. Nor do I discuss why our schools have different career consequences for different groups of students. These are important issues, of course, and have engendered heated debates. For my purposes, however, discussion of these issues would divert attention away from the ever increasing gulf between the worlds inside and outside schools. As I have said, this gulf, which has always been with us, dramatically widened after World War II and, therefore, requires special scrutiny.

This book is not a polemic and it does not contain a blueprint. What we call a "blueprint" has to be seen as one in a series of blueprints all of which were preceded by sketches, a form of "playing around" with the ideas and problems initiated by the need to create something. To the extent that the rationale for the blueprint is understood and accepted by those with a vested interest in the final outcome, that outcome stands a chance of achieving desired goals. The major purpose of this book is to put forward the argument that a particular axiom about education requires serious challenge. If this argument gains currency, one may then hope that different people in different places will engage in a sketching process from which will emerge the foundation for appropriate action. A blueprint, whether for a building or an institutional change, has a concreteness that too frequently facilitates rejection: either the plan strikes one as strange or, as is sometimes the case, it gets a quick acceptance that deprives one of both the benefits of the sketching process and the chance to gain understanding and acceptance from those who will be affected by implementing the blueprint. So, if this book does not provide a blueprint, it is because the substance of the issues has hardly been glimpsed. I do not derogate those with different views or those who will make short shrift of my position. In this particular arena *argumentum ad hominems* may be titillating but they are a distraction from the fact that what is at issue is the nature of our world view, a problem in cultural change and social-intellectual history, not in a narrow psychology.

The stakes are high and they go far beyond scientific illiteracy. Indeed, I do not consider it at all encouraging that current talk about schooling derives from concerns that, however important, have the effect of narrowing both the scope of the problem and the range of its possible solutions. In science, the significance of a contribution is in part proportional to how much it renders previous contributions obsolete. In the arena of societies and their major institutions, contributions are significant if they illuminate how what appears to be an obsolete past is nevertheless present and, precisely because it is unobtrusive, profoundly influential. Improving schools is, unfortunately but inevitably, not a matter of social engineering. When a major societal institution like schools appears unamenable to change, when more people than ever before are unperturbed by the suggestion that we should cut our losses and do as little as possible, when puzzlement about past failures degenerates into apathy, the red lights should start flashing to warn us that we may be taking something for granted that deserves our closest attention.

EXPERIENCES IN AND OUTSIDE SCHOOL

What students learn and experience in school should stand in some relationship to what they learn and experience outside school. If that statement seems obvious both as a value and as a goal, it nevertheless has features of the untestable abstraction because when people nod agreement to the statement, it is not clear what is being agreed to. Do we mean, for example, that what a kindergartner learns and experiences in school should stand in some *current* relationship to what is being learned and experienced outside school? Or do we have in mind *future* learning and experience outside school? Similarly, is what a high school student learns in a math or social studies class to stand in relationship to current or future experience outside school? What about the *past?* When a student is in a history or literature class, is what he or she is learning to stand in relation to a "dead" past that was once outside or to one that has continuity with the outside present and future? Some people would argue that they mean all of the above, as if such comprehensiveness either settled the problem or contributed a great deal of meaning. If one were to ask what such a statement means in terms of what one should be able to observe in and out of schools in order to conclude that these statements of goals and values are being appropriately implemented, the answers would not come easily and, if my experience is not atypical, would be generalizations by no means clear in meaning.

When I pose this question, I do not expect the answers to resemble a teacher's daily lesson plan. Rather, I expect concrete examples or detailed descriptions that allow one to compare the answer to what one would observe in a modal classroom or school. More correctly, the answer should permit one to contrast proposed inside-outside relationships with those relationships as we would observe them in our schools. If, as is unlikely, the two pictures are highly similar, we have to look elsewhere for the sources of disappointment with our schools. But if those pictures diverge, especially if they diverge a great deal, we have to pursue the reasons therein, on the assumption that whatever contributes to the divergence may be relevant to our disappointment. It is, of course, possible that faced with obvious divergences, some people would make the judgment, for any number of reasons, that the "theoretical" picture is utterly impractical and that the "actual" picture of these inside-outside relationships is now both more understandable and more acceptable. In that event, we not only have to temper criticism but also have to concede that our social world is not organized to make it practical to implement the theoretical picture to a desired degree. The initial assumption would have to be restated: what students learn and experience in school will, unfortunately, stand in a limited relationship to what they learn and experience outside school. And these limitations, it would be apparent, derive not only from what schools and school personnel are but also from the traditions and attitudes that bulwark our society and its structures. What some people regard as impractical because it may require significant and difficult changes inside and outside schools can be a goad to those for whom the impractical is a welcome challenge.

There are other possible reactions to divergence, but at this point I wish to stress only that the first task is to recognize that the assumption in any of its forms leads us to look at and far beyond schools. How learning and experience in schools should relate to what is learned and experienced outside schools cannot be answered by looking only at schools. However obvious this point may seem, it is remarkable how different critics have examined the assumption primarily by looking at schools. What is even more remarkable to me, taking into account the unanimous acceptance of the assumption of inside-outside relationships, is how unclearly and unsystematically that assumption has been posed and discussed. That lack of clarity has not been helped, indeed it has been aggravated, by the attention that has been given to another and far more circumscribed assumption to which we now turn. Here, too, the assumption has all of the characteristics of a glimpse of the obvious but, unlike the first assumption, it is taken seriously, so seriously that it deflects attention away from the first assumption even though the two revolve around the same issues and principles.

The second assumption is: that which a student learns and experiences at any one point in his or her schooling should stand in some relationship to a later point in schooling. The later may be tomorrow, next month, next year, or five years in the future but it is a point that is, in terms of time and place, within the school. When a school says, for example, that it has a mathematics curriculum, it means that there is a graded sequence spanning several grades and that there is a rationale justifying that sequence. Likewise, if you ask why kindergartners engage in activities A, B, and C, the answer will be phrased in terms of skills, knowledge, and attitudes that are necessary for the transition to first grade and the mastery of the beginning phases of reading, arithmetic, writing, and other subjects. Every teacher knows that whatever he or she is requiring students to learn is preparation for, and organized in relation to, what the student will be asked to learn and experience the next semester or year. In fact, one of the sources of friction among teachers in adjacent grades is the claim that teachers in the lower grade are not preparing students well for the next grade. And, as the reader undoubtedly knows, colleges blame high schools, which blame parents. (This approach has given rise to a flourishing curriculum publishing industry, journals devoted to the theory and evaluation of curricula, and sustained controversies about the substance and adequacy of different curricula—their psychological underpinnings, the demands they place on teachers, and their interest value for students.) If for any one year one were able to list every workshop, lecture, or graduate course designed for school personnel—and the list would run into the thousands—the percentage that would explicitly concern curriculum would be very large. And there would be little or nothing said on those occasions that bears on the relationship between learning and experience inside and outside of schools.

Schooling is seen as a continuous, integrated process in which learning and experience at different points in time become fused in a more complex and differentiated pattern of knowledge, skill, and conception. As a goal that view is unchallengeable. But the question that has to be asked is: what price do we pay when that goal is in practice defined primarily in terms of within-school learning and experience? More concretely, does that definition permit us to understand better not only some major criticisms of schools but also why efforts to change and improve schools have been disappointing both to critics and to the public? Is it not possible that the perceived problematic relationship between what students learn and experience in and outside schools is in part a consequence of the unreflective emphasis on learning and experience within schools? Can the issues surrounding the integration of learning at two different points in time within schools be discussed, let alone resolved, without attention to *concurrent* learning and experience in and out of school?

There is no group more preoccupied with making schools more interesting places than curriculum developers. The "making school interesting" industry received its greatest impetus from the American uproar following the launch of the first sputnik, as I suggested earlier. Our country, the critics said, was behind the Soviet Union in the quality of education and a contributing factor was the inadequacy of curricula. School learning, we were told, could be interesting, enjoyable, and mind expanding. Turned off students could be turned on by better curricula. It is my impression that the new math curricula that were introduced at the time received more play in the mass media than any curricula before or since (with the possible exception of curricula for sex education). What got conjured up in people's minds was a picture of somnolent students waking up to a fairyland of intellectual delights. I am not being facetious or disdainful but rather trying to convey how the assessment that schools were uninteresting places was (and is) a central feature of the diagnosis of the ills of our educational system. And this feature was found at all levels of schooling. The problem was most clear at the high school level because our society was starting to see that it had a problem on its hands: disaffected youth, many in number, varied in their expression and style, and heterogeneous in background. High schools were beginning to be declared disaster areas that could not be ignored. As a high school principal said to me at the time, "We have several types of students. Those who do not come to school. Those who come to school but who hang around, make trouble, and don't go to classes. Those who come to class but whose minds are elsewhere. And then there are those, a minority to be sure, who come to class and their minds are there."

(A digression: as I was writing these words in March 1982 I received a call from the head of staff development at a modest-sized school system in a nearby state. The community had, I was told, a per capita expenditure for its schools that put it in the top 2 percent of all school districts in the country. I was asked whether I could recommend resource people who could help the system with some problems: absenteeism in the high schools, drugs, and discipline. This person said that the district's problems were not severe, comparatively speaking, but pressure was mounting from within and without the schools to do something. I relate this telephone conversation because it was less discouraging—not more encouraging—than my contacts with school settings usually are.)

Let us begin to examine these questions by focusing on an observation about which there is a consensus: schools are not very interesting places for most of the people in them. That is indisputably the case for high and middle or junior high schools, especially in our metropolitan areas. In fact, the post-World War II era has spawned a sizable literature on how stultifying schools can be. From the standpoint of eliciting and studying student attitudes toward schooling, the most systematic and comprehensive study is that by Buxton (1973). His report does not, to indulge understatement, lead to reassuring conclusions. But Buxton, a longtime colleague of mine at Yale, is a sober, "hard-nosed" type of psychologist who would not be regarded as flaming liberal or radical intent on redoing society or its major institutions. He came to his study because of a long-standing interest in adolescents, and he was not bent on criticizing schools. In fact, Buxton was both surprised and perturbed by his findings. I point these things out because so much of the literature sharply critical of high schools has been based on participant-observation by social scientists of reformist or radical leanings. That statement should in no way be taken as a criticism by me because their descriptions of how people in schools feel and act not only have a ring of truth but also do not conflict with the conclusions of Buxton's study.

Two things are noteworthy about our unsuccessful efforts to make schools interesting. The first is the assumption that students are truly interested in the subject matters, e.g., math and social studies—or, more correctly, that the ways in which children normally and spontaneously think about and experience these subject areas are similar in content and form to the ways in which they are or should be presented in the curriculum. It is one thing to say that in the course of development the phenomenology of children contains a good deal of questioning and answering about numbers, human relationships, spatial relationships, the physical world, causality, biological functions, and other matters that Piaget's work did so much to illuminate. It is quite another to say that the characteristics of this questioning and self-generated answering—as well as the characteristics of the occasions in which they emerge—are highly similar to those that the curriculum seeks to re-create or to capitalize on. So, the curriculum developers are correct in assuming that children are interested in these matters, but not necessarily in assuming that they are addressing these matters in ways attuned to the phenomenology of the student. It would be fair to say that curriculum developers spend a lot of time trying to figure out how to interest students in what the curriculum developers believe is the appropriate content and form of the subject matter. It is also fair to say that they have fallen far short of their mark. The second assumption underlying these efforts is that it is possible to engender interest within the confines of a classroom or school (more correctly, within the confines of the classroom and the division of the day into periods, each of which is devoted to a particular subject or activity). That assumption, rarely articulated, has a compelling surface validity despite the fact that students and teachers have long experienced school in ways that should have brought the assumption into serious question. That assumption has been seriously questioned in recent decades in relation to high schools. Critiques have encompassed any or all of the following observations:

1. Schools are very uninteresting places for both students and teachers.
2. Students are capable of, and would be eager to accept, more responsibility for their own learning. This is a matter not of empowerment based on abstract principles but of capitalizing on the motivations of students. Students, sometimes vaguely, sometimes clearly, resent and are bored with the passive role assigned to them.

3. Students have strong interests in and about the world but that world is not related to the one they experience in school.
4. Students do experience the outside world in ways that are intellectually, educationally, and personally productive.
5. Only to a very limited degree can that outside world be re-created or simulated in a classroom or school.

These critiques do not come from people who overidealize youth. Nor do they come from people who believe that children have the capacity and wisdom to go their own ways, as if the role of adults were to insure that nothing gets in the way of children's self-direction and self-expression. And they do not come from people who downplay the goal of attaining structure and direction in experience. What these critiques have in common is the observation that schools are uninteresting places, the emphasis on learning and experience over time *in* school is misplaced and self-defeating, and we can no longer ignore the importance of integrating concurrent learning in and out of schools. They also have in common the belief that the problem of interest cannot be resolved by curricula riveted on the traditional classroom.

Let me illustrate some of these points with an example that I use less because it is typical and more because it has been described and evaluated in an atypically comprehensive and judicious fashion.[2] I refer to Project City Science, a program carried out by New York University in conjunction with several junior high schools in poor New York neighborhoods. Funding came from the National Science Foundation. The purpose of the project was "to help bring about a major, lasting and self-perpetuating improvement, principally in New York City, in the teaching of science in the middle grades between elementary and high school" (Longo, 1979, p. 12). Longo went on to state:

> While the rationale for placing primary emphasis on science rather than on other subjects, such as reading and mathematics, is not clearly stated, it is

---

[2] Paul Longo of Queens College directed the evaluation and report, which is in three volumes. Despite its intimidating size, the report is quite instructive and very readable. Anyone interested in what efforts at educational changes are like, how they are formulated and implemented, and what obstacles they encounter in an uncontrollable, unpredictable world will find this report very informative. I am sorry that I was unaware of this document when I wrote the second edition of *The Culture of the Schools and the Problem of Change* (Sarason, 1982) because it beautifully confirms how I conceptualize and judge modal attempts at educational change, attempts that have brought disillusionment with, and criticism of, schools in their wake. These attempts begin by viewing schools as places of salvation and end by scapegoating them. Longo's evaluation is refreshingly far more balanced in this regard.

evident that the proposers of [Project City Science] PCS feel that science is an area in which instruction is particularly ineffective. It is noted that:

> science teaching at the middle school level in New York City and many other cities can only be regarded, on the whole, as gravely inadequate. . . . [Furthermore], science education in the city elementary schools remains woefully weak, when not absent altogether.

Having concluded that, "improving elementary school science in the cities seems to be an intractable problem of massive proportions" project staff apparently decided that the middle school (i.e. grades 6-9) should become the logical focus of their efforts. The reasons offered for this appear to be three-fold. First, a large fraction of inner city youth do not go on to attend high school, and so efforts made at a later stage would be too late. Second, by the time students reach high school, a deep antipathy toward the study of science has already developed, and so they will usually not choose to take courses in science; and, third, even though many educators agree that the junior high school years may be critical for students, very little emphasis has been placed on developing procedures that improve instruction or modernize curriculum at this level—particularly in science.

The proposal goes on to clearly emphasize its junior high school focus.

> For many city youngsters, junior high school provides the only formal instruction in science they receive in their lives! . . . it constitutes quantitatively the most science they will formally encounter.

Project emphasis was not solely upon the direct improvement of science instruction in the school, but upon the development of a model program for training junior high school science teachers as well. The intent was to both provide science teachers for the New York City middle schools, and to develop a training model with widespread potential. The then Project Director, interviewed for an article about PCS, indicated what the program's major concerns were:

> First, we're doing in-service training of teachers who are already in the schools. Second, we're designing a training program for the whole next generation of junior high school teachers. Third, we're working to analyze instructional problems and devise system-wide solutions. . . . Over the long run, [the director] can envision Project City Science helping to effect a new kind of science teaching. . . . If Project City Science succeeds, and if it is duplicated in other cities, in ten years we could replace up to 40 percent with a cadre of science teachers trained for the job. . . . What we want to develop is a design that can be used in city schools throughout the country, something that can be adopted quickly by other universities and other school districts. (pp. 12–13)

One more quotation is relevant to the major problems the project was created to address:

> Assuming, then, that there is an especially urgent need to improve science instruction during the transition years, what are the particular problems that must be solved or at least ameliorated? The 1974 proposal

explicitly claimed, and Project experience has subsequently supported, *that three major problems exist:*

1. *The failure of teacher training,* both preservice, and inservice, to prepare science teachers to deal effectively with the early adolescent child in the inner-city situation.
2. A continuing reliance on *science programs that do not reflect* sufficiently what has been learned in the last decade or so about science curricula and new approaches to teaching science.
3. *A scarcity of systematic knowledge* about the age group and about what conditions and techniques best promote an *interest in a learning of science* at that age and in inner-city circumstances.

Implicit in the proposal and accentuated by Project experience is a fourth problem: *The failure* on all sides to identify, organize, and bring *to bear in a coordinated way* the not inconsiderable *material and human resources* of the state, city, district schools, universities, and community at large. Related to this is the problem of establishing a self-sustaining system for continuing reform rather than merely instituting this or that improvement, regardless of how alluring a given reform seems to be in the short run, or however much desired by one or the other agency or institution. (Longo, 1979, p. 14)

The problems were many but it was recognized that among the most crucial was how to engender in pupils an interest in science. More correctly, how first to overcome *antipathy* and then to engender and sustain interest.

I have gone into detail about this project to make a point that, once made, will seem obvious. Indeed, the point is so obvious that it apparently required no statement or examination by the creators of the project or, for that matter, by the people at the National Science Foundation who decided to fund this and similar efforts. (Let us not scapegoat the project directors. We can assume that the project was scrutinized by a variety of specialists for whom the obvious also was literally unremarkable.) *Insofar as the schools were concerned, the emphasis was exclusively on the classroom—that was where interest was to be engendered and productive learning to take place. It was in the classroom that success would be judged by changes in test scores over time. For all practical purposes, learning and experiencing science outside school—utilizing "the not inconsiderable material and human resources of the state, city, district schools, universities, and community at large"—were not in the picture.* We can assume that Project City Science did engender more interest in students but there is nothing in the evaluation to suggest that it was other than a sometime thing.

I am not suggesting that it is impossible for classroom learning to be interesting. I have seen classrooms, albeit a very small percentage of the classrooms I have observed, in which teachers and students experience and sustain interest, even excitement, in learning. Very few of these unusual classrooms are in high or junior high schools; by far, the majority are in elementary schools. What is common to these classrooms is the ability of the teacher to create an atmosphere that approximates that of outside situations that stimulate and elicit a child's attention and interest—really, anybody's attention and interest.

Imagine that two criteria could be met. The first is that we can get agreement about the characteristics of "real-life" situations that elicit children's interest. The second is that we can reliably rate classrooms for the degree to which they contain these characteristics. My experience suggests that the more a classroom contains the characteristics of outside-school situations, the more the people in that classroom will experience and sustain interest. This very observation has led to the criticism that there is nothing wrong with schools that better selection of teachers could not cure. And it is this observation that has powered funding for in-service programs to improve the quality of teaching. After all, the reasoning goes, if a few teachers can do it (regardless of what *it* may be), why can't others learn to do it? That is a legitimate question in the sense that it emerges from observation and deserves scrutiny. But it has always seemed strange to me that those who ask this question have inordinate difficulty recognizing another legitimate question: is there something about encapsulated classrooms and schools—spaces, places, and social organizations that are physically and psychologically separate from the outside world—that makes it extraordinarily difficult for them to be interesting? Should not the fact that so few teachers meet our expectations cause us to examine the basis of our expectations? Are we putting students and teachers into a situation that far from engendering and sustaining interest contains, by virtue of its isolation and internal structure, nearly insurmountable obstacles to such interest?

I cannot refrain from relating the following story. I was trotting out these arguments to a friend who had long worked with prison inmates, staff, and administrators. I did not get very far when he stopped me and, much like a father patting a child on the head for trying to think like an adult, he said in essence:

> What you are trying to say is in principle on all fours with the history of attempts to humanize prisons. You can always point to a few prison personnel who truly can relate to prisoners in very helpful, sensitive ways. There are even a few prisons you might be tempted to say are humane. So why can't we select our personnel better and have less junglelike prisons? Why is our track record poor even in those few instances in which bleeding hearts like me had the opportunity, to a modest degree, to make these changes? We did some good and if given new opportunities I would break my neck to do better. But, it took me a long time to recognize that it is the nature of prisons that sets drastic limits to achieving my

goals. There is a part of me that still gets angry as hell when I see brutality or insensitivity on the part of prisoners or staff. There is another part of me that says that the problem is as much in what prisons are as in personality makeups. That is a hard fact to which to adjust because there is no way that the public is going to give up its belief that the problem resides primarily in what people *are*. That's the essence of the problem. Plato still lives!

Over the decades I have worked with school personnel in classes, workshops, and inservice training meetings. Whenever possible I request that participants take a few minutes to ponder this question: think of two instances—they could be from any time in your life, they could have occurred anyplace, and they could have lasted from a few minutes to hours, days, or months—during which your interest in something was kindled to a degree and in a way that allows you to say that the episode had an influence on you. I then ask each member of the group briefly to describe the instances in such a way as to highlight their major characteristics. A number of features always come up: the occasion contained an element of novelty; it bore strongly on an existing (sometimes subliminal, sometimes explicit) need or interest; it was not planned or predictable but simply happened; it involved another person, usually older, with mentorlike qualities; it was marked by a sense of excitement, or exploration, or "new meanings"; it stuck in memory, sometimes with few or no apparent sustained behavioral consequences, sometimes with life-changing consequences; it was recalled with pleasure and nostalgia. Now, two other characteristics: the instances tended to occur in adolescence or early adulthood and only a small number occurred in a school setting.

After each person describes his or her instances and the characteristics common to them are recognized by the group, I ask, "How frequently have you had experiences in school as a teacher that were interesting?" The immediate response usually is a subdued ripple of anxious laughter. Three statements can summarize the discussion that typically follows. First, the frequency of interesting experiences is very low. Second, the organization of a school does not make it likely that the characteristics of interesting experiences can occur. Third, within the classroom, school teachers are too isolated from each other and from the world at large; i.e., the social contexts from which interesting experiences might emerge are not likely to be found in schools. In one of these groups, at a point at which the participants were both puzzled and bothered by what was being discussed, one teacher said, "But that does not mean that we do not get satisfaction from what we do." To which another teacher replied, "You're right, but how long can you go without an interesting experience? If it were not for the kicks I get from interesting experiences outside of school, my level of satisfaction would be a lot less than it is now." My impression from these discussions is that high and junior high school teachers, in contrast to those in elementary school, report less satisfaction from their work and more bitterness about the infrequency of interesting experiences.

I sometimes pose a second question: how frequently do you think students have interesting experiences in school? Here one must immediately separate elementary from high or junior high school personnel because the latter typically raise the problem of student uninterest, to which I respond, "Granted that it would be quite unfair to place blame for this exclusively on junior high and high schools, what is it about these places that may be aggravating the problem?" The inevitable answer is: these schools have too many students; the way the school day is organized makes it impossible for teachers to remember the names of all students, let alone get to know other than a handful; teachers are, depending on where the school is, at best monitors and at worst police in training; these places are more like factories than schools. The reader will remember that earlier in this chapter I related that while I was writing I received a telephone call for assistance from a high school in a very affluent town in a nearby state. Discipline, drugs, and absenteeism were the problems with which they were unsuccessfully coping. I was asked to make a visit, I said yes, suggested a date, and was told that I would be contacted in a few days to confirm the appointment. The call came canceling the appointment. The person calling me was embarrassed and even angry because the task of getting a "resource person" had been dumped into his lap and he was told to act quickly. He went on to tell me that he had just found out that the immediate stimulus for the first call had been a stabbing, and that the superintendent had decided that what was needed was a new principal and not an outside consultant. I give this account not to paint high schools as armed camps, which most are not, or to suggest that there are really no differences between schools in ghettos and affluent suburbia, which would be ridiculous, but rather as a way to convey to readers who have no contact with junior high and high schools how bothered, bewildered, and despairing school personnel are about their efforts to understand, stimulate, and manage students. Stabbings are rare—absenteeism, discipline problems, and drugs are not. Junior and high schools can be exciting places but it is the kind of excitement no one wants. That they are uninteresting places for those who populate them—that, too, no one wants but no one seems to know what to change and how to change it.

As I have stressed in this book, schools are uninteresting places. But the word "places" does not capture the core of the problem as seen by school personnel. It is *people,* the students, who are uninterested, and that is to teachers and other staff the important etiological factor. As a superintendent of schools said:

Kids enter kindergarten and first grade with interests. They are motivated to be and learn in school. As they go through the grades they seem to lose more and more interest and most of them slip over into the uninterested category. So the dropout rate is scandalous, or most who graduate have really learned to dislike learning. If it weren't for that small minority who are really interested, who occasionally brighten your day so that you can come to work the next day, schools would explode. At least the teachers would.

When I asked him whether it is possible that our traditional concept of school as *the* place in which students and teachers can have interesting educational experiences may be getting in the way, he was very puzzled and finally said, "Where else would schooling take place?" The inability to generate other than a very limited universe of alternatives (or any alternatives) in the face of an intractable social-institutional problem is a sign of how effectively tradition and culture function to blind us; but more about that later.

Some readers will find themselves saying to me, "You may be right about *public* schools as uninteresting places. And you may be right that whatever we have done to improve matters is no cause for enthusiasm or encouragement. But how do you account for the fact that *private* schools are more interesting places than public schools, regardless of their use of classrooms?" I do not regard it as a fact that private schools are more interesting for either students or teachers. It may be that students in private schools are more motivated for academic achievement. And it may be that they do better on achievement tests, pose fewer disciplinary problems, and have a lower rate of absenteeism.[3] But that says nothing about educational experiences being more interesting in private schools. Although my experience in and with private schools is less than that in and with public schools, my observations do not support the conclusion that they differ in terms of being interesting places. In fact, in my talks

---

[3] With the publication of Coleman's *High School Achievement* (1982) comparing public and private schools—in which public schools came out a poor second—the critics of public schools were confirmed in their opinions, especially those critics in favor of a voucher system that would allow parents to shop around to find a school appropriate to their children. These critics and the public at large will probably not hear either about what critics of that report have written or about the statistical analyses that suggest that differences between public and private schools may be minuscule or even nonexistent. Rejoinders to, or retractions of, what makes front-page headlines are never published on the front page. However, for my present purposes this controversy is not important because neither the report nor its critics are at all concerned about how interesting schools are, although I would guess that none of the participants in the controversy would rate public or private schools as places that their occupants find interesting.

with private school personnel the usual problem comes up: how, as one teacher put it, can you light an intellectual fire in the bulk of students for whom learning is such a bore?

But why, some readers will wonder, do I stress the notion of schools as interesting places? Is it not the primary goal of schooling to foster the acquisition of knowledge and skills and only secondarily to provide an interesting context for this to happen? Is it the goal of the school to be a happy place? Are schools supposed to be centers for entertainment, suppliers more of what students want than of what they need in this world? Granted that schools should be more interesting places than they are, are you not diverting attention from their deficits in regard to academic achievement? Is not the return to basics in part a reaction to what happened when schools introduced all kinds of gimmicks and frills that catered to students' interests?

Let me begin my answer by noting that I do not use the word "interesting" as a synonym for "happy." When students *and* school personnel complain about schools as uninteresting places, they are complaining not about the absence of happiness but rather about boredom and the lack of the sense of personal challenge and meaning (i.e., the sense that one is engaged in a process that pulls one willingly to a desired future, to a tomorrow that will add to one's knowledge, outlook, worth, and mastery). To be engaged in serious learning—which is tantamount to experiencing change—is to encounter difficulty, frustration, challenge, excitement, questioning, and satisfaction. It is not a happy process, although the feeling of happiness is occasionally there. The complaint of students and teachers is that school learning is not a satisfying experience and, therefore, it is uninteresting. To assume that students and teachers seek happiness is at best a caricature of their complaint and at worst a total misunderstanding of what they seek.

Another part of the answer is that my emphasis on schools as uninteresting places rests on what students and teachers have for decades reported. What their reports demonstrate is that regardless of the substance or content of the curriculum, there is something about schools that does not engage the interest of most students. And that lack of engagement forces one to predict that the current back-to-basics movement will be no more successful than the emphases it presumably seeks to remedy or replace. The problem does not inhere in the curriculum but in the limits that the organization and culture of the school place on engaging the interest of students; as long as we continue to view education as something that should take place in a school building, we drastically restrict the opportunities for students and teachers to experience serious, interesting learning. That conclusion, as we shall see in later chapters, has long been recognized by schools as valid for certain types of students, a small minority, but its applicability to all students has not been noted. For example, that conclusion has long been considered valid for the least and the most educationally talented students for whom what was available in the school was considered to be insufficiently appropriate and interesting. Several times during the year one can count on reading newspaper accounts of so-called gifted students for whom the school (or parents) arranged serious educational experiences in diverse community settings. And one can also count on reading about students, who are clearly not educationally talented, who are engaged in some hands-on experience in the community. Historically, the creation of vocational schools was in part a recognition that for some students the academic aspects of schooling hold no interest; they require an educational setting that will engage what is thought to be their practical interests. I need not belabor the point that school personnel have long been sensitive to the fact that without student interest productive learning does not occur. Someone once said that a teacher's definition of paradise is a classroom with one half the students he or she now has. It would be nearer the truth to say that teachers fantasize paradise as a place with classrooms of students who are interested and eager to learn. One of the delights of fantasy is that it gets us away from the nature and demands of reality. And the reality that the fantasies of school personnel avoid confronting is that the traditional classroom is not, has not been, and cannot be a very interesting place for the bulk of students and school personnel. Whatever schools are or have been, they are not and have not been interesting places.

The final part of the answer is usually given not by me but by those who wonder why I stress the idea of schools as interesting places. The fact is that those who question my emphasis frequently (and quickly) convey in indirect ways that they know that to argue against the centrality of the concept of interest is like arguing for sin and against virtue. (One person said to me, "I feel I am arguing in favor of a motorless car. It looks good, sounds good, but moves you nowhere.") Usually, those who question my stance see me as advocating permissiveness and downplaying the so-called basics, a devotee of process over substance. I am able to convince most of these critics that I am not doing either of these things but rather emphasizing how central interest is in learning *anything* one thinks worthwhile. Once they understand what I am saying, they have less difficulty facing up to two things: school tended to be uninteresting for them and schools have been resistant to efforts to make them interesting places. So what do we do? Get rid of schools? The second question, we shall see, is a trap because it suggests a flight into action that temporarily may dilute the sense of frustration at the same time that it adds confusion to apathy and despair. It would also be a trap if advocating such an action could be interpreted as giving school personnel their final comeuppance, because it suggests that school personnel are to blame if schools are uninteresting places. That would be an instance of blaming the victim because school personnel, no less than we and a good deal more than most of us, have been socialized to define education as that which takes place *in* schools. That such a definition, literally poured into concrete, may be drastically limiting to efforts to make education interesting is hard for any of us to seriously consider, not only because it requires us to think in new ways but also because subliminally we know that the obstacles to society's acceptance of the implications of these ways of thinking would be many and strong. After all, when we talk about schools we are talking about institutions that in their size, structure, stated purposes, internal dynamics, and relation to the social surround reflect this country's social, intellectual, religious, political, and economic history. That it reflects these factors is easy to state and document. What is extraordinarily difficult is to become aware of the degree to which our communities depend on schools being where they are, bounded as they are, and organized as they are. That dependence is not a willed one or the result of a conspiracy—such oversimplifications obscure more than they clarify. For my present purposes it is sufficient to say that it is not until you come to see how self-defeating it is to continue to expect that schools can be truly interesting places (and then come to see the necessity of expanding one's conception of where and how serious learning can occur) that you will begin to glimpse how much of the way our communities are organized and function depends on schools being where they are, set off from the community as they are, and organized internally as they are.

I have argued that if schools are, by and large, uninteresting places, part of the explanation is in the emphasis on learning in the bounded classroom and school. Not only does that emphasis place definite limits on the degree to which schooling can be interesting, but also it permits us to avoid a critical question: can students experience schooling as interesting if their teachers do not? Let me try to throw light on that question by a comparative approach. If you were to ask, as I have, a university professor to justify the existence of a university, one of the most frequent answers would be, in one form or another, that a university is a place that creates the conditions in which its faculty can learn, change, and grow. If university faculty are to contribute to knowledge, then the university has to be organized on a basis and structured in a way to support faculty in their investigations, learning, and changing. In fact, as I pointed out earlier, the university assumes that to the degree that it creates the conditions that nurture the development of its faculty, students will experience learning as both interesting and productive. But, some professors will note, you can have a university without students; i.e., the primary justification of a university is its obligation to faculty. That justification arouses ambivalence in many people. On the one hand, they interpret that justification as a form of unde-served (or enviable) indulgence of narcissism, social irresponsibility, or sheer laziness. On the other, they cannot ignore—living as we do in a culture that respects practical knowledge and people with know-how—the fact that university faculty have served society well by these criteria (not all fields represented in the university, of course, but enough to keep the ambivalence in check). The idea that the primary function of a university is to support the development of its faculty receives grudging acceptance on the part of the public. If university faculty justify the existence of the university as they do, and if they are aware that this justification is rare in the bulk of other work settings, they are aware also that the way they justify the university makes it a very vulnerable institution in our society. After all, to be part of an institution whose obligation is to create the conditions that further your development (and make it interesting) produces if not guilt then at least the sense that one is fortunate.

Now, if you ask school personnel to justify the existence of schools, the answer is always that schools are for the pupils: their needs, their development. That justification, of course, is dramatically different from the one given by university faculty. Can teaching be interesting and personally and intellectually productive if school teachers are not provided the conditions that contribute to their own learning and personal and intellectual change and growth? If the needs of pupils and teachers are not co-equal—if meeting the needs of the former is seen as a necessity while those of the latter are either not recognized or viewed as a luxury or indulgence or frill—can teachers sustain those conditions that contribute to an interesting educational experience for pupils?

One of the unverbalized assumptions undergirding the organization and thrust of our schools is that the conditions that make schools interesting places for children can be created and sustained by teachers for whom those conditions exist only minimally, at best. There is nothing in theory, research, or practice that lends credence to that assumption. On the contrary, whatever we have learned about what makes for interesting experiences, about what makes for boredom in and disaffection from learning, about the features of settings that elicit and sustain interest—all of this and more underline the importance of symmetry in making life interesting for teacher and pupil. If schools are uninteresting places, it is in part because we have focused only on what we think pupils are and need, totally ignoring what teachers are and need. I have never met anyone who denied that children are curious about a lot of things, that they strive to achieve a sense of mastery, that they want to feel as propelled from within as stimulated from without, and that they know the difference between learning that is interesting and learning that is stultifying. In short, as they grow older, students increasingly appreciate the difference between labor and work, i.e., between end products that in no way bear the stamp of the producer and end products that do bear such a stamp (if only partially). Put another way, no one asserts that students do or should experience every minute of every day as fascinating; at the same time, however, no one asserts that for most of the school day students should be either bored or passive. And in what way are teachers different from children in terms of needs and expectations? Are teachers people whose curiosity has been satisfied? Are they people who feel no need to deepen their understanding or expand their mastery? Are they by nature devotees of ritual, far more interested in being laborers than workers? Are teachers allergic to change and growth and exploration? (Do not many critics impugn the very motivations and behavior on the part of teachers that the latter attack in their students?)

In this chapter I have discussed several factors that help explain not only why efforts to change and improve schools have been disappointing but also why future efforts are likely to fail. That conclusion derives from a rejection, in total or in part, of four interrelated assumptions. First, schools are or should be the primary places in which education takes place. Second, it is possible to create within schools the conditions that make for interesting experiences. Third, schools are primarily for students. Fourth, it is possible in school for teachers to create and sustain for students the conditions of productive and interesting learning when those conditions do not exist for teachers.

The conclusion I have come to will be resisted in diverse ways, all of which I have encountered in myself in my efforts over the years to understand why schools have not been amenable to change. What might be some of the basic but unverbalized assumptions without which the organization, thrust, and problems of schools are incomprehensible? It was not until I was able to ask and pursue this question that I began to see how amazingly effective our socialization is—so effective that we are unable to formulate, let alone challenge, these undergirding assumptions. But even if one begins to see and to take faltering steps to overcome what our socialization has made it unnecessary for us to verbalize, our socialization immediately confronts us with a fact that we knew in some abstract way but never understood in terms of what it meant vis-à-vis the way in which society is organized. And that fact is that when you begin to challenge the assumptions on which our schools are based, you begin to see how much our society depends on schools continuing to be what they are and where they are.

The idea that there must be things we can do inside schools that will make them more interesting places and instill in the unformed minds of students a respect for learning, even a hunger for learning, a sense of mastery over self and one's world and a sense of purpose that pulls one to a tomorrow built on the achievements of today and yesterday—put whatever way you wish for students in language flowery or mundane, the idea that they can be achieved will die hard, if it dies at all. That is not a gloomy forecast but a recognition that our world views change very slowly. Nor is this prediction gloomy in the sense that it implies a lack of alternatives. Inevitably, as one's world view starts to change, the elements of a new view come to the fore; the consequences and pace of such developments are not predictable except in barest outlines. As we shall see in later chapter, some of those elements are already on the scene waiting, so to speak, for their general significance to be recognized. New world views—whether they be literally about the world or about a major institution, and the two are always interrelated—do not appear full-blown, discontinuous with the old ones. It takes future historians to discern that the seeds of a new world view were imperceptibly sprouting in the old. So, for example, today we know that our world view has changed and continues to change in regard to men and women, race, and the family. Our libraries are being enlarged daily by books trying to describe how and why this world view came about, why it took so long to unfold, and what it portends for the future. And if there is any consensus about these matters it is in regard to two facts: the strength of unverbalized assumptions about the way the world is and should be and the extent to which the socioeconomic and political organization of society depends not only on those assumptions but also on their remaining unchallenged.

Our schools have not been exempt from challenges to traditional world views. Since the adoption of compulsory education in the nineteenth century and with ever increasing intensity down to the present, the place and function of our schools in society are issues that have never been off the societal agenda. And when future historians write their accounts of the post-World War II era, they will give a good deal of attention to the dissatisfactions that surfaced about schools, the efforts to transform and improve them, and the malaise and puzzlement that were consequences of the failure of these efforts. It is the malaise and puzzlement that suggest that in regard to schools we are still in the grips of unverbalized assumptions some of which I have presented in these pages. Compared to other changes that are taking place in our world view, changes in our schools have to be regarded as minimal at best. (I hasten to point out that I do not equate change with good and resistance to change with bad; such thoughtless equations seem with some people to take the place of reflective thinking.) That changes in schools have been minimal, on a comparative basis, seems satisfactory to no one. Indeed, there are those who would be delighted with proof that schools have hardly changed because they are convinced that schools have changed a good deal but for the wrong reasons and in the wrong directions.

CHAPTER
13

REFLECTIONS

I end this book by reprinting the last half of a chapter (similarly titled) in my most recent book *Parental Involvement and the Political Principle: Why the Existing Governance Structure of Schools Should Be Abolished* published in 1995 by Jossey-Bass. The reason I end with that material is that it expresses well why I have come to believe that desired school change cannot occur unless governance structure is radically altered. In other words, whatever changes I have previously recommended stand no chance of being productively implemented unless governance structure changes. I should have realized this a long time ago. Like everyone else, I unreflectively assumed that improvement could come about with minor changes in governance structure. I am hard put to say why it took me so long. Was it that I was educated in that structure and assumed that it was locked in concrete? Whatever the reason or reasons I regret the fact that it took me so long to see what I now regard as obvious: you can change the actors, even the way they think, but if all this takes place in a governance structure that is an obstacle to creativity and risk taking, we will end up again proving that the more things change the more they remain the same.

A colleague of mine who read this book (all but this chapter) in manuscript said, "I would have started out by asking the reader, as you have in other of your books, what they mean by productive thinking, its cognitive characteristics and the contexts which stimulate and sustain them, what I think you mean when you say a child should *want* to learn more and more.[1] Then I would have summarized what scads of studies have demonstrated on these points. Would that not have forced the reader to own up to the obvious fact that those contexts simply do not and cannot exist in the way schools have been and are organized and run? It is an open and shut case. I agree with you on the political principle but I would not have started with it because it does not bear directly on productive thinking which is really what you are after." That gave me pause, and not only because the thought of reorganizing this book was more than I could tolerate. Why did I start with the political principle? It did not take much soul searching—I am not that unknown to myself—to get the answer. In terms of human degradation, war, murderous dictatorships, and lesser forms of man's inhumanity to man, this may be the worst century in human history. I have lived through most of it. If it has not been easy, if there have been countless times I have been tempted to throw in the towel and give up on the human race, I took solace from the fact that at the core of these dispiriting events was the question: did *individuals* have rights and interests that should be respected in ways that allowed them to feel that they literally had some kind of voice, that they could represent those rights and interests even though it meant that their views *may* not prevail? When we accord respect to an individual's rights and interests, should we not expect that we will hear things we do not want to hear, that what we hear may conflict with our views, that we will tend to seek ways that violate the spirit of respect? In this century it became all too easy to violate that spirit, and in a large part of the world that violation continues.

What I have just said is painfully true on the stage of world events. But I have never been an actor on that stage. I, like you, am a member of a society where respect for individual rights and interests is embodied in our constitution, an inheritance for which we should be eternally grateful. But, as a friend of mine said, that inheritance can also be and has been, "one grand pain in the neck." He is a historian who said to me, "You can write the history of our country as a litany of moral horrors. You can also write it as a glorious history of attempts to protect individual rights and interests. At least in the United States you can write two histories; for most people on this earth there is only one miserable history." The thrust of his remarks was that what happened (and is still happening) on the world stage con-

---

[1] The text beginning with this sentence and continuing to the end of this chapter is reprinted from *Parent Involvement and the Political Principle: Why the Existing Governance Structure of Schools Should Be Abolished,* 1995. San Francisco: Jossey-Bass. Copyright 1995 by Jossey-Bass Inc., Publishers. Reprinted by permission.

tains issues with which we in this country are confronted as individuals and organizations. They are not issues only "out there" beyond our borders but "here" as well, albeit getting played out in an infinitely less disastrous way. That is to say, we are not off the hook. Although I have long been committed to the political principle I confess that its significance for me in the arenas I have worked was not always as clear to me as it should have been. I do not feel guilt about that, I certainly feel more humble, and I have much greater appreciation for those who have difficulty accepting the principle. I am referring specifically, of course, to those in the educational community. That explains only in part why I began this book with a discussion of the political principle. Together with that was my feeling that in regard to our schools we have been and continue to be on a course that is doomed to result in failure, a course with percolating, destabilizing societal consequences. This is not to say that if the political principle is taken seriously educational outcomes will necessarily be more satisfactory, for reasons I gave earlier. But I strongly believe that those outcomes will be more likely if the existing governance structure is abolished and replaced by one more congenial to the consideration of a reordering of purposes. School systems will not change from within. They will only change in a truly meaningful way when dissatisfaction from within stimulates and coincides with pressures from without. Unfortunately, the dissatisfactions from within our schools have been kept "within" even though more than a few leaders and rank- and-file people know full well that the stultifying features of the governance structure are a mammoth obstacle to the raising and discussion of ideas that challenge that governance structure. Numerous times in earlier pages I emphasized a point both those in and out of the educational community have been unable to perceive: the political principle is violated in the relationships among the layers of the system's hierarchy just as educators violate that principle in their relationships with parents and community, and in both instances the justifications offered are identical.

I started with the political intuitively. That is to say, my entire adult life forced on me the bedrock significance of the political principle in human affairs: personal, social, political, national and international. What would have surprised me is if I had begun this book with other than a discussion of the political principle. It did not occur to me to start otherwise. From my perspective I was asking the reader "to return to the basics." My colleague was right, except in one respect: what I was really after in this book was to get the reader to accept, in letter and spirit, the legitimacy and wisdom of the political principle. Our founding fathers knew that in 1787, which is why they scrapped the Articles of Confederation and wrote a new constitution.

A penultimate comment. In the *Harvard Business Review* for January–February of 1994 there is an article by Bernard Avishai with the title

"What is Business's Social Impact?" It is well worth reading. One of the thrusts of the article stems from Avishai's reaction to a visit to a small auto supplier with a reputation for quality.

> The company made fuel injector components and component manufac-turing equipment, about $50 million in sales. It was housed in the same square building it had taken over in the 1950s, still looking very much like an oversized garage. But instead of the classical factory scene of lath-es spinning or pallets shuttling about, with one man drilling and anoth-er grinding, the floor looked more like the operating room of a makeshift hospital, with a scattering of people speaking in quiet tones to one anoth-er. The master schedule and customer and quality information were dis-played on screens; operators were monitoring them with obvious seri-ousness. Off to the side was a small room with a glass door, and sitting inside was a lanky blond man wearing a ponytail, moving the mouse on a CAD–CAM system.
>   A talk with the company's CEO brought its own surprises. "The problem with this country is that the schools don't teach," he said. "I would pay more taxes if people were ready for work. We send a $250,000 machine to a GM plant, and in six weeks it is trashed—it is like sending a Mercedes to Zaire." What of his own company? The problem too is finding people. That young man with the ponytail was at the heart of the company. "Nobody cares about his hair anymore," said the CEO.
>   This was my introduction to a burgeoning system of production that would change what was meant by the crisis of capitalism. We were entering an age when the problem would not be worker unemployment but rather worker *unemployability.* (p. 44)

Having said that, it is no surprise that the author goes on to say,

> New hires will have to present themselves for work knowing how to keep learning and how to get the best from other people. They will need to speak others' (at times, foreign) languages. They will be undaunted by change and failure. In short, they will integrate to organize the cre-ation of value for customers, using dispersed parts of the value chain. (pp. 45–46)

Avishai then discusses and quotes from Ray Marshall and Marc Tucker's *Thinking for a Living: Education and the Weather of Nations* (1992).

> Marshall and Tucker insist that business leaders need to "face the chal-lenge," to acknowledge that public education is worth investing in as a business decision. Next, businesses need to focus on how fit existing schools are for delivering on these goals. Just how should the schools be restructured? Marshall and Tucker borrow heavily from the experi-ence of major U.S. technology companies, suggesting that the schools

need to undergo a quality revolution much like the ones led by David Kearns at Xerox and Bob Galvin at Motorola—both of whom, in the authors' view, personify business's enlightened commitment to the reform of public education.

The agenda for reform is ambitious: performance measures, a new curriculum, devolution of authority onto school principals and local administrators, elimination of school board bureaucracy, and the provision of a "whole new set of incentives and accountability measures that provide real rewards for school staff whose students make real progress." In all of these initiatives, business—and Marshall and Tucker really seem to mean big business—would be a kind of activist partner, providing funds for the work of educational foundations, working with community colleges on curriculum, offering a new language of explanation for city school boards (thus, for instance, students are "customers," failing students are "defects"), and even innovating with institutions of higher education of their own.

Schools, feeling the ambient pressure of business, would undergo a quality change something like the one other suppliers to big business have experienced over the past ten years. Companies would present school boards not with "design specifications"—in other words, the elements of a standard curriculum (read, write, and account)—but with "performance specifications," targets of competence all students must meet. As suppliers, individual schools would take the initiative on how to meet the general standard, while the "customer," the school board, would take the initiative on qualifying the supplier, much like an original equipment manufacturer. Meanwhile, businesses, the next customer in the value chain, would help the school board set appropriate standards: "Many firms would have to help build the science and math curriculum; set technical standards for apprenticeship programs; offer opportunities for on-the-job training; [and] provide mentors, job opportunities and personal support to disadvantaged students." (p. 46)

Avishai does not think that Marshall and Tucker have gone far enough because they are wedded to a notion of education in familiar public classrooms. "When we explode our concept of education to include transforming media and information technologies, both of which are driven by private competitors, the meaning of educational institutions is clearly not going to stay the same." Indeed, he goes on to suggest that our secondary schools, which he describes as "mass-production skill factories," will be a relic of the past.

Some readers, I assume not few, will have reacted to the above as a vision of an Apocalypse where business "finally" controls the education of our youth, molding them to fit in ways that make for "bottom lines" that warm the cockles of the hearts of executives and stockholders. I entreat such readers to set aside that vision, for the moment at least, and try to answer the question: what is the private sector responding to? Is it only

simple greed masked by pieties about social responsibility? Is it only ignorance of the "true" purposes of education? Is it another example of science and technology running rampant over issues of values and individual purposes? Is it confirmation of Karl Marx's argument that in a capitalistic
society people are objects and things, never fully or partly human?

Before responding to those questions I must tell the reader that in no
way will I be suggesting that business (especially the Fortune 500 types)
is now comprised of leaders lacking in narrow self-interest or now possessed of a semi-sophisticated understanding of matters educational.
What I believe and do suggest is that *some* of these business leaders have
learned a good deal about the contexts that make for productive learning, contexts absent in our schools. Let me list some of the things some
of them have learned:

1. The adversarial relationship between labor and management,
between the layers of the organizational structure, were counterproductive to the overarching goal of being efficient and profitable.

2. The day was past when those at or near the bottom layers would
passively accept cipherdom, lack of recognition, lack of worthiness, the
role of asset poor, deficit rich, dispensable drudges who, like old man
river, just kept rolling along.

3. The consequences of points 1 and 2 were intractable to remediation by the traditions, spirit, and letter of the existing governance structure. In almost all of these instances (and it is probably all) they were sufficiently puzzled, frustrated, and desperate as to seek outside help.
Someone said that nothing focussed the mind more than the knowledge
that you will be executed tomorrow. These executives saw the equivalent of execution coming down the road.

4. I am making it sound too simple, rational, and cookbookish when
I say that two major changes occurred: governance structure changed,
and people in all layers of the organization participated *in some way* in
planning and decision making. Put in another way, there were now
incentives *to want* to learn, change, feel more competent, more necessary
to organizational goals. Issues surrounding the allocation and distribution of power decreased in frequency and in untoward consequences.

5. All of the above interacted with the most obvious change demanding feature of the modern era: the work place would be transformed by
information technologies for which the existing governance structure and
customary personnel relationships were, to say the least, self-defeating. In
the abstract, technology is neutral; in practice it challenges, upsets, and
exacerbates the messy problem of values, outlooks, the way we define
ourselves in relation to others, and how much that we accord to ourselves
we should feel obliged to accord to others. If you compare the average

work place before World War II to that of today, it is like comparing apples and oranges (both of which are fruit and that is where the resemblance ends). In the lifetime of current business executives they have learned five things: change is the name of the game, the game seems always to change, learning is a lifetime affair, the alternatives *to wanting to learn* are kinds of living deaths, and the organization that does not create and sustain contexts for productive learning is missing the point and probably the future.

As I said, I am not suggesting that, *generally speaking*, business executives have experienced an "enlightenment" that goes beyond rhetoric and narrow self-interest. That, however, should not obscure the fact that some very influential and articulate business leaders know that the game has changed and should change. The crucial point is that, again generally speaking, business executives, *aware as they are of the changes their organizations have had to make in structure and process, cannot understand why schools have remained what they were and are despite the lack of desirable outcomes.* As one executive said to me, "For a long time American business and industry were based on the stance that if it ain't broke don't fix it. Then we had our comeuppance. It was broke and we had to fix it. Schools are broke and they need to be fixed."

But there is more to their argument. Here is the first paragraph of Avishai's article.

> Our cities are in trouble, and business managers are understandably torn about what to do. They are exhorted to be good corporate citizens and know they command extraordinary resources. Vaguely, managers feel that a once clear separation between public and private sectors has broken down, that they are spending heavily on such things as education and training, and that this may not be their responsibility. At the same time, the financial uncertainties that press on them are stronger than ever before. There are the uncertainties of global competition and new technologies that undermine their sense of command. The new financial industry challenges their governance when the stock price gets even temporarily soft. What, in this context, are business's social responsibilities? Have they changed? (p. 38)

To say that our cities are in trouble may well be the most egregious understatement of the past half century. Later in his paper Avishai, in one sentence, states what is the source of the most anxiety arousing concerns in people generally: the problem is less one of unemployment than it is of *unemployability,* a problem whose percolating, destabilizing consequences confront but go far beyond the self-interests of the private sector.

What the reader has to do is to separate Avishai's specific possibilities for transforming schools from the issue of whether he is correct in concluding that schools must undergo as radical a transformation as business and industry are experiencing. Is he right for the right reasons or right for the wrong reasons? That he is right I have no doubt, as I have argued in this and previous books, especially in *Schooling in America: Scapegoat and Salvation* (1983). In fact, in that book I present a cognitive-educational rationale for what Avishai proposes but one that takes explicitly and seriously the overarching purpose I discussed in the previous chapter; a purpose barely alluded to in his paper. However, slighting that purpose is one thing, but what is no less troubling is that he talks *only* about schools, as if what happens in schools is completely independent of the preparatory programs from which school personnel come. And that is my point: Avishai's diagnosis is very wrong to the extent that it is woefully incomplete, i.e., it commits the error of misplaced emphasis. Of course *schools* are part of the problem, but so are university preparatory programs, as John Goodlad has eloquently said countless times. Furthermore, as I read his paper I found myself expecting that the logic of his argument would lead him to recommend a dramatic change in governance structure of our schools. I was disappointed. Essentially, he accepts the existing governance structure despite his knowledge of the challenges to and changes in the governance structure that the private sector has and continues to experience.

I had to conclude that Avishai and many "enlightened" executives are dogooders. I define a dogooder as someone who with the best of motives simply does not know what in hell he or she is getting into. Possessed as they are with rescue fantasies they enter the fray armed with good (indeed the best of) intentions only later to be disarmed by the consequences of their ignorance. *That is true not only for many in the private sector but for many reformers in the educational community; the former are latecomers to the scene.* So, for example, Avishai says that his proposals would transform secondary schools. *"Primary schools may well stick to something like classroom-based teaching, if only to help small children master simple courtesies."* I confess that when I read that sentence I felt like the man who had broken several ribs. When a friend asked him how he felt, he replied, "It only hurts when I laugh." With that kind of conception of young children—loveable pets who have to be tamed—the failure of educational reform is guaranteed.

Finally, in earlier chapters I noted that you could find exceptions here and there to generalized criticisms of schools. I bring the reader's attention to one such exception. It is contained in a paper "Enhancing Motivational Opportunity in Elementary Schooling. A Case Study of the Ecology of Principal Leadership," authored by Barbara Butterworth and Rhona Weinstein. (It is as yet unpublished but copies can be obtained from Professor Weinstein, Department of Psychology, University of California at Berkeley.) I cannot do justice to their description of this school.

Here are some of its features:

1. It is a small, K–6, private elementary school with somewhat more than a hundred students. Class size averages between sixteen and eighteen students.

2. One third of the students are from relatively poor economic minority backgrounds. The school depends completely on tuition. It is in all respects what has been called an "undermanned setting," i.e., it lacks the financial, spatial, and personnel resources such settings ordinarily have or are expected to have.

3. Precisely because it is such a setting the accomplishment of its educational objectives requires that everyone—teachers, parents, *and* students—perform a variety of functions. The following provides glimpses of what their fuller description contains:

> Admissions to the school were largely non-selective (on a first-come, first-serve basis), except in the case of ensuring ethnic minority representation. An active scholarship program resulted in minority representation in each class at a higher level than its surrounding public school district (approximately 30%). An afterschool program also drew single parent and two-worker families from a wide variety of socioeconomic positions. As a result, the population of children attending the school was as varied as the local public schools. Thus, there are elements in its design that are similar to and can be generalized to the public sector.
>
> In addition to the regular academic program (which differs perhaps by virtue of specialist teaching in the elementary grades and by the requirement of a second language), there existed a variety of additional programs which enhanced the daily classroom activities. These included student government, a school economy, publishing, theater performances, an outdoor education program, community experiences, an afterschool program, and holiday celebrations.
>
> The school had a system of student government in which a mayor, vice-mayor, secretary, treasurer, and social coordinator were elected by the whole school twice a year. Each individual running for office appointed a campaign manager who, along with the candidate, prepared a speech as well. Representatives from each class completed the membership of the governing body. Two teachers helped the students plan activities and fund-raisers for the school.
>
> The school also had an economic system in which children held regular jobs around the school and were paid a weekly salary in the local scrip, keybucks. Jobs ranged from aiding in the classroom or office to maintenance around the school grounds: adults in the school supervised jobs related to their interests and classroom/subject area needs. Jobs were listed, students wrote applications, and were interviewed for positions. Students could save keybucks in the bank (run by the sixth grade) or spend keybucks at the school store (run by the fifth grade) or book-

store (run by the fourth grade) and for field trips and the use of special equipment like computers.

Publishing was a third area of activity for the school. A student newspaper was published monthly, staffed by students from all the grades, and a literary magazine was published twice a year by the fourth grade. A yearbook with photographs was also published by a student staff with teacher help. The principal wrote a weekly Wednesday letter to parents and children and classroom teachers routinely sent home newsletters about class activities.

During the year, two school-wide performances were held, a musical for the holiday season, and a dramatic or musical comedy at the end of the year. Scripts were modified so that every child in the school performed in the play. In addition, each grade put on a play for the school and for parents.

An outdoor education program involved fourth–sixth graders in a five day camping trip to an area of ecological importance and younger children in one night camping trips. Class visits to community theatre, concerts, and museums were also regular parts of the program. Students brought their own performances to local homes for the aged. Community resources also visited the school, for example, two architects collaborated with fifth grade students in designing a model community for their social studies assignment.

The year was also punctuated by celebration—Halloween parades, Thanksgiving luncheon, Martin Luther King's Birthday, Grandparent Day, Graduation dinner to list a few. These traditions have developed rich, elaborate rituals which brought energy to the school periodically during the year and warmly involved the family community.

Before school opened and after school hours, a rich and varied program was available for children whose families sign them up at an additional cost. Staffed by adults as well as local high school and college students, activities included a study hall for homework, art projects, films, and sports program and leagues with other schools. Signups were for single days or on a regular basis. The afterschool program expanded its hours for school half–day closings when teacher-parent conferences were held. (pp. 14–17)

That is what I mean by taking the overarching purpose of schooling seriously. But that is not why I have presented it here; I am sure that there are other exceptions. I presented it to deal with the question: Since this is a private school, can its features be replicated in a public school? Part of the answer has already been given in that this was not the kind of school we ordinarily think of as a well-heeled private school containing youngsters only from secure economic backgrounds, witness the fact that it had more minority students than surrounding public schools. What distinctively characterizes this school is its perception and thorough-going *redefinition* of who in the school *and* community were assets and resources for educational purposes. *And that included the children.* Clearly, the school had many important purposes but, equally clearly, the overarching one was reinforcing children's *wanting to learn,* as the words in the paper's title ("Enhancing Motivational Opportunity") say.

Replicating in one setting what happened in another is literally impossible, a fact the elaboration of which would require another book. You can read the Butterworth and Weinstein paper and point to this or that of the school's features that would make replication difficult, although in my opinion the number of those features would not exceed one, perhaps two. The point is that when people talk of replication, they almost always mean replicating what people *do,* i.e., the overt, describable goings on. In that sense replication is impossible, it can only be approximated, i.e., things will look and happen differently. What is absolutely crucial in replication is that the assumptions, conceptions, values, and priorities undergirding what you seek to replicate are clear in your head and you take them seriously, you truly accept and believe them, *they are nonnegotiable starting points.* "How to do it" is one thing. "How to think it" is another. One of the things replicators have learned, usually after failure, is that there are minimal conditions which if not met means that replication stands no chance of even being somewhat approximated. And one of those minimal conditions is that you have thought through and accepted the rationale, the "how to think and believe it" process, to the point where you know what other minimal conditions need to exist if you are to stand a chance of being consistent with that rationale.

The Butterworth and Weinstein rationale is no great mystery. It is a distillation of what has long been known about productive learning, its processes and contexts. They took it seriously and literally created the appropriate contexts. Is this rationale applicable to and replicable in public schools? The answer is "yes," it is applicable; the answer is "no," it is not replicable given the way our schools are organized and governed. That is not my opinion alone. I asked four elementary school teachers to read the Butterworth and Weinstein paper, and to answer the question, "Could this be done in your public school?" They did not laugh in my face, if only because the article reminded them of the gulf between what they had read and what they daily experienced and did. But one of them did say something that plaintively summarized what all of them felt: "Since when are schools places congenial to the vision and persistence of the writers of that article?" Translating it into my words, "Since when have schools been organized and run informed by what we have long known about productive learning?" They have never been so organized and run. Today, however, the societal stakes are much higher than ever before.

REFERENCES

Ausubel, D.P. (1967). Crucial psychological issues in the objectives, organization, and evaluation of curriculum reform movements. *Psychology in the Schools, 4,* 111–120.

Avishai, B. (1994). What is business's social impact? *Harvard Business Review,* 38–46.

Blom, G. (1979–1980). Heather's story: A handicapped person's rights to as normal a life as possible. *American Examiner, 8*(1), 35–56.

Butterworth, B., & Weinstein, R. (Unpublished study). Enhancing motivational opportunity in elementary schooling. A case study of principal leadership.

Buxton, C. (1973). *Adolescents in Schools.* New Haven: Yale University Press.

Coleman, J.S., Hoffer, T., & Kilgore, S. (1982). *High School Achievement.* New York: Basic Books.

Cuban, L. (1984). *How Teachers Taught.* New York: Longman.

Farber, B. (1991). *Crisis in Education: Stress and Burnout in the American Teacher.* San Francisco: Jossey-Bass.

Fehr, H.F. (1966). Sense and nonsense in a modern school mathematics program. *The Arithmetic Teacher, 13,* 83–91.

Flexner, A. (1960). *Medical Education in the United States and Canada: A Report to the Carnegie Foundation for the Advancement of Teaching.* Washington, DC: The Carnegie Foundation for the Advancement of Teaching. (Originally published in 1910.)

Freud, S. (1925). Analysis of a phobia in a five-year-old boy. *Collected Papers, Vol. 3.* London: Hogarth Press.

Ginzberg, E., & Bray, D. (1953). *The Uneducated.* New York: Columbia University Press.

Goodlad, J. (1984). *A Place Called School.* New York: McGraw-Hill.

Goodman, A.W. (1965). *The Pleasures of Math.* New York: Macmillan.

Gunther, J. (1936). *Inside Europe..* New York: Harper.

Jensen, A.R. (1979). *Bias in Mental Testing.* New York: Free Press.

Kanner, L. (1943). Autistic disturbances of affective contact. *The Nervous Child, 2,* 217–250.

Kaplan, F., & Sarason, S.B. (Eds.) (undated). *The Psycho-Educational Clinic: Papers and Research Studies.* Boston: Department of Mental Health, Commonwealth of Massachusetts.

Lane, H. (1976). *The Wild Boy of Aveyron.* Cambridge, MA: Harvard University Press.

Longo, P. (1979). *Program Evaluation: Project City Science Final Report.* New York: Queens College, Department of Education.

Marshall, R., & Tucker, M. (1992). *Thinking for a Living: Education and the Weather of Nations*. New York: Basic Books.

Rossiter, C. (1966). *1787: The Grand Convention*. New York: New American Library.

Sarason, S.B. (1944). Dreams and thematic apperception test stories. *Journal of Personality, 39*(4), 121–126.

Sarason, S.B. (1969). *Psychological Problems in Mental Deficiency* (4th ed.). New York: Harper & Row.

Sarason, S.B. (1972). *The Creation of Settings and Future Societies*. San Francisco: Jossey-Bass.

Sarason, S.B. (1980). Review: Jensen's bias in mental testing. *Society, 18*(1), 93–98.

Sarason, S.B. (1982). *The Culture of the School and the Problem of Change* (2nd ed.). Boston: Allyn & Bacon. (Originally published in 1971.)

Sarason, S.B. (1983). *Schooling in America: Scapegoat and Salvation*. New York: Free Press.

Sarason, S.B. (1985). *Psychology and Mental Retardation: Perspectives in Change*. Austin, TX: Pro–Ed.

Sarason, S.B. (1986). *Caring and Compassion in Clinical Practice*. San Francisco: Jossey-Bass.

Sarason, S.B. (1993). *The Case for Change: Rethinking the Preparation of Educators*. San Francisco: Jossey-Bass.

Sarason, S.B. (1993). *You Are Thinking of Teaching? Opportunities, Problems, Realities*. San Francisco: Jossey-Bass.

Sarason, S.B. (1993). *Letters to a Serious Education President*. Newbury Park, CA: Corwin Press.

Sarason, S.B. (In press, 1995). *Parent Involvement and the Political Principle: Why the Existing Governance Structure of Schools Should Be Abolished*. San Francisco: Jossey-Bass.

Sarason, S.B., Carroll, C., Maton, K., Cohen, S., & Lorentz, E. (1977). *Human Services and Resource Networks*. San Francisco: Jossey-Bass.

Sarason, S.B., Davidson, K., & Blatt, B. (1986). *The Preparation of Teachers: An Unstudied Problem in Education*. Cambridge, MA: Brookline Books.

Sarason, S.B. & Doris, J. (1969). *Psychological Problems in Mental Deficiency* (4th ed.). New York: Harper & Row.

Sarason, S.B. & Doris, J. (1979). *Educational Handicap, Public Policy, and Social History: A Broadened Perspective on Mental Retardation*. New York: Free Press.

Sarason, S.B., Levine, M., Goldenberg, I.I., Cherlin, D.L.,& Bennett, E.M. (1966). *Psychology in Community Settings: Clinical, Vocational, Educational, Social Aspects*. New York: John Wiley.

Sarason, S.B., & Lorentz, E. (1979). *The Challenge of the Resource Exchange Network*. San Francisco: Jossey-Bass.

School Mathematics Study Group, Stanford University (1961). *Newsletter*, No. 10.

Westbrook, R.B. (1991). *John Dewey and American Democracy*. Ithaca, NY: Cornell University Press.

Whitehead, A.N. (1929). The mathematical curriculum. In *The Aims of Education*. New York: Mentor Books. (Originally published by Macmillan in 1929.)

ABOUT THE AUTHOR

Seymour B. Sarason is professor of psychology emeritus in the Department of Psychology and at the Institution for Social and Policy Studies of Yale University. In 1962 he founded and directed the Yale Psycho-Educational Clinic, one of the first research and training sites in community psychology. Fields in which he has made special contributions include mental retardation, culture and personality, projective techniques, teacher training, anxiety in children, and school reform. His numerous books and articles reflect his broad interests.

Dr. Sarason received his Ph.D. degree from Clark University in 1942 and holds honorary doctorates from Syracuse University, Queens College, Rhode Island College, and Lewis and Clark College. He has received awards from the American Psychological Association and the American Association on Mental Deficiency.